THE ECONOMY AND POLITICAL CULTURE IN NEW DEMOCRACIES

To Jane and John Broderick

The Economy and Political Culture in New Democracies

An analysis of democratic support in Central and Eastern Europe

KRISTIN J. BRODERICK
Kutztown University, USA

LONDON AND NEW YORK

First published 2000 by Ashgate Publishing

Reissued 2018 by Routledge
2 Park Square, Milton Park, Abingdon, Oxon OX14 4RN
711 Third Avenue, New York, NY 10017, USA

Routledge is an imprint of the Taylor & Francis Group, an informa business

Copyright © Kristin J. Broderick 2000

All rights reserved. No part of this book may be reprinted or reproduced or utilised in any form or by any electronic, mechanical, or other means, now known or hereafter invented, including photocopying and recording, or in any information storage or retrieval system, without permission in writing from the publishers.

Notice:
Product or corporate names may be trademarks or registered trademarks, and are used only for identification and explanation without intent to infringe.

Publisher's Note
The publisher has gone to great lengths to ensure the quality of this reprint but points out that some imperfections in the original copies may be apparent.

Disclaimer
The publisher has made every effort to trace copyright holders and welcomes correspondence from those they have been unable to contact.

A Library of Congress record exists under LC control number: 00134487

ISBN 13: 978-1-138-73814-0 (hbk)
ISBN 13: 978-1-138-73807-2 (pbk)
ISBN 13: 978-1-315-18503-3 (ebk)

Contents

List of Figures   *vii*
List of Tables   *ix*
Acknowledgements   *xi*

Introduction   1

PART I: EMPIRICAL STUDY OF DEMOCRATIC SUPPORT

1 Democratic Consolidation and Mass Support   7

2 Measurement and Data   27

3 Findings and Analysis   39

PART II: CASE STUDIES

4 Introduction to Case Studies   57

5 The Czech Republic   62

6 Slovakia   88

7 Lithuania   115

8 Russia   144

Conclusion   177

Appendix One: Economic Reform Index   *181*
Appendix Two: Data   *184*
Bibliography   *186*

List of Figures

Figure 1.1	System Support Model	24
Figure 3.1	Democratic Satisfaction and Financial Evaluations 1994	44
Figure 3.2	Democratic Satisfaction and Market Reform 1994	45
Figure 3.3	Predicted Level of Democratic Satisfaction Over Time	51
Figure 5.1	Democratic Satisfaction for the Czech Republic and Central and Eastern Europe	63
Figure 5.2	Percentage Change in Real GDP for the Czech Republic and Central and Eastern Europe	65
Figure 5.3	Democratic Satisfaction and Percentage Change in Real GDP for the Czech Republic	66
Figure 5.4	Inflation for the Czech Republic and Central and Eastern Europe	68
Figure 5.5	Democratic Satisfaction and Inflation for the Czech Republic	69
Figure 5.6	Financial Evaluations for the Czech Republic and Central and Eastern Europe	70
Figure 5.7	Democratic Satisfaction and Financial Evaluations for the Czech Republic	71
Figure 6.1	Democratic Satisfaction for Slovakia, the Czech Republic, and Central and Eastern Europe	89
Figure 6.2	Percentage Change in Real GDP for Slovakia, the Czech Republic, and Central and Eastern Europe	91
Figure 6.3	Democratic Satisfaction and Percentage Change in Real GDP for Slovakia	92
Figure 6.4	Inflation for Slovakia, the Czech Republic, and Central and Eastern Europe	93
Figure 6.5	Democratic Satisfaction and Inflation for Slovakia	94
Figure 6.6	Financial Evaluations for Slovakia, the Czech Republic, and Central and Eastern Europe	95
Figure 6.7	Democratic Satisfaction and Financial Evaluations for Slovakia	96
Figure 7.1	Democratic Satisfaction for Lithuania and Central and Eastern Europe	116

Figure 7.2　Percentage Change in Real GDP for Lithuania and Central and Eastern Europe　118
Figure 7.3　Democratic Satisfaction and Percentage Change in Real GDP for Lithuania　119
Figure 7.4　Inflation for Lithuania and Central and Eastern Europe　120
Figure 7.5　Inflation and Democratic Satisfaction for Lithuania　121
Figure 7.6　Financial Evaluations for Lithuania and Central and Eastern Europe　122
Figure 7.7　Democratic Satisfaction and Financial Evaluations for Lithuania　123
Figure 8.1　Democratic Satisfaction for Russia and Central and Eastern Europe　145
Figure 8.2　Percentage Change in Real GDP for Russia and Central and Eastern Europe　146
Figure 8.3　Democratic Satisfaction and Percentage Change in Real GDP for Russia　147
Figure 8.4　Inflation for Russia and Central and Eastern Europe　148
Figure 8.5　Democratic Satisfaction and Inflation for Russia　149
Figure 8.6　Financial Evaluations for Russia and Central and Eastern Europe　150
Figure 8.7　Democratic Satisfaction and Financial Evaluations for Russia　151

List of Tables

Table 2.1	Example of Weighted Average of Democratic Support for Albania 1994	29
Table 2.2	Example of Weighted Average of Financial Evaluations for Albania 1994	34
Table 2.3	Correlation Matrix of Economic Independent Variables	36
Table 3.1	Cross-sectional Regression for 1994	43
Table 3.2	Pooled Cross-sectional, Times-Series Model	48
Table 3.3	Least Squares Dummy Variable Model	49
Table 5.1	Democratic Satisfaction for the Czech Republic and Central and Eastern Europe	63
Table 5.2	Percentage Change in Real GDP for the Czech Republic and Central and Eastern Europe	65
Table 5.3	Inflation for the Czech Republic and Central and Eastern Europe	67
Table 5.4	Financial Evaluations for the Czech Republic and Central and Eastern Europe	70
Table 5.5	Czech Perceptions of History (October 1968)	83
Table 5.6	Czech Evaluations of Historic Personalities (1946)	84
Table 5.7	Czech Evaluations of Historic Personalities (1968)	85
Table 6.1	Democratic Satisfaction for Slovakia, the Czech Republic, and Central and Eastern Europe	89
Table 6.2	Percentage Change in Real GDP for Slovakia, the Czech Republic, and Central and Eastern Europe	90
Table 6.3	Inflation for Slovakia, the Czech Republic, and Central and Eastern Europe	92
Table 6.4	Financial Evaluations for Slovakia, the Czech Republic, and Central and Eastern Europe	95
Table 6.5	Occupational Structure in 1910 by Nationality	101
Table 6.6	Slovak Perceptions of History: Question One (October 1968)	110
Table 6.7	Slovak Perceptions of History: Question Two (October 1968)	111
Table 6.8	Slovak Evaluations of Historic Personalities (October 1968)	112

Table 7.1 Democratic Satisfaction for Lithuania and Central and Eastern Europe	116
Table 7.2 Percentage Change in Real GDP for Lithuania and Central and Eastern Europe	117
Table 7.3 Inflation for Lithuania and Central and Eastern Europe	120
Table 7.4 Financial Evaluations for Lithuania and Central and Eastern Europe	122
Table 7.5 Lithuanian Response to Systems Support/Alienation Items (1990)	140
Table 8.1 Democratic Satisfaction for Russia and Central and Eastern Europe	144
Table 8.2 Percentage Change in Real GDP for Russia and Central and Eastern Europe	146
Table 8.3 Inflation for Russia and Central and Eastern Europe	148
Table 8.4 Financial Evaluations for Russia and Central and Eastern Europe	150
Table 8.5 Russian Response to Systems Support/Alienation Items (1990)	174

Acknowledgements

I owe thanks to many friends and colleagues who have unselfishly given their time and energy toward this project. Foremost, I am grateful to Thomas C. Muller for his analytical, editorial, and technical assistance. Special thanks to Noreen Boyle-Tunney, Elaine Tallman, and Lori Ann Vandermark for production help. I would also like to thank Sam Martineau for assisting with various reference materials and editorial comments.

I am extremely fortunate to have had friendship and professional advice from Richard I. Hofferbert, James P. Young, Eduard Ziegenhagen, and Stuart A. Bremer. And, I am heavily indebted to Robert Compton, Jenny Heyl, Susan Metz, David H. Sacko, and Eric J. Kimmelman for their technical advice, moral support, and friendship.

Introduction

The collapse of Communism in Central and Eastern Europe poses both theoretical and empirical challenges to social scientists. Beyond the immediate significance of the demise of totalitarianism in the region, the democratic transitions have worldwide implications. For some, the fall of Communism signifies the triumph of liberal democracy and the 'end of history' (Fukuyama, 1992). For others, it represents a movement towards world peace (Maoz and Russett, 1993). Regardless of the ideological connotations of these arguments, it is undeniable that the transitions in Central and Eastern Europe are part of a greater global movement toward democracy. They are the culmination of the 'third wave' of democratization, which constitutes by far the largest expansion of democracy in world history (Huntington, 1991). Accordingly to Doh Chull Shin, the number of democratic regimes has more than doubled since 1972. Today, nearly 60 percent of the countries of the world are democratic.

Corresponding to this global expansion of democracy, a significant amount of research concerning the forces that propel democratization has emerged. The research not only has examined the socio-economic and cultural factors that influence the development of democracy, but also has explored how new democracies can be maintained and consolidated. An understanding of the consolidation process is crucial in view of the frequency of reversal, which has demonstrated the precarious nature of some new democracies. The failure of democratic regimes is often attributed to the lack of necessary conditions for consolidation. Shin asserts that 'empirically, newly democratizing countries tend to lack many factors that facilitate the process of democratization, including market economies and civic organizations' (1994, 137). If social scientists can achieve a greater understanding of the consolidation process, perhaps they can assist the new democracies in surviving in the face of economic, social, and cultural obstacles.

This research investigates the consolidation of the new democracies in Central and Eastern Europe. Unlike many other countries that have experienced transitions towards democracy, the Central and Eastern European states face the additional hurdle of transforming their economies. The rigors of economic transition, coupled with the underdevelopment of civil society and the legacy of a half century of state socialism, pose major impediments to the preservation of democracy in the region. It is still uncertain whether these countries will continue along the path of consolidation or regress into authoritarian regimes (Schmitter, 1994). An examination of the relationship between the economic environment and popular support for democracy can contribute to a better understanding of those factors, which, in turn, could assist the process of democratic consolidation.

The purpose of this research, then, is to examine the effect of economic factors on popular support for democracy in Central and Eastern Europe. It rests, both theoretically and empirically, on the assumption that democracy can survive and consolidate only if the public is committed to it. It may be that the transitions in Central and Eastern Europe were initiated by elites; however, a democratic regime, by definition, can continue only through citizen support, which therefore qualifies as a legitimate focus in examining democratic consolidation. What factors influence citizen commitment to democratic regimes in Central and Eastern Europe? How does economic performance affect support for the regimes? What strategies can policymakers implement to promote the democratization process in this region?

My research also examines the effect of free-market transitions on the consolidation of the newly emerging democracies in Central and Eastern Europe. There is widespread agreement among social scientists that the success of liberal democracy in the Central and Eastern European countries will depend largely upon the success of the mutually reinforcing processes of economic and structural change (Huntington, 1991; Przeworski, 1991). The central question that I explore is: what are the effects of economic policy, economic conditions, and economic perceptions upon citizen support for the new democracies? Specifically, what role does the economy play in the survival of the new democracies? I argue that citizen perception of well-being is the most important element influencing political support.

In addition to economic factors, what other influences affect democratic support? I argue that political culture can hinder or assist democratic consolidation. Although all of these states endured long-term Soviet domination, they exhibit significant differences in their political culture. Thus, previous political experience, political development, and attitudes toward politics play an important role in the consolidation process.

The book is organized into two parts. Part I consists of the first three chapters, which offer the theoretical framework, measurement, and a generalizable cross-national empirical model of the effect of economic factors upon democratic support. Part II (Chapters Four through Nine) contains four country case studies that investigate the political development of each state and assess how democratic support has been affected by the political culture of the state.

Chapter One reviews the predominant theoretical frameworks of the study of democratization, examines the linkage between democratic consolidation and mass support for democracy, offers a systems approach to investigating democratic support, and discusses the role of economic factors and political culture as an explanation for support. Chapter Two provides a discussion of data, measurement, and research design and presents the conceptualization and operationalization of democratic support. In addition, it addresses the economic factors (both economic conditions and perceptions) that are hypothesized to affect the support for democracy. Also, Chapter Two examines the extent of economic reform and its relationship to democratic support, which provides a linkage between the economic transitions and democratic consolidation. Following the operationalization of each economic factor, hypotheses concerning the expected relationship to democratic consolidation are offered. Finally, Chapter Two evaluates how differences in political culture can affect democratic support and how these differences can be included in empirical tests.

Chapter Three presents the empirical model that explains democratic support in Central and Eastern Europe. The relationship between economic factors and support for democracy is assessed. A cross-sectional analysis of 1994 is used to examine the relationship between the extent of economic reform and support for democracy. In addition, a pooled cross-sectional design is implemented to capture patterns across countries and over time. Problems with the pooled cross-sectional analysis are discussed and addressed in a revised Least Square Dummy Variable Model. The empirical analyses are followed by a discussion of the implications of my findings in terms of economic policies for the Central and Eastern European countries.

Chapter Four serves as a brief introduction to the subsequent case studies. Chapters Five through Eight examine four countries: the Czech Republic, Slovakia, Lithuania, and Russia. These cases were chosen on the basis of the empirical model presented in Chapter Three. Each of these chapters investigates the economic factors for the particular country to see how well the country fits the general empirical model and its hypothesized relationships. Following that analysis is an assessment of that state's political culture as an additional explanation for democratic support.

4 *The Economy and Political Culture in New Democracies*

Chapter Nine discusses general conclusions drawn from both the generalized empirical model and the case study analysis. Policy implications, specifically in terms of economic policy, are offered that may aid the new democracies in their consolidation.

PART I
EMPIRICAL STUDY OF DEMOCRATIC SUPPORT

1 Democratic Consolidation and Mass Support

Introduction

The primary purpose of this research is to investigate the relationship between economic conditions (including popular perceptions of financial wellbeing) and mass support for democracy in Central and Eastern Europe. I argue that such support is necessary for the Central and Eastern European countries to remain democratic. Thus, this research falls under the broad rubric of the study of democratization.

The literature that examines democratization covers a plethora of definitions, explanatory factors, historical forces, and processes.[1] Why has so much of the scholarly community turned its attention to the study of democratization? In part, the focus is due to the undeniable empirical global trend toward democratization, which permits social scientists to reexamine the established theories regarding democratization as well as to develop strategies that might encourage the consolidation of newly democratic regimes. Furthermore, as Huntington (1991, 58) argues, democracy is 'the only legitimate and viable alternative to an authoritarian regime of any kind'.

Many theoretical, conceptual, and methodological issues surround the analysis of democratization. Definitions and measurements of democracy or democratization often vary according to what question is posed and what approach is taken. This chapter analyzes the literature that concentrates on the democratic consolidation process and the role of mass support in that process. It concludes with a systems approach toward the analysis of democratic support in Central and Eastern Europe.

Theoretical Frameworks of the Study of Democracy

The study of democracy is broad in scope; however, some predominant approaches have emerged in the literature. Shin asserts that 'there are four stages in democratization: 1) decay of authoritarian rule, 2) transition, 3) consolidation, and 4) the maturing of democracy' (1994, 143). This delineation is useful in its abstract logical sequencing; however, it is important to keep in mind that not all democratizing states follow this linear sequence. Rather, as Diamond argues (1992), some transitions fail immediately, while others decay rather than consolidate. Research has addressed all the stages of democratization, and the stage under examination is determined by the question that is posed. Reisinger asserts that 'the study of democratization is actually the study of two potentially distinct questions: What facilitates the replacement of one or another form of authoritarian rule with democratic institutions, norms, and procedures? And, what facilitates the consolidation of democracy?' (1997, 53). Thus, the following literature review will concentrate on the prevailing theoretical groupings that address these questions. (My research clearly focuses on the second of Reisinger's questions.)

Democratic Pre-Conditions

In the mid-1960s comparative sociology and politics began a reassessment of the study of social and political change. Currently, the predominant framework for examining the relationship of economic development, socio-cultural progress, and political institutional change is offered by the Modernization school. Seymour Martin Lipset's 'Some Social Requisites of Democracy: Economic Development and Political Legitimacy' posits that socio-economic development is a 'requisite' to democracy (1959). Lipset's (1960) findings indicate that societies characterized by higher levels of industrialization, urbanization, education, and wealth tend to be democratic. This hypothesis is supported by many empirical studies (Lipset,1959; Jackman, 1973; Bollen, 1979, 1983; Bollen and Jackman, 1985; Brunk, Caldeira, and Lewis-Beck, 1987; Arat, 1988; Gosnick and Rosh, 1988). In short, these scholars argue that the higher the level of socio-economic development, the more democratic the state. These studies have largely focused upon the institutional components of democratic systems.[2]

The empirical connection between socio-economic development and democracy has become what Burkhart and Lewis-Beck describe as an 'iron law' of political sociology (Burkhart and Lewis-Beck, 1994, 903). They argue that 'economic development consistently emerges as a statistically and substantively significant influence on democracy' (1994, 903). In addition, Brunk, Caldeira, and Lewis-Beck contend that economic development accounts for more variation in democracy than any other independent variable

(1987, 468). The most commonly cited reason for the importance of economic development is that well-being for the mass public increases the demand for political advantages of democracy (Dahl, 1989). Development, particularly economic development, creates a more complex and diverse society in which authoritarian rule is difficult to maintain (Lipset, 1960; Dahl, 1989; Huntington, 1991). In other words, as the masses reap the rewards of economic prosperity, they become less concerned with survival and more concerned with political freedom. Thus, a population's wealth becomes a calling card for democracy.

This 'liberal' Modernization hypothesis has withstood examination of increasingly sophisticated statistical analysis, and, as Brukhart and Lewis-Beck conclude, 'it is clear that economic development substantially improves a nation's democratic prospects'. However, exceptions to this empirical pattern have led some scholars to question the applicability of the thesis outside Western Europe and North America (O'Donnell, 1973, Diamond, 1992). Diamond (1992) argues that Lipset's own data reveal that Central and Eastern European states had achieved greater economic development than Latin American democracies. Prior to the collapse of Communism, the cases of Central and Eastern Europe were considered anomalous to the Modernization hypothesis. The Central and Eastern European states had achieved high levels of economic development, but they were non-democratic. However, the transitions of 1989 corrected for these anomalous cases.

The Modernization school appears to have two weaknesses with regard to examining the relationship between economics and democracy in Central and Eastern Europe. First, Lipset's hypothesis failed to explain why the Central and Eastern European countries did not become democratic until 1989. Why is it that the democratic transitions did not occur earlier? Second, more importantly, the Modernization school fails to account for democratic regime persistence; rather, it concentrates upon the emergence of democratic institutions. This criticism was leveled at the Modernization school in the 1970s when the second 'wave' of democracy was followed by a 'reverse' wave of democratic breakdown.

In what way can the Modernization school's view of the relationship between development and democracy further our understanding of the consolidation process in Central and Eastern Europe? Dahl (1971, 78)) argued that

> as countries with hegemonic systems move to high levels of economic development (for example, the USSR and the Eastern European countries) a centrally dominated social order is increasingly difficult to maintain. For if our argument

is correct, economic development itself generates the conditions of a pluralistic social order. The monopoly over socioeconomic sanctions enjoyed by the hegemonic leaders is therefore undermined by the very success of their economy: the more they succeed in transforming the economy (and with it, inevitably, the society) the more they are threatened with political failure.

This analysis can be appropriately applied to the collapse in 1989; however, it lacks explanatory and predictive power regarding consolidation. The Modernization hypothesis applied to Central and Eastern Europe is, according to Reisinger (1997, 58), that 'the most economically developed Eastern European and post-Soviet societies should have been the first to experience public pressure for democratization and should possess the best prospects for consolidating their democratic systems'. However, this has been only partially supported.[3] By extending the hypothesis to include consolidation, it can be argued that those states that were highly developed before transition contained the necessary preconditions for the continuation of democracy. Thus, development under Communist rule would have provided fertile soil for the maintenance of democracy.

Structural and Historical Approaches

The literature in this grouping is quite diverse theoretically and empirically. It has moved away from the necessary and sufficient conditions put forth by Modernization research. In general, this grouping examines the relationship of the state to society and/or the relationship of political change to external factors. Thus, this literature can be broken into a two sub-categories: 1) theoretical arguments addressing internal, domestic factors (such as civil society, the market, and class divisions) that foster democracy, and 2) studies that investigate external factors (international and economic pressures and 'snowballing' or diffusion) that lead to a breakdown in authoritarianism and the facilitation of a democratic regime.

The first set of theoretical arguments concerns the relationship between the state and society. Civil society is often pointed to as a necessary ingredient for both the breakdown of authoritarianism and the consolidation of democracy. Civil society, as defined by Keane (1988, 14), is 'an aggregate of institutions whose members are engaged primarily in a complex of non-state activities – economic and cultural production, household life and voluntary associations – and who in this way preserve and transform their identity by exercising all sorts of pressures or controls upon state institutions'. In terms of the removal of authoritarian regimes, the necessary pre-conditions that

Lipset spoke of – economic development, industrialization, urbanization, and education – lead theoretically to a strengthening of the independent organizations and associations. Civil society offers individuals alternative means of pursuing interests and eventually challenging authoritarian rulers, who consequently find it increasingly difficult to control their societies. Thus, civil society plays a critical role in the breakdown of authoritarianism (Diamond, 1992; Ekiert, 1991; Inkeles, 1991; Karl, 1990; Putnam, 1993).

Tocqueville considered civil society to be the foundation of democracy and believed it plays a clear role in the maintenance of a democratic regime. The existence of non-state associations and organizations helps to counterbalance the power of the state. Reisinger (1997) points out that 'modern state institutions concentrate so much potential power in the hand of top officials that corruption and other abuses of power become very tempting' (59). A strong, developed civil society offsets state power and allows for a continuation of democratic competition.

The role of the market in society-state relations is similar to that of civil society. Resinger argues that 'the private sector' is one distinct component of civil society (1997, 60). Regardless of whether it is part of or distinct from civil society, the theoretical argument concerning the market's influence is similar. Non-governmental economic activities foster competition among enterprises and among individuals for economic gain. The economic realm, therefore, provides a source of status and power apart from the state. And, as Ware (1988) asserts, non-state economic activities limit the state's ability to exclude groups from the political process. This argument, of course, is rebutted by those within the Marxist paradigm. Gramsci (1971), for example, argues that civil society strengthens state power and that wealth generated in the private economic sphere supports the state. He also asserts that independent societal associations serve to fortify the capitalist state and protect it from socialist influences. Similarly, Miliband (1973) maintains that the '"engineering of consent" in capitalist society is largely an unofficial enterprise' (165).

As previously mentioned, failed democratic transitions are often blamed on the fact that countries lack the necessary pre-conditions, such as a market economy and civil society, to remain democratic (Shin, 1994). In the case of Central and Eastern Europe, a market economy was nonexistent prior to recent restructuring efforts. Thus, drastic reform was required, even though the short-term economic and social costs of such efforts can be enormous and, ironically, can undermine democratic consolidation. At the same time, few independent civic organizations existed in Central and Eastern Europe, with the notable exceptions of the Catholic Church and Solidarity in Poland. In addition, the citizens in the region lacked the experience and widespread democratic values that abet the formation of such organizations. Thus, the countries were in a precarious position regarding consolidation.

Comparative historical studies have also focused upon the role of class in political change (Moore, 1966; Rueschemeyer, Stephens, and Stephens, 1992). Barrington Moore Jr.'s classic study *Social Origins of Dictatorship and Democracy* examines the historical relationship between 'landed nobility and the peasantry in the transformation from agrarian societies ... to modern industrial ones' (xi). Moore delineates three paths: 1) capitalist revolution from below that culminates in democratic social systems, 2) capitalist revolution from above that results in fascism, and 3) peasant revolution that produces communist societies. The first path requires a bourgeois revolution that leads to an industrial revolution in which 'a key feature ... is the development of a group in society with an independent economic base' (xv). This was experienced by states such as Great Britain, France, and the United States. In the second path, the revolution is led by the nobility rather than the bourgeois class, and industrialization takes place under their control. In such cases, democracy can be stillborn, and in some instance, such as Germany and Japan, 'abortive bourgeois revolutions' led to fascism (xvii). Russia and China exemplify Moore's third path of development. In those states, 'great agrarian bureaucracies' restrained commercial development to the point where 'urban classes were too weak to constitute even a junior partner' in the process of modernization. A huge peasantry continued to exist, and peasant revolution led to communism (xvi-xvii). Rueschemeyer, Stephens, and Stephens (1992) use Moore's framework to analyze democratization in Western Europe and Latin America. They examine class relations, state institutions, and international influences. Reisinger (1997, 63) summarizes their argument in terms of class:

> ... democratization is pushed by the subordinate classes in a society as a means to increase their power relative to the dominant class or classes. When conditions such as capitalist economic development provide a formerly nonexistent or politically uninvolved class with growing social power, that class will struggle to advance democratic forms of governance since those reduce, though by no means eliminate, the political power held by the upper classes.

Rueschmeyer, Stephens, and Stephens argue that an organized working class is critical to the development of democratic institutions. Their analysis, however, sets aside the Modernization assumption of the existence of a single set of causal factors. Thus, their rich theoretical development is achieved at the expense of generalizability. This is the major weakness of the historical approach in which 'each case is unique' (Skocpol and Somers, 1980, 192). In other words, 'historical cases may be used to point out the limits of received general theories, but for the most part the focus is not on theories or hypotheses or explanatory problems. Rather it is on the cases themselves and the contrast between and among them that underlie the uniqueness of each' (Skocpol and Somers, 192). And, as Frentzel-Zagorska points out, 'there are enough different theoretical approaches to the concept of "civil society" and enough varying historical contents of the notion to turn every work dealing with this subject into a philosophical and/or historical treatise devoted to conceptual variations and subtleties' (1992, 40).

For Central and Eastern Europe, the historical approach can assist us in understanding the present political dynamics. The suppression of civil society in these states by their totalitarianism regimes provided a common experience among the states, which allows for generalizability across the post-Communist systems. Thus, we can look for patterns across the present system, and we can also identify differences that may be attributed to a country's particular historical political development. For example, the historical approach applied to the Central and Eastern European states can aid our understanding of the political culture as well as the emerging party systems in these countries.

In addition to domestic internal factors, international influences of different kinds have both hindered and promoted democracy. Huntington (1991) and Whitehead (1986) argue that the international influences become important through the interaction of internal and external forces. It is obvious that some types of external influence, such as invasion and occupation, alter the existing regime. The most frequently noted example is the imposition of democracy upon Germany and Japan following WW II. In terms of hindering democracy, the Soviet invasions of Hungary in 1956 and Czechoslovakia in 1968 are clear cases. Soviet domination kept any democratization efforts in Central and Eastern Europe from coming to fruition during the Cold War at least until the late 1980s when, as DiPalma (1990, 184) argues, the USSR 'removed the veto'. However, the Soviet Union's role in democracy should not be underplayed by that phrase; rather, the liberalization efforts of Soviet leader Mikhail Gorbachev in an attempt to save Communism through reform had greater consequences than originally envisioned. The necessity for Gorbachev's reforms stemmed from a bankrupt, inefficient, centrally planned economy. The intensification of the arms race in the 1980s further strained economic productivity and available resources in the Soviet Union. Thus, US military buildup had an indirect, though salient, role in the collapse of the Soviet Union.

Research on international influences on democratization has examined the role of foreign policy, non-state international actors, and diffusion. American foreign policy analysts have argued that it is desirable for the United States to promote democracy internationally (Muravchik, 1991; Diamond, 1992, Allison and Beschel, 1992; Mroz, 1992/93; Lowenthal, 1991). This argument is based on both moral and realistic grounds. The moral ground – that democracy and, by extension, human rights are foreign policy goals in and of themselves – has been strongly supported in American political rhetoric (Whitehead, 1986; Huntington, 1991). The realist view in American foreign policy has posited that the promotion of democracy increases US national security and economic prosperity. The national security argument clearly suits the proponents of the view that democracies don't fight each other (Maoz and Russett, 1993; Mousseau, 1997). In addition, the promotion of the market in post-Communist states is viewed as aiding the international political economy. Regardless of the intentions behind the foreign policy goals, it is evident that the United States has played a role in the democratization of a number of states.[4] In addition, Western European countries have aided the newly democratizing states by offering 'financial assistance, technological advice, and constitutional guidance' (Grey, 1997, 250).[5]

Intergovernmental organizations as well as non-state transnational actors have also played a prominent role in the breakdown of authoritarianism and the promotion of democracy. Countries in transition have received direct support from groups such as the European Union (EU), the Organization of American States (OAS), and the World Bank (Shin, 1994; Lowenthal, 1991; Pastor, 1987). Along with financial aid, these organizations also furnish political incentives for countries to remain democratic. For example, one of the membership criteria for admittance to the EU is democracy. Democracy can be viewed as the only political alternative to gain membership in the elite international community. As Han (1990) puts it, 'democratization is the necessary ticket for membership in the club of advanced nations' (341). Furthermore, transnational actors, such as the Catholic Church, have played a role in furthering democracy, particularly in Latin America (Huntington, 1991; Grey, 1997). Grey (1997, 264) points out that although the suppression of religion under Communism made the Church less of a force in the Central and Eastern European transitions, its role in Poland has been similar to that in Latin America.

Yet another view of the international effects on the breakdown of authoritarianism and the spread of democracy is the diffusion effect (Huntington, 1991; Scalapino, 1992; Starr, 1991). This 'snowballing' has been observed in regions where democratic transitions in one state serve as a model for other transitions in the same region. The diffusion is clearly seen in the Central and Eastern European states, where democratic transitions took place in quick succession.

Transitions and Elite Bargaining

Research on transitions has concentrated on short-term political change and the role of individual leaders and elites in this process. The role of leadership in the initiation of transition is vital in that 'democratic regimes that last have seldom, if ever, been instituted by mass popular action' (Huntington, 1984, 212). This approach pushes aside the implied determinism of the structuralists and argues that states can achieve democracy without the necessary preconditions as long as there is agreement among elites. Reisinger asserts that this approach makes 'a genuine contribution by combating a sense of determinacy' (1997, 68).

Research in this area examines the transition stage as a series of steps in the bargaining of elites. Thus, democratization is characterized by the relationship between key individuals and the progressive sequencing of decisions made by these individuals. For democratization to take place, a sufficient number of elites must agree that democratic competition is the preferred means of decision-making. Burton, Gunther, and Higley (1992, 3) argue that 'a key to the stability and survival of democratic regimes is...the establishment of substantial consensus among elites concerning rules of the democratic political game and the worth of democratic institutions'. Ultimately, a winning coalition is needed which 'can emerge through settlement (a compromise) or convergence (intra-elite differences grow smaller)' (Reisinger, 1997, 66). O'Donnell, Schmitter, and Whitehead (1986), in investigating Latin American transitions, refer to these compromises as *pacts*, or *pactadura*. However, to achieve democracy, there can be little compromise about the rules of the game. As Przeworski (1986) points out, 'democracy means that all groups must subject their interests to uncertainty. It is the very act of alienation of control over outcomes of conflicts that constitutes the decisive step toward democracy' (58). Because of the uncertainty of policy outcomes inherent to the democratic process, elites must agree upon the institutions. Przeworski (1986, 60) addresses this critical agreement:

What is possible are institutional agreements, that is, compromises about the institutions that shape prior probabilities of the realization of group-specific interests. If a peaceful transition to democracy is to be possible, the first problem to be solved is how to institutionalize uncertainty without threatening the interests of those who can still reverse the process. The solution to the democratic compromise consists of institutions.

Reisinger points out that the uncertainty of outcomes raises the question of 'why should those in a position of authoritarian power ever agree to a new institutional arrangement that places them in a competitive situation, as democratic procedures must?' (1997, 67) He offers a number of scenarios in which elites may believe democracy is a necessary solution: 'a defeat in battle, enduring economic stagnation, vanishing popular legitimacy, a domestic guerrilla force, and the like' (1997, 68). Moreover, political incentives for democracy, such as foreign aid or the lure of positions of power in the new democratic regime, may prompt elites toward pacts. Research regarding elite bargaining, with its focus on individuals, has been important in understanding the political dynamics of transition. It has also led scholars to differentiate types of transitions (Huntington, 1991; Karl and Schmitter, 1991).

Huntington distinguishes among transitions from above (transformations), from opposition gaining control (replacements), and a combination of the two (transplacements). Karl and Schmitter (1991) also identify four 'modes' of transitions by determining whether they are mass or elite initiated and whether they come about by force or compromise. These modes of transition result in different regime types.[6] Karl finds that transitions that are elite directed and result through pacts are the most stable.

This elite bargaining approach has been applied to the transition of the Soviet Union (Bova, 1991). Bova analyzes the Soviet case by looking at four sets of actors: hard-liners, opponents of the regime, centrists for liberalization, and centrists for democratization. He asserts that the liberalizing reforms of Gorbachev led to a split in the elites in the USSR. Liberalization can release forces in which politics become radicalized – the center drops out and the situation becomes polarized between the hard-liners and opponents of the regime. Thus, Gorbachev's centrist position lost out to Yeltsin's more radical platform. Much of the literature using this framework has focused upon transitions in Latin America. Thus, more work can be done in exploring the applicability of this approach to Central and Eastern Europe.

In addition to examining transitions, research has also focused on the 'crafting' of democracies, emphasizing the importance of constitutional design for democratic consolidation (Lijphart, 1992). Reisinger argues that 'constitutional design is intimately connected to the intra-elite bargaining dynamic [in that]... the long-term goal of building an effective, stable, and democratic political order can serve as a public good that most of the competing elites hope will result from their bargaining' (1997, 71). The notion that institutions should match the conditions of any given society is not new. In his *Spirit of the Laws* Montesquieu argues that the 'general spirit' of a nation should be reflected in both the type of government and the laws that govern. More recently, Powell (1982) and Lijphart (1984) examine the relationship between institutional arrangement and how well a democracy performs. Decisions regarding the choice of a parliamentary or a presidential system, federal or unitary system, and the specifics of the electoral system are of vital importance to democratic consolidation, particularly in highly divided societies. Thus, the choice of institutions in Central and Eastern Europe is a salient issue.

Role of Mass Support

The Modernization school concerned itself with the necessary conditions for the emergence of democratic institutions, while transition research has focused on the role of leaders. However, my research concentrates on the consolidation process. Political leaders may be vital in the transition stage, but it is ultimately the masses that determine consolidation. Although the last thirty years have witnessed the largest wave towards democracy, democratic transitions have also tended to collapse (Huntington, 1984). The failure to consolidate is attributed to the lack of legitimacy for the regime (Arat, 1991), resulting from an incompatibility between the institutions and the values and norms of the society and/or the inability of the regime to meet social or economic needs of the citizens (including the failure to handle economic crisis effectively). Therefore, regime legitimacy is an integral part of consolidation.

In the cases of Central and Eastern Europe, it is important to examine not only the implementation of democratic institutions but also the support for democratic regimes. Many of the legal-institutional elements of democracy have been put in place formally in the Central and Eastern European countries. Rather than examining those institutions, my research focuses on mass support for democracy to gauge the consolidation process.

Legitimacy and Democratic Consolidation   To investigate democratic consolidation, one must examine the legitimization of democratic regimes, since authority ultimately depends upon the support of its citizens. What is legitimacy? Lipset offers this definition: 'the capacity of the system to engender and maintain the belief that the existing political institutions are the most appropriate for the society' (1959, 77). Juan Linz suggests a similar definition: 'the belief that in spite of shortcomings and failures, the political institutions are better than any others that might be established, and therefore can demand obedience' (1988, 65). Both of these definitions refer to 'belief' by the citizenry that the political system is an authority and should be obeyed. However, this belief is never unanimous within the population; rather, legitimacy should be thought of in terms of degrees along a continuum. Linz (1988, 66) asserts that 'no political regime is legitimate for 100 percent of the population, nor in all its commands, nor forever, and probably very few are totally illegitimate based on coercion'. In a democratic system, legitimacy must be widespread for regime survival.

It is the essence of democracy that a diversity of opinions and interests may be expressed and channeled through the political system. Some citizens may be satisfied and others dissatisfied with the current politics and/or government. However, dissatisfaction within a large segment of the populace with governmental performance does not necessarily indicate regime illegitimacy. As Lipset (1959) suggests, legitimacy entails popular support for the existing political system even when this support may not necessarily extend to particular incumbent political leaders. Changes in government occur through peaceful means and do not threaten the legitimacy of the system. The maintenance of legitimacy is less important for authoritarian regimes, since authority is not based on public support but, rather, on force. By examining legitimacy in terms of a continuum, a comparative analysis of the new democracies can be performed. The question becomes: How do new democracies foster support and, by extension, legitimacy for the regime? Two predominant frameworks address this question of mass support: the Culturalist approach and the Policy Outputs approach.

Political Culture and Support

The Culturalist approach emphasizes the congruence between mass values and political institutions. In other words, legitimacy results when institutions correspond to the social and political values of the citizens. For example, in long-standing Western European democracies, the social and political values have evolved over centuries to produce very stable, legitimate democratic institutions. There is widespread agreement among the people as to the appropriateness of their governmental institutions. Gabriel Almond and Sidney

Verba (1963) refer to the mass values of a political system as a country's political culture. This term political culture encompasses 'everything from beliefs in the legitimacy of the system itself to beliefs about the adequacy and appropriateness of political input structures, government policies, and the role provided for the individual in the political process' (Dalton, 1996, 263). Numerous definitions of political culture have appeared since the 1960s. Kavanagh (1983) counts more than 30 different ways of defining the concept. For political scientists, the dominant conceptualization is Almond's (1965) formulation: 'The political culture of a society consists of the system of empirical beliefs, expressive symbols, and values which define the situation in which political action takes place. It provides the subjective orientation to politics' (Pye and Verba, 1965, 513). However, political culture can also be thought of in an objective sense, i.e., in terms of political behavior (Fagen, 1969; Tucker, 1973). My preferred conceptualization is Archie Brown's (1984) definition of political culture: 'the subjective perception of history and politics, the fundamental beliefs and values, the foci of identification and loyalty, and the political knowledge and expectations which are the product of the specific historical experience of nations and groups' (2). This conceptualization allows not only for the subjective perceptions of politics but also for the historical aspect of political culture.

How is political culture linked to democracy? In *The Civic Culture* Almond and Verba analyze the impact of political culture on the stability and effectiveness of democracy across five states (US, Great Britain, West Germany, Italy, Mexico). They search for 'a democratic political culture – a pattern of political attitudes that foster democratic stability, that is some way "fits" the democratic political system' (1963, 473). Political culture involves the beliefs, attitudes, and orientations toward the politics and political system of a particular country. More specifically, Almond asserts that political culture consists of three components: 'system' culture, 'process' culture, and 'policy' culture (1980, 28). Almond defines these components as:

> The system culture ... includes the sense of national identity, attitudes toward the legitimacy of the regime and its various institutions, and attitudes toward the legitimacy and effectiveness of the incumbents of the various political roles. The process culture of a nation would include attitudes toward the self in politics (e.g., parochial-subject-participant), and attitudes toward other political actors (e.g., trust, cooperation, competence, hostility). The policy culture would consist of the distribution of preferences regarding the outputs and outcomes of politics, the ordering among different groupings in the population of such political values as welfare, security, and liberty.

The most important aspect of political culture for regime legitimacy is the 'system' culture or system affect. These attitudes towards the political system as a whole have a profound effect upon the fragility of democracy. Almond and Verba argue that regime support is necessary for democratic stability. They present empirical evidence that system affect is prevalent in the long-standing democracies (US and Britain). They further argue that it is the affective feelings that legitimize the regime and constrain expressions of discontent. For democratic consolidation, the most important of these attitudes is the generalized feelings toward the political system or system affect.

Ronald Inglehart defines culture as 'a system of attitudes, values, and knowledge that is widely shared within a society and transmitted from generation to generation' (1990, 18). The importance of this statement, in terms of analysis in Central and Eastern Europe, involves the transmission of attitudes and values over time. Inglehart's statement implies that the political culture of any particular state is relatively stable. Furthermore, Inglehart asserts that 'cultural theory implies that culture cannot be changed overnight ...but changing basic aspects of the underlying culture will take many years' (1990, 19). In addition, change in political culture is likely to occur intergenerationally rather than 'by the conversion of already-socialized adults' (1990, 19). In terms of the mutability of political culture, much has been made of the West German case. In a 1959 survey, for example, Almond and Verba found very low levels of system affect as measured by pride in governmental and political institutions. This low level of system affect (as compared to Great Britain and the US) led Almond and Verba to be skeptical in regards to the long-run stability of postwar democratic Germany. However, surveys conducted in 1978 demonstrated an increase in system affect in West Germany.[7] Thus, the political culture had changed over the nineteen-year period from one of widespread distrust in the system to one of greater pride in the system. In addition, Conradt (1980) argues that this change was due to favorable economic performance. 'Thus a system's high level of performance, its output, can over time "take on a life of its own," that is, become a symbol aiding in identification with the political institutions and processes of the regime' (Conradt, 1980, 222). In other words, positive economic performance altered the German political culture to one that is supportive of the democratic regime.

In applying this approach to Central and Eastern Europe, the idea of the relative stability of political culture over time needs to be considered. The Soviets subjected these states to resocialization and re-educational policies in an attempt to change divergent cultures toward a political culture of the 'socialist man'. However, Inglehart states that this effort was only partially successful.[8] And, 'despite massive efforts, these cultures showed considerable resistance to change; moreover, these changes took considerable time, largely occurring as intergenerational population replacement took place' (Inglehart, 1990 20). One would expect that these policies had some effect upon the traditional political cultures in these states, although the extent has not been clearly determined. In addition, if intergenerational change has occurred, we would expect, given fifty years of Communist rule, that the bulk of the population has been affected by these policies. This is not to say that traditional political cultures have been eliminated. On the contrary, since liberalization, states have looked to the past for national, cultural, and ethnic identity. This is evidenced by the number of national movements that emerged in the late 1980s as well as the resurgence of historical political parties. Thus, I expect that differences in traditional political cultures across Central and Eastern Europe will affect the support for the new democratic regimes. States in which the Soviets were less successful in their resocialization efforts will exhibit greater support for democracy, as will those with traditional political cultures that contain pluralistic values. Conversely, states in which the Soviets were more successful and/or in which traditional political cultures contain elements of authoritarianism will have low levels of support for democracy.

A second matter of importance in the political culture framework is the idea of change through favorable governmental performance. If the Central and Eastern European states can successfully transform their economies and foster positive economic performance, then those states lacking a democratic political culture can develop the norms and values congruent to the democratic institutions. The Policy Outputs approach examines the impact of economics on support.

Policy Outputs and Support

The Policy Outputs approach argues that governmental policies affect the level of support for a regime. Easton develops a framework for analyzing political support (1965, 1975), which distinguishes between objects of support (political authorities, the regime, and the political community) and types of support (specific and diffuse) within and for a political system. Political authorities are political elites and officeholders. Support is directed at particular individuals or groups of individuals. Regime support involves citizens' attitudes towards governmental institutions and procedures rather than the individuals that hold office. In addition, regime support encompasses citizens' attitudes towards the principles of the regime, such as beliefs in pluralist democracy.

Easton argues that this distinction between objects of support is crucial because of the political implications of citizen dissatisfaction. For example, dissatisfaction with political authorities may lead to an election loss for incumbents. Loss of support for officeholders does not indicate dissatisfaction with the institutions and/or political system as a whole. However, negative attitudes regarding the regime and/or political community may have much more severe political implications. Easton asserts that 'not all expressions of unfavorable orientations have the same degree of gravity for a political system. Some may be consistent with its maintenance; others may lead to fundamental change' (Easton, 1975, 437). Weakening of regime support and/or support for the political community may result in a challenge to the institutional structures and possibly revolution or civil war. In a democratic system the consequences of dissatisfaction with the regime may be an increase in repression and a backsliding towards authoritarianism. In terms of democratic consolidation, the most important political consequences are those that halt the consolidation process and lead to the breakdown of democracy.

Along with the differentiation between objects of support, Easton delineates two types of political support: specific support and diffuse support. This distinction is important in terms of political consequences. Specific support corresponds to evaluations of political authorities. It involves citizens' assessment of both the policies and performance of political elites. Thus, governmental officials are held responsible for particular policy decisions.

Accountability research, specifically in terms of 'economic voting' literature, suggests that economic downturns punish incumbent governments. This proposition is well tested in the case of American politics (Key, 1966; Fiorina, 1978, 1981; Kinder and Kiewiet, 1979, 1981; Kiewiet, 1983; Kramer, 1983; Markus, 1988). However, the accountability of particular governments for poor economic performance does not necessary indicate a decline in support for the regime. Although specific incumbent governments may be punished for poor economic performance, long-standing, effective democratic regimes can withstand short-term economic downturns. In other words, the performance of a government may be deemed unsatisfactory, but the 'rules of the game' and the appropriateness of the system do not come under question.

In order for consolidation to continue, the political system must have what Easton terms diffuse support. Diffuse support involves the generalized attitudes toward the political system or a 'commitment to the political system that transcends the actual behavior of government' (Dalton, 1996, 264). If diffuse support exists, regimes are able to weather periods of dissatisfaction. The Central and Eastern European states have no track record of long-term effectiveness to carry the regimes through periods of economic crises. Thus, it is reasonable to assume that not only specific governments but also the regime itself will be held responsible for economic performance. In other words, the performance of the economy will influence citizens' evaluations of the political system in its entirety as well as incumbent governments (Anderson and Guillory, 1997).

Adam Przeworski applies the Policy Outputs approach to Central and Eastern Europe by examining the relationship between economic reform and democratic consolidation. He argues that successful market transition is necessary for regime consolidation and, after examining the types of economic reform strategies, concludes that radical reform achieves not only economic success but also democratic legitimacy in the long run. However, the short-run consequences of economic restructuring can threaten the consolidation process. Tóka (1996, 355) summarizes Przeworski's model of the relationship between Policy Outputs and democratic consolidation as:

> popular dissatisfaction with Policy Outputs → introduction of economic reforms → dissatisfaction with the initial results of reforms → slow down of reform → declining efficiency of economic policy decisions → popular dissatisfaction with economic Policy Outputs → loss of legitimacy → which leads (under certain circumstances) to serious challenges to democratic consolidation.

This model assumes that support and legitimacy are derived from specific policies and their consequences. Other recent research has also investigated the relationship between economic reforms and democratic consolidation (Pereira, Maravall, and Przeworski, 1993; Haggard and Kaufman, 1992; Geddes, 1995; Nelson, 1994). These studies argue that the social and economic consequences of economic restructuring threaten the democratic consolidation process. Latin American cases suggest that economic restructuring can lead to internal political conflict and deterioration of democracy (Haggard and Kaufman, 1992; Pereira, Maravall, and Przeworski, 1993). In addition, market-oriented austerity measures often entail decreases in state social spending, which can lead to civil discontent (Nelson, 1994). Thus, a linkage between economic reforms (and the resulting social and economic consequences) to democratic support and consolidation is established.

Model for Central and Eastern Europe

A synthesis of the Culturalist and the Policy Outputs approaches must be made in order to understand and to explain democratic support. Easton's general political system model offers a framework for incorporating both approaches. In Easton's model, specific support for political authorities results from the government's Policy Outputs that satisfactorily meet the demands of the populace. However, in the new democracies, where the basic political attachments are not deeply rooted, I expect that the Policy Outputs will affect not only specific support but also diffuse support. Thus, the Easton model is modified in that the Policy Outputs have a direct and real effect upon the regime support.

Figure 1.1: System Support Model

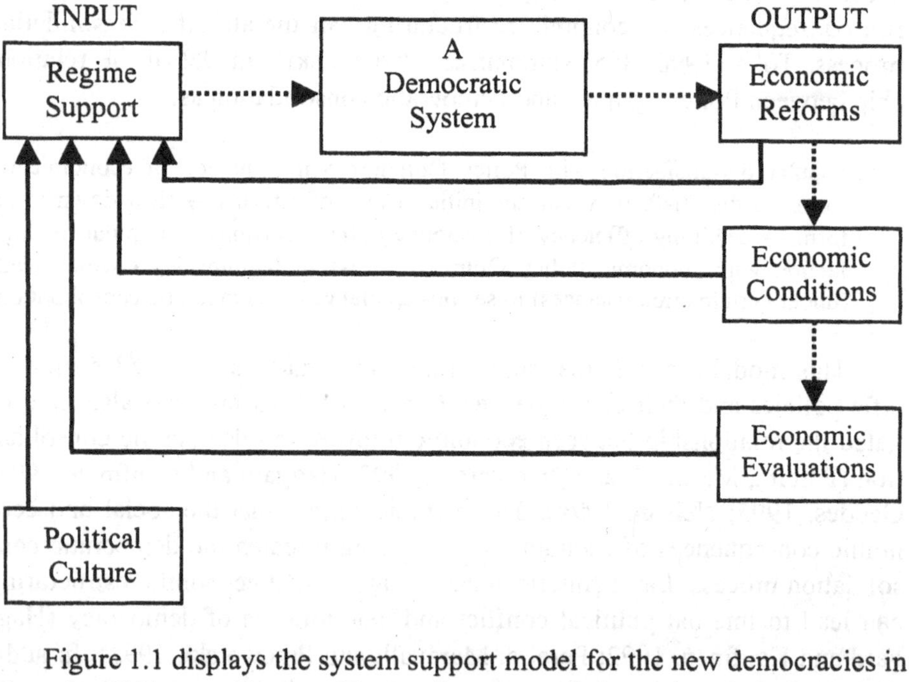

```
   INPUT                                           OUTPUT
 ┌──────────┐      ┌──────────────┐          ┌──────────┐
 │ Regime   │·····▶│ A Democratic │·········▶│ Economic │
 │ Support  │      │   System     │          │ Reforms  │
 └──────────┘      └──────────────┘          └──────────┘
      ▲                                            │
      │                                            ▼
      │                                      ┌──────────┐
      │◀─────────────────────────────────────│ Economic │
      │                                      │Conditions│
      │                                      └──────────┘
      │                                            │
      │                                            ▼
      │                                      ┌──────────┐
      │◀─────────────────────────────────────│ Economic │
      │                                      │Evaluations│
      │                                      └──────────┘
      │
 ┌──────────┐
 │ Political│
 │ Culture  │
 └──────────┘
```

Figure 1.1 displays the system support model for the new democracies in Central and Eastern Europe. The performance of the regime is indicated by the economic reforms, the economic conditions, and the citizens' evaluations of their financial situation. The economic reforms refer to the Policy Outputs of the new democratic system. In Central and Eastern Europe, the economic reforms are aimed at a complete restructuring of the collapsed command economy, which provides a basis for citizens' judgments about how well the regime is performing. Economic well-being is measured by the citizens' evaluations of their financial situation. Thus, using this system model of regime support, hypotheses are derived regarding the relationships between the economic policies and support, the economic conditions and support, and the economic evaluations and support.

H_1: *If the level of economic reform increases, then satisfaction with democracy decreases.*

H_2: *If economic conditions deteriorate, then satisfaction with democracy decreases.*

H_3: *If citizens' evaluate their financial situation optimistically, then satisfaction with democracy increases.*

H_4: *If future financial uncertainty increases, then satisfaction with democracy decreases.*

These hypotheses express the expected relationships of the Policy Outputs approach to democratic support. Detailed explanations of the hypothesized relationships are presented in Chapter Two. I expect, given the austerity of the reforms and the severity of the conditions, that economic factors are the primary determinants of regime support. However, these political systems do not exist in a vacuum. Easton argues 'it would be wrong to consider that the level of support available to a system is a function exclusively of the outputs in the form of either sanctions or rewards' (1965, 397). Furthermore, he argues that system support flows from 'the process of politicization', which involves the basic political attachments and values and norms of the society, or political culture.

The incorporation of political culture as an additional explanation for democratic support has been neglected somewhat in research examining the new democracies of Central and Eastern Europe, largely due to the Communist legacy and the collateral assumption of the dearth of 'alternative' political cultures. However, I anticipate some impact from traditional values and norms, which I expect to differ to a certain extent across the region. In addition, the political cultures across this region vary, and I anticipate that these differences will translate into higher or lower levels of support for democracy. Political culture can serve as a reservoir of support in difficult economic times. Countries that have had some past experience with the democratic regime or that have pluralistic traditional values are likely to have higher levels of regime support than those that lack experience and/or are more authoritarian in their values and norms. Thus, the Culturalist approach to democratic support is incorporated into the Policy Outputs model to obtain a fuller explanation of democratic support.

Notes

1. Scott Mainwaring (1992) refers to the study of democracy and democratization as a 'veritable growth industry' in 'Transition to Democracy and Democratic Consolidation: Theoretical and Comparative Issues,' in *Issues in Democratic Consolidation*, Scott Mainwaring, Guillerimo O'Donnell, and J. Samuel Valenzuela, eds.
2. Numerous measures of democracy have been constructed (Cutright, 1963; Cutright and Wiley, 1969; Banks, 1971; Dahl, 1971; Bollen, 1980; Gastil, 1987). These measures consist primarily of institutional practices and guarantees such as free elections, effective parliaments, political rights, and civil liberties. In addition, many of these measures combine political democracy and stability. That is, they merge the measure of democracy with years of democracy (democratic experience) into a single index (Lipset, 1959, 1981; Cutright, 1963; Cutright and Wiley, 1969; Coulter, 1975; Muller, 1988).
3. Reisinger argues that 'the early establishment of democratic movements in Poland, Hungary, and the Baltic countries as well as the relatively late appearance of democratic pressure in the Balkan and Central Asian regions and that ... democratic movements in Armenia and Georgia got underway before those in more industrialized and better educated Russia, Ukraine, and Byelarus' provides for only a weak relationship between economic development and democracy (1997, 58).
4. Shin (1994) states that 'US diplomatic and economic pressure has been critical to the democratization of a number of countries, including Bolivia, Chile, El Salvador, Honduras, Kenya, Korea, Nigeria, and the Philippines' (153).
5. Other recent research that examines Western European aid to Central and Eastern Europe includes: Höhmann, Meier, and Timmerman, 1993; Koch, 1993; Pridham and Vanhanen, 1994; Pridham, Herring, and Sanford, 1994.
6. The four types of regimes are: conservative democracy, corporatist democracy, competitive democracy, and one-party dominant regimes.
7. David Condradt's 'Changing German Political Culture' in *The Civic Culture Revisited* (Gabriel A. Almond and Sidney Verba, eds.), states that 'the most striking feature of these data is the increase in pride in the political system and institutions in the Federal Republic from only 7 percent in 1959 to 31 percent in 1978'.
8. Research on Communist political cultures has addressed the compatibility between 'traditional' political cultures and the Communist political culture as well as the success of adapting the Communist political culture to states (Barghoorn, 1965; Fagen, 1969; Solomon, 1971; Tucker, 1973, 1987; Brown, 1979; 1984; White, 1979). Brown argues that the Soviets were less successful in states such as Czechoslovakia, where the traditional political culture is pluralistic in nature. In addition, White (1979) argues that the Soviets were able to utilize aspects of traditional Russian political culture to legitimize the Communist regime.

2 Measurement and Data

Most Similar Systems Design

This chapter presents the conceptualization, operationalization, and measurement of support for democracy and the factors that are hypothesized to influence it. The Central and Eastern European transitions offer an opportunity to investigate the practical and theoretical significance of dual transformations. In limiting my sample to the Central and Eastern European region, my analysis does not allow for a truly comparative study, in the sense that findings pertain to this region alone. Many would argue that this study is not generalizable to all states consolidating democracy. However, by examining these cases, a step can be made toward a more general theory of transitions.

This study utilizes the most similar systems design (Przeworski and Teune, 1970), which allows the investigator to examine a particular set of states with intermediary factors that may influence the occurrence of particular phenomena. In the case of Central and Eastern Europe, the intermediary factors include: 1) Communist control for at least forty years, 2) domination of the Soviet Union both politically and militarily, and 3) isolation from the West. By examining countries that fall within this particular set, one can control for these intermediary factors. The most similar systems design is a first step in a more generalizable theory of democratic consolidation, in that factors influencing the consolidation process in Central and Eastern Europe may also be evident in post-transitional states in other regions.

Use of the most similar systems design makes it possible to look for patterns across states. This study investigates the pattern of economic influences on democratic consolidation. In addition, it is a 'systems' design, meaning that it analyzes the aggregate level. By using a cross-national, aggregate level design, one can uncover patterns across the region of post-Communist countries. Measurement of variables must be reflective of the type of design. This study aggregates the Central and Eastern Euro-Barometer surveys by constructing a weighted average, which provides a country/year measure. Thus, the unit-of-analysis is country/year in the analysis for democratic support.

Democratic Support

Conceptualization

Most empirical studies of democratization, as evidenced by the Modernization school, have focused on the presence of democratic institutions. This legal/institutional framework is reflected in the various measures of democracy, which can be utilized to assess the progress of political transitions in Central and Eastern Europe. However, my research does not investigate the drawing up of constitutions or the granting of civil liberties. Rather, I assume that most democratic political institutions have been established. Of course, not all institutions have been put in place in all the Central and Eastern European countries, and questions have been raised about the fairness of some elections and the human rights practices in some states. However, democratization is an evolutionary process, and it is reasonable to argue that these states are functioning democracies.

Rather than concentrating on the legal/institutional framework, I have adopted a second perspective to analyze the legitimacy of the democratic regime. In terms of democratic consolidation, I argue that the extent of legitimacy can be assessed by examining the extent to which citizens support democracy. Since, in the long run, democratic institutions can only be sustained if they are accepted and supported by the citizens, mass support of the citizenry is an appropriate indicator of the level of legitimacy of a particular regime.

Measurement of Democratic Support

The conceptualization of democratic consolidation in terms of mass support requires a measure that is distinct from institutional or procedural measures. Because democratic consolidation is linked to the legitimacy of the regime, the measurement should attempt to capture citizens' attitudes toward the regime. Dogan (1994) argues that 'the concept of legitimacy can be tested empirically by survey, research on confidence in institutions, trust of leaders and support for the regime'. I measure democratic support by using surveys administered in the Central and Eastern European countries. The data are obtained from the Central and Eastern Euro-Barometer 1-5: 1990-1994. These data are multistage national probability samples. Specifically, democratic support is measured from the question that asks:

How satisfied are you with democracy? very satisfied, fairly satisfied, not very satisfied, not at all satisfied.

Thus, citizen support for democracy is measured by the level of satisfaction with the regime. A weighted average for each country/year is created as a composite score. This was done by assigning a weight for each category.

Table 2.1 Example of Weighted Average of Democratic Support for Albania 1994

Categories	Weight	# of Respondents	% of Respondents
Very Satisfied	4	74	7.16
Fairly Satisfied	3	276	26.69
Not Very Satisfied	2	484	46.81
Not at all Satisfied	1	186	17.99
Total		1020	98.65

Demo. Satisfaction = (Weight)(# of Respondents) / total # of Respondents
= (4*74) + (3*276) + (2*484) + (1*186) / 1020
= 2.23

From the example, we see that the aggregate response score of democratic satisfaction for Albania in 1994 is 2.23. The theoretical range for the average democratic satisfaction measure is from 1 to 4. An aggregate score of 1 indicates that all respondents are not at all satisfied with democracy in that particular country and year and that support for the regime is nonexistent. Similarly, an aggregate score of 4 indicates that all respondents are very satisfied with democracy for that particular country and year and the regime is strongly supported and legitimate. The actual range of the data is 1.54 (Bulgaria 1994) to 3.21 (Czechoslovakia 1990). The average aggregate score of democratic satisfaction for the entire sample is 2.11. Because the unit of analysis is country/year, the weighted average provides a measure of the overall level of democratic satisfaction of the citizens of a given country. This makes it possible to examine support across post-Communist states. This weighted average is calculated for all countries included in the Central and Eastern European Euro-Barometers.[1] It indicates that, on average across Central and Eastern Europe, there is room for improvement in citizens' satisfaction with the new democratic regime.

Determinants of Regime Support

I expect that support for democracy in Central and Eastern Europe is determined by the level of economic reform, economic conditions, citizens' evaluations of their own financial situation, and the subjective norms and values of a particular society. Given the Policy Outputs approach, I expect that the economic factors will be the primary determinants of democratic support in Central and Eastern Europe. In addition, I expect that specific political cultures that are overtly authoritarian or pluralistic in nature will influence support for democracy [See Figure 1.1].

Citizens, in evaluating the effectiveness of the regime, respond to the economic environment, which includes the economic reforms (success or failure), the objective economic conditions, the citizens' evaluations of their own financial situation, and the perceived financial uncertainty. The following section discusses the measurement of the economic environment. The expected relationship between each of the economic variables and support for democracy is given. Five economic variables are operationalized: level of economic reform, change in percentage real gross domestic product (GDP), consumer prices (inflation), citizens' personal financial evaluations, and personal financial uncertainty.

Economic Reform

The Policy Outputs approach argues that support for the democratic regime is affected by dissatisfaction resulting from economic restructuring. Since the post-Communist states faced conversion of their economies from a centrally planned to a market system, they were required to undergo large-scale economic reforms. Przeworski (1991) argues that, in the short term, citizens will be dissatisfied with such economic restructuring because of the resulting economic dislocations. Although the economic reforms are necessary in the long run, the short-term social and economic disruptions threaten democratic support and the consolidation process. I expect those states that are further along in the economic transition to have less support for democracy in the short run; however, they will have greater support in the long run. Since this research analyzes the relationship between economic reform and democratic support for 1994, I expect that the short-term relationship will hold. In other words, I anticipate that greater levels of economic reform result in less support for democracy.

Measurement of Economic Reform A reform index measures the extent that the Central and Eastern European countries have transformed their economies. The data for this measure are taken from the *Transition Report* (October 1994) issued by the European Bank for Reconstruction and Development (EBRD). Bank experts rate progress toward a market economy in 25 Central and Eastern European countries. They evaluate six economic areas: 1) privatization of large-scale enterprises, 2) privatization of small-scale enterprises, 3) restructuring of companies, 4) price liberalization and competition, 5) trade and foreign exchange system, and 6) banking reform.[2]

Each category is rated on a scale of 1 to 4. A score of 1 indicates little progress in terms of reform. A score of 4 indicates that the economic area has been transformed to a market economy. An index of extent of reform toward the market is created by adding the scores across all six areas. The theoretical range for the economic reform index is 6 to 24. A score of 6 indicates little progress in economic transition. A score of 24 indicates full transition to a market economy. The actual range of the economic reform data is 8 (Ukraine and Georgia) to 21 (Czech Republic). The mean score of economic reform is 15.94. The data are available only for the year 1994.

Theoretically, I expect that the greater the amount of reform toward the market the higher democratic satisfaction will be in the long run. Those states that make the economic transition quickly and have a functioning market in place are likely to rebound economically from the restructuring and are better able to weather the short-term costs. However, while the amount of reform toward the market is an indicator of successful governmental performance, the social and economic costs of restructuring can initially lead to citizen dissatisfaction with the democratic regime. Since the long-term consequences of the economic restructuring remain to be seen in most of Central and Eastern Europe, I expect that the economic transitions will, in the short term, produce a negative evaluation of democracy. Thus, the amount of reform toward the market should negatively effect the level of democratic satisfaction. This relationship is expressed in the following hypothesis:

H_1:   *If the level of economic reform increases, then satisfaction with democracy decreases.*

Objective Economic Conditions

The economic environment can either promote or compromise support for democracy. Favorable economic performance not only benefits particular governmental officials but also gives credence to the effectiveness of the regime. As in the case of postwar West Germany, long-term economic achievements can help to legitimatize the regime. Given that the Central and Eastern European democracies do not have the benefit of long-term effectiveness, I expect the regime to be particularly sensitive to economic conditions. The new democracies do not have a reservoir of legitimacy to fall back upon in times of economic crisis. Thus, the state of the economy is one means for the populace to judge the regime.

Two variables are used to measure aggregate economic conditions: percentage change in real GDP and inflation. Although both indicators are macroeconomic, inflation affects individuals directly. Sources for both indicators are: The International Monetary Fund (IMF); the World Bank; the Organization for Economic Cooperation and Development (OECD); and the EBRD.[3]

Gross Domestic Product The GDP measure is the percentage change in real gross domestic product. GDP measures the macroeconomic situation for each country for each year (1990-1994). Because of the economic transition, output has fluctuated dramatically in Central and Eastern Europe. The percentage change in real GDP ranges from -52 percent (Armenia 1992) to 11 percent (Albania 1993). The reported mean percentage change in real GDP is -9.58, indicating that, on average, output in Central and Eastern Europe has dropped significantly. This measure demonstrates the magnitude and direction of change in economic output.[4]

Consumer Prices Inflation is measured by annual percentage change in retail consumer prices. The range for the increase in consumer prices is 9 percent (Slovakia 1992) to 10,996 percent (Armenia 1993). The reported mean inflation is 849 percent. There are two extreme cases of hyperinflation: 1) Armenia 1993 (10,996 percent), and 2) Ukraine 1993 (10,155 percent). If these cases are excluded, the mean is 545.13 percent. We see that even with the extreme cases removed, hyperinflation has been prevalent in post-transitional Central and Eastern Europe.

Given the poor state of the transition economies, I expect that the citizens will have a negative evaluation of the regime's performance. The expected statistical relationship between economic conditions and democratic satisfaction is positive. This is expressed in the following hypotheses:

H_2: *If economic conditions deteriorate, then satisfaction with democracy decreases.*

H$_{2a}$: *If percentage change in real GDP decreases, then satisfaction with democracy decreases.*

H$_{2b}$: *If inflation is high, then satisfaction with democracy decreases.*

Citizens' Evaluations of Financial Situation

Two variables are used to measure individuals' perceptions of economic conditions: personal financial evaluations and personal financial uncertainty. Citizens' perceptions of their own economic situations impact their satisfaction with both the government and the regime. Moreover, individuals' evaluations of the economic situation may not be reflective of the actual state of the economy and may have even greater impact upon support for the government and democracy than the actual economic conditions. Perceptions of poor economic conditions may become exaggerated. Negative economic evaluations may be much greater than the actual existing economic conditions. In addition, negative perceptions may linger in citizens' minds after the actual economic conditions have begun to improve.

Citizens' Financial Evaluations The first variable that is used to measure perception of economic conditions is citizens' financial evaluations. Like democratic support, the measure of financial evaluations is obtained from the Central and Eastern Euro-Barometer 1-5 (1990-1994). The data are collected from the question that asks:

Compared to 12 months ago, do you think the financial situation has gotten: a lot better, a little better, stayed the same, a little worse, a lot worse?

The weighted average is an aggregate level measure for current financial evaluation. Because the unit of analysis is country/year, the weighted average provides a measure of the level of financial evaluation for all respondents. The weighted average is calculated for all countries included in the Central and Eastern European Euro-Barometers.

Similar to the measure of democratic support, a weighted average for each country/year was created as a composite score. This was done by assigning a weight to each category. The theoretical range for the aggregate current financial evaluation measure is from 1 to 5. An aggregate score of 1 indicates that all respondents perceive their financial situation as having gotten a lot worse in the last 12 months in that particular country. Similarly, an aggregate score of 5 indicates that all respondents perceive their financial situation as having gotten a lot better in the last 12 months in that particular country. The actual range for financial evaluations is 1.67 (Ukraine 1993) to 3.51 (Albania 1992). The reported mean for the data is 2.37. This indicator provides a measure of the aggregate of individuals' perceptions of their current financial situation in comparison to the previous year.

Table 2.2 Example of Weighted Average of Financial Evaluations for Albania 1994

Categories	Weight	# of Respondents	% of Respondents
A Lot Better	5	88	8.51
A Little Better	4	479	46.32
Stay the Same	3	290	28.05
A Little Worse	2	116	11.22
A Lot Worse	1	55	5.32
Total		1028	99.42

Financial Evaluations = (Weight)(# of Respondents) / total # of Respondents
$$= (5*88) + (4*479) + (3*290) + (2*116) + (1*55) / 1028$$
$$= 3.42$$

I expect that financial evaluations have an effect on governmental support, as they do on regime support. I expect a positive statistical relationship between financial evaluations and satisfaction with democracy. The relationship is expressed in the following hypothesis:

H_3:   *If citizens evaluate their financial situation optimistically, then satisfaction with democracy increases.*

Citizens' Financial Expectations The second variable of citizens' perceptions of the economic situation is uncertainty of their financial situation. This variable is derived from a survey question that asks how individuals expect their financial situation to be in the next 12 months. This indicator is also obtained from the Central and Eastern European Euro-Barometer 1-5 (1990-1994). The data are collected from the question which asks:

In the next 12 months, do you expect your financial situation to get: a lot better, a little better, stay the same, a little worse, a lot worse ?

Initially, a weighted average as an aggregate level measure for citizens' financial expectations was constructed. However, measurement and utility problems arose in the use of this expectation variable.

In terms of measurement, each of the weighted averages for the variables taken from the Euro-barometer surveys is formulated from respondent categories for each question. However, the surveys also included an additional category of *don't know*. When creating these measures the respondents answering *don't know* were excluded from the weighted average. This is common practice when formulating composite scores from survey data (Warwick and Lininger, 1975). As a rule-of-thumb, *no answer* or *don't know* categories are excluded as long as the percentage of respondents for these categories do not exceed 10 percent. The process of eliminating *no answer* and *don't know* categories in coding survey data is know as 'zeroing out' (Warwick and Lininger, 1975). However, if the percentage of respondents answering *don't know* or *no answer* is large, it may be an indication of uncertainty. This appears to be the case in the measurement of personal financial expectations.

For each year, the average percentage of *don't know* for all countries exceeds the 10 percent cut-off: 11.3 percent for 1990, 15.1 percent for 1991, 12.4 percent for 1992, 12.4 percent for 1993, 12.4 percent for 1994. The percentage of *don't know* responses is as high as 26.2 percent for Russia in 1993. Conventional coding practices suggest that an additional category may be needed to cover all possible answers for a given question. However, the categories (a lot better, a little better, the same, a little worse, a lot worse) used in the surveys can be assumed to be exhaustive and mutually exclusive. Thus, the high percentages of *don't know* suggest a degree of uncertainty regarding future financial situation. This conclusion is reasonable given the questions surrounding the transition economies.

Other than the issue of high percentages of *don't know* answers, the expectation survey question closely corresponds to the evaluations survey question. The weighted averages for financial evaluations and financial expectations are correlated to determine how closely related they are. A correlation matrix for all of the economic independent variables checks for multicollinearity between the variables. The four economic independent variables (GDP, inflation, financial evaluations, financial expectations) are correlated and displayed in Table 2.3.

From the correlation matrix, it should be noted that financial evaluations and financial expectations are highly correlated (.915). This high correlation indicates that the two independent variables are extremely close in measurement. Indeed, the use of only one of these variables is sufficient. When two independent variables are highly interrelated, the second will be explaining the same variation as the first (Blalock, 1979). Therefore, the financial expectations variable, measured as a weighted average, is dropped from the regression analyses in Chapter Three. However, the *don't know* category of responses, discussed below, raises some interesting theoretical possibilities.

Table 2.3 Correlation Matrix of Economic Independent Variables

	GDP	Inflation	Financial Evaluations	Financial Expectations
GDP	1.000	-0.611	0.612	0.568
Inflation	-0.611	1.000	-0.453	-0.522
Financial Evaluations	0.612	-0.453	1.000	0.915
Financial Expectations	0.568	-0.522	0.915	1.000

Future Financial Uncertainty A great deal of political and societal uncertainty exists in states that recently have undergone a regime transition. The collapse of political and economic structures removes feelings of security held by the populace and replaces them with doubt and suspicion. For the new democracies of Central and Eastern Europe, this insecurity may be particularly prevalent. Under Communism the state provided basic needs such as housing, job security, and health care. However, in the post-transitional era, these 'securities' no longer exist. Consequently, financial uncertainty among the populace may be very significant in terms of governmental and democratic support. Thus, the second variable of citizens' perceptions is future financial uncertainty. It is measured as the percentage of respondents answering *don't know* to the Euro-Barometer question which asks:

In the next 12 months, do you expect your financial situation to get: a lot better, a little better, stay the same, a little worse, a lot worse, don't know?

A high percentage of respondents answering *don't know* indicates that individuals are uncertain in regards to their future financial situation. The theoretical range for financial uncertainty is 0 percent to 100 percent. No respondents answering *don't know* indicates perfect certainty of future financial situation. One hundred percent of respondents answering *don't know* indicates perfect uncertainty of future financial situation. The actual range of the data is 2.3 percent (Hungary 1990) to 26.22 percent (Russia 1993). The mean future financial uncertainty is 12.74 percent.

I expect that uncertainty about the future will affect regime support. I expect a negative statistical relationship between financial uncertainty and satisfaction with democracy. This relationship is expressed in the following hypothesis:

H_4: *If uncertainty over the financial future increases, then satisfaction with democracy decreases.*

Control Variables

Political Culture The relationship between a particular political culture and a given political system can be viewed in terms of compatibility. The likelihood of successful democratic consolidation increases in countries in which the values and beliefs of the citizenry are congruent with the democratic institutions. The most similar systems design suggests that the history of Soviet domination is controlled for across the set of post-Communist states. However, this design does not control for cultural differences or political attitudes across these countries. Although I expect the economic factors to be the primary influence on democratic satisfaction, the Culturalist approach offers an alternative rival hypothesis for regime support. Lacking an adequate measure of democratic political culture, I attempt to control for cultural influences with dichotomous variables for each country. The expectation is that states with a traditional dominant political culture that is harmonious with a democratic political system are likely to have higher regime support. Conversely, states in which the Communist political culture was successfully adopted and/or the traditional political cultural is dissonant with the democratic system are likely to have lower regime support.

Time In Central and Eastern Europe, I expect that legitimacy will be at its highest immediately following transition, regardless of the economic performance. Moreover, public support for the regime will decay, rather than accumulate, over some short period of time. During the initial period of economic restructuring, the new democracies may experience a 'honeymoon period', in which the regime is not held responsible for economic malperformance (Balecerowicz, 1995). Weil (1989, 695) defines this honeymoon period as the equivalent of an accumulated reservoir of regime support, which may have two sources. First, inefficiency, mismanagement, and corrupt practices within the centrally planned economic structure may lead the populace initially to place the blame for economic woes on the Communist regime. Second, Weil argues that citizens 'may extend credit to an unproven regime or make "advance payment" to the reservoir' of regime support (Weil, 1989, 699). This 'extended credit' may be a result of the Communist's discredit. However, memories are short-lived, and this extended credit is limited. Thus, a decline in democratic satisfaction is expected shortly after the honeymoon period expires.

A control variable for time is included in the analysis to test for a decline in support. Theoretically, I expect that democratic satisfaction is highest at the time of transition. Citizens are carried away on a wave of euphoria, and this euphoria is manifested in the honeymoon period. As the euphoria wanes, we would expect a natural decrease in satisfaction level. This relationship is expressed in the following hypothesis:

H_5:   *As time from transition increases, satisfaction with democracy decreases.*

Of course, this hypothesis is conditioned on the time frame of this particular study. Over a longer period, I would expect democratic satisfaction to rise. It is likely that this hypothesis applies only to the first decade following transition.

Notes

1   The weighted averages are reported in Appendix Two.
2   Appendix One provides the rating categories for the economic reform index.
3   These data are reported in Appendix Two.
4   This percentage change in real GDP is used in the cross-sectional analysis for 1994. Since the cross-sectional analysis is a snapshot for 1994, percentage change is appropriate in measuring the strength or weakness of economic output for that year. However, this variable is transformed for the pooled, cross-sectional, times-series design and the Least Squares Dummy Variable (LSDV) model. Both of these analyses look across the states and time (1990-1994). Thus, the GDP variable is transformed through the addition of t-1. For example, GDP for state A in 1991 is equal to percentage change of real GDP 1990 added to the percentage change of real GDP 1991.

3 Findings and Analysis

Introduction

This chapter tests the relationship between economic factors and democratic satisfaction in the post-Communist countries. Economic performance and evaluations serve as means for assessing regime performance, as reflected in the level of popular support. The new democracies require complete restructuring of their economies. Thus, austere economic measures coupled with the harsh conditions of the transition economy can translate into a negative regime evaluation and a decline in support.

Chapter Two presented the operationalization and measurement of democratic support as well as the economic factors that are hypothesized to influence it. This chapter attempts to test the Policy Outputs approach to democratic support by examining the relationship between the economic environment and popular support at the systems level. The Policy Outputs approach argues that governmental policies affect the level of support for a regime. and examines the role of economic conditions, particularly economic crises, and economic policy on regime support. This model assumes that mass support and legitimacy are derived from specific policies and their consequences. However, it does not examine the role of political culture in the consolidation process.

The second approach, the Culturalist approach, argues that the values and political attitudes of the citizenry can foster or hinder popular support for a nation's institutions. For the new democracies, it suggests that those states in which the norms and values are compatible with the democratic institutions are likely to have higher levels of democratic support. Conversely, those states in which norms and values are antithetical to democracy will have lower levels of popular support.

A forging of these two distinct approaches to support gives us a fuller understanding of democratic consolidation. In general, I expect that economic conditions and evaluations of those conditions are the primary determinants of democratic satisfaction in Central and Eastern Europe and that attitudes toward the political system play a secondary role. Thus, the following analyses seek to uncover a generalized pattern of the effect of economic conditions and evaluations on democratic support in Central and Eastern Europe. However, I expect some variation across states due to distinct historic experiences, ethnic differences, and diverse political cultures. I attempt to address these differences across the post-Communist states in the empirical analysis. This provides a means of examining the Policy Outputs approach in conjunction with the Culturalist approach.

Sample

The primary focus of my research is the effect that economic policy, economic conditions, and citizens' perceptions of their own economic situation have on democratic consolidation. The sample is drawn from the 24-country population of Central and Eastern European countries. The sample examines 18 of the 24 states. These countries are determined by the country sample used in the Central and Eastern European Euro-Barometer surveys 1-5; 1990-1994. The sample size in the analysis varies for each time point.[1]

Methods

Statistical Designs

These data are analyzed using three tests: cross-sectional regression for 1994; pooled, cross-sectional, time-series regression; and Least Squares Dummy Variable (LSDV) analysis. All three tests investigate the relationship between economic factors and democratic support. The cross-sectional regression for 1994 is used to test for a relationship between economic policy and democratic support. The measure of market reform is available only for the year 1994; therefore, it cannot be included in the pooled, cross-sectional, time-series regressions. The cross-sectional analysis only tests for the effect of the economic factors on democratic support. In other words, the cross-sectional design examines only the Policy Outputs approach to democratic support.

The pooled design is used in order to examine effects across both time and space. Because the length of the time series is abbreviated ($t_1:t_n = 5$) and the sample of cross-sections is modest (N<30), pooling is particularly useful in testing for statistical significance. In addition, the pooled design offers the advantage of capturing variation across different units in space as well as variation that emerges over time (Sayrs, 1989). This design also tests the Policy Outputs approach by looking at the economic conditions and citizens' perceptions of their financial situation on popular support for democracy. The Culturalist approach is incorporated in the Least Squares Dummy Variable model, which controls for differences across states.

The Least Squares Dummy Variable model has both statistical strengths and weaknesses in addressing the Culturalist approach with this sample of countries. The strengths of this model can be viewed as two-fold: 1) it addresses the problem of autocorrelation, and 2) it allows the independent variable of political culture, which is often termed *unmeasurable*, to be incorporated. The pooled, cross-sectional, time-series design imposes a restriction of homogeneity on all cross-sectional units. In other words, the pooled design ignores any differences across countries and time. Autocorrelation is often a problem for this design type because it does not address the unique variations of the individual states. Incorporating dummy variables for both the countries and the time points accounts for the individual and time-series effects.

The second, and more important, strength of this model is its ability to include a theoretically viable independent variable. This design allows for the inclusion 'of important variables whose explicit inclusion in the model was not possible' (Deilman, 1989, 49). Thus, the concept of *political culture*, which statistically is otherwise unmeasureable at the systems level, can be accounted for.

The weaknesses of this design lie in the number of parameters to bc estimated and the interpretation of the results. Because the dummy variables for each country and time point increase the number of parameters to be estimated, this design reduces the degrees of freedom in the estimated equation. The total N for the pooled, cross-sectional, time-series and the LSDV model is 64. The inclusion of the dummy variables greatly reduces the degrees of freedom.

Truncated Dependent Variable Regressions

All three designs (cross-sectional; pooled, cross-sectional, time-series model; and LSDV model) use the dependent variable of democratic satisfaction. As discussed in Chapter Two, democratic satisfaction is a weighted average constructed by assigning weights to the categories of responses. Because the number of responses are exclusive (four), the range of the dependent variable is 1 to 4. Since the dependent variable (democratic satisfaction) is bounded between 1 and 4, the classical linear regression may provide biased estimates.[2]

Data and Analysis

What is the effect of economic conditions on support for democracy in Central and Eastern Europe? According to the Policy Output/support hypothesis, I expect economic conditions to have a positive relationship with democratic support.

Five indicators have been selected to examine the impact of economics on democratic consolidation in Central and Eastern Europe:

- percentage change in real GDP
- inflation
- financial evaluations
- financial uncertainty
- economic reform

Model I: Cross-sectional Regression 1994

A cross-sectional analysis is performed for 1994. This model tests for the effects of the economic variables and the effect of the level of economic reform on democratic satisfaction. The cross-section tests the following hypotheses:

H_1: *If economic conditions improve, satisfaction with democracy will increase.*

H_2: *If citizens' evaluations of their financial situation improve, satisfaction with democracy will increase.*

H_3: *If citizens' financial uncertainty increases, satisfaction with democracy will decrease.*

H_4: *If the level of economic reform increases, satisfaction with democracy will decrease.*

The specified model, incorporating both the economic variables and the economic reform index, estimates the following equation:

Democratic Satisfaction = $\alpha + \beta_1$ GDP - β_2 Inflation + β_3 Financial Evaluations - β_4 Financial Uncertainty - β_5 Economic Reform

The results of the cross-sectional regression are reported in Table 3.1.

Table 3.1 Cross-sectional Regression for 1994

Variable	Coefficient	Std. Error	T-ratio	Probability
Intercept	0.591	0.40	1.49	0.14
% Δ GDP	-0.285	0.67	-0.42	0.67
Inflation	0.183	0.27	0.07	0.95
Financial Evaluations	0.389*	0.86	4.52	0.00001
Financial Uncertainty	0.875	0.51	0.17	0.86
Economic Reform	0.331*	0.11	3.10	0.002

N = 17
Adjusted R^2 0.56
Durbin Watson Statistic   1.97
Log-Likelihood   10.38
*p < .01

Results corrected for Heteroskedasticity

In this model, two independent variables (Financial Evaluations and Economic Reform) have statistically significant coefficients. This indicates support for the Policy Outputs approach. For Financial Evaluations, we see that the coefficient is positive and significant beyond the .01 level. This supports the expected hypothesis that as financial evaluations improve, democratic satisfaction increases. The insignificant findings in regards to the actual economic conditions (GDP and inflation) are interesting in light of the significance of financial evaluations. The cross-sectional regression indicates that what is influencing democratic satisfaction is the citizens' attitudes toward their own financial situation rather than the actual state of the economy. Perceptions matter more than actual economic conditions. If this is accurate, an argument can be made that regimes can weather economic crisis by successfully convincing the population that they are not worse off.

Figure 3.1 presents the scatter plot for financial evaluations and democratic satisfaction with the predicted regression line. It shows where the individual countries fall in relation to the regression line. The Czech Republic, Lithuania, and Poland display higher regime satisfaction than their financial evaluations indicate. Conversely, Armenia, Bulgaria, and Russia demonstrate less democratic satisfaction than their financial evaluations indicate. Interestingly, Albania, in which the economic conditions are particularly adverse, shows both favorable financial evaluations and a high level of democratic satisfaction.

Figure 3.1: Democratic Satisfaction and Financial Evaluations 1994

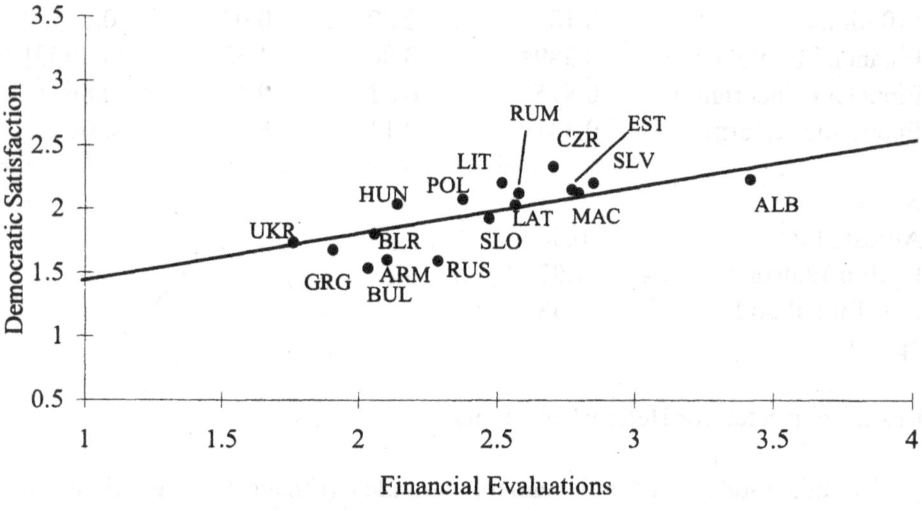

Figure 3.2 displays the scatter plot for democratic satisfaction and market reform with the regression line. It shows the regression line in relation to the actual data plotted for democratic satisfaction and level of economic reform. Albania, Lithuania, Slovenia, and the Czech Republic show higher levels of democratic satisfaction than the predicted level. Similar to the instance of financial evaluations (Figure 3.1), the Czech Republic and Lithuania have higher satisfaction levels than is predicted by their financial evaluations and levels of market reform. This suggests that

there are non-economic factors that are promoting regime satisfaction in these two cases. In addition, Armenia, Bulgaria, and Russia exhibit lower democratic satisfaction than predicted. As with financial evaluations, these three states should have higher regime satisfaction. This implies an additional hindrance to regime support for these states.

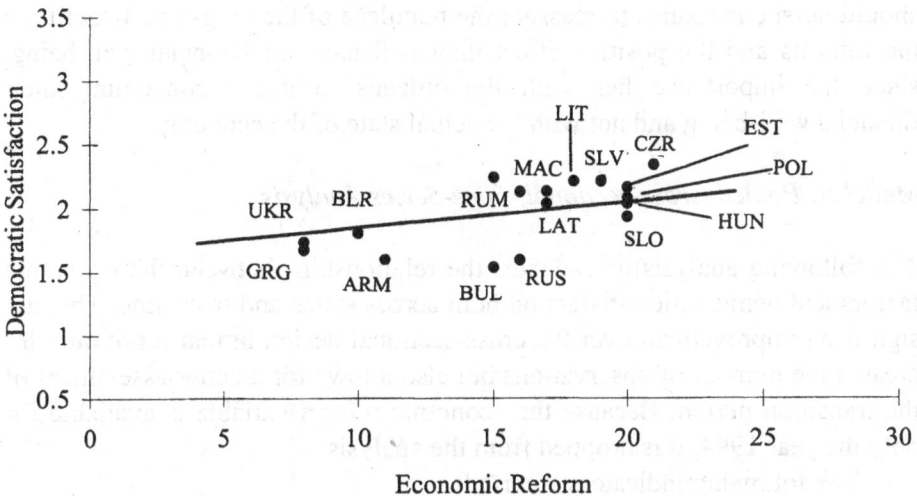

Figure 3.2: Democratic Satisfaction and Market Reform 1994

Given Przeworski's argument that the short-term effects of the economic transition carry high social costs, I expected a negative relationship between economic reforms and democratic satisfaction. However, the findings do not support this; rather, the economic reforms produced greater regime satisfaction. The positive relationship between the level of economic reform and democratic satisfaction suggests that successful transition toward the market aids the democratic consolidation process. Przeworski (1991) argues that states that have implemented more reforms or engaged in 'shock therapy' will have a decline in support in the short term; however, the long-term benefits of the radical reform will be further consolidation of the regime. It seems likely that citizens in those states in which the economic transition is nearly complete believe that the reforms are necessary and that the economic problems will be short-lived. At the same time, citizens in states that have made little progress with their economic transition may hold the regime responsible for continued dislocations. Thus, the positive statistical relationship exists.

The more interesting implication of this finding is that policy can be an instrument to increase support. Since the level of economic reform has a direct positive relationship with the level of support, the recommended policy prescription is acceleration in economic restructuring. And, because the findings indicate that the actual economic conditions do not affect support, the governments should proceed with the reforms regardless of the ensuing severity of the economic environment. However, the governmental elites should pursue measures to reassure the populace of the long-term benefits of the reforms and the positive effect they will have on financial well-being, since the importance lies with the citizens' attitudes concerning their financial well-being and not with the actual state of the economy.

Model II: Pooled Cross-sectional, Time-Series Analysis

The following analysis investigates the relationships between the economic factors and democratic satisfaction both across states and over time. This design is an improvement over the cross-sectional design in that it not only increases the number of observations but also allows for a better assessment of the transition period. Because the economic reform variable is available for only the year 1994, it is dropped from the analysis.

The following indicators are used:

- time from transition
- percentage change in real GDP
- inflation
- financial evaluations
- financial uncertainty

And, the following hypotheses are tested:

H_1: *As time from transition increases, satisfaction with democracy decreases.*

H_2: *If economic conditions improve, satisfaction with democracy will increase.*

H₃: *If citizens' evaluations of their financial situation improve, satisfaction with democracy will increase.*

H₄: *If citizens' financial uncertainty increases, satisfaction with democracy will decrease.*

With the exception of H_1, the hypothesized relationships are identical to those for the cross-sectional test. The pooled cross-sectional design allows for a test of the existence of the 'honeymoon period'. Thus, theoretically, I expect that democratic support will decline after the time of transition. Table 3.2 reports the results from the pooled cross-sectional, time-series regression.

For Model II, I estimate the following equation:

$$\text{Democratic Satisfaction} = \alpha - \beta_1 \text{ time} + \beta_2 \text{ GDP} - \beta_3 \text{ Inflation} + \beta_4 \text{ Financial Evaluations} - \beta_5 \text{ Financial Uncertainty}$$

Like the results for the 1994 cross-sectional analysis, citizens' financial evaluations are positive and statistically significant. Again, this establishes that what is important is citizens' attitudes toward their own well-being. This linkage between the citizens' economic attitudes and regime satisfaction neatly fits the Policy Outputs approach. The citizens' attitudes serve as the evaluation of the performance of the regime, and thus are directly connected to the level of support. The economic variables (GDP and inflation) are not statistically significant. Again, this suggests that it is not the actual state of the economy that the populace uses to measure regime performance; rather, it is the citizens' belief regarding the state of their own financial situation.

In addition, the coefficient for time is negative and statistically significant. This supports the notion of a honeymoon period or a period of extraordinary politics. The existence of this time of extraordinary politics suggests to policy makers that necessary economic reforms should be implemented as soon as possible following transition in order to take advantage of the high level of support for the regime. Democratic satisfaction across the states is highest at the beginning of regime transition and declines thereafter. This suggests that the regime has some base of legitimacy at the outset that may be due to the discredit of the Communist regime. The shortcomings of the old regime are fresh in the minds of the citizenry, and legitimacy of the new regime is extended on credit. As time from the transition increases, the memories of the old regime begin to fade and the political, social, and economic problems of the new democratic regime gain dominance.

Table 3.2 Pooled Cross-sectional, Time-Series Model

Variable	Coefficient	Std. Error	T-ratio	Probability
Intercept	186.240*	43.05	4.33	0.00002
Time	-9.276*	0.22	-4.29	0.00002
% Δ real GDP	0.139	0.15	0.09	0.93
log Inflation	-0.193	0.15	-1.26	0.21
Financial Evaluations	0.356*	0.65	5.51	0.00000
Financial Uncertainty	-0.509	-0.41	-1.25	0.21

Adjusted R^2 0.56
Durbin Watson Statistic   1.4
Log-Likelihood   21.94
*p < .01

Results corrected for Heteroskedasticity

Model III: Least Square Dummy Variable Analysis

Model III incorporates the country dummy variables to control for differences in political culture across the states. Model III is an attempt to incorporate the Culturalist approach with the Policy Outputs approach to support. Expectations regarding the economic variables remain the same as in the cross-sectional times-series design. Expectations regarding particular country dummy variables are not specified; rather, the empirical analysis is looked upon as exploratory in nature, with the hope that it will provide further insights into regime support in post-transitional countries.

For Model III, I estimate the following equation:

Democratic Satisfaction = α - β_1 time + β_2 GDP - β_3 Inflation + β_4 Financial Evaluations - β_5 Financial Uncertainty +/- β_k country variables

Table 3.3 reports the results of the LSDV model.

Table 3.3 Least Squares Dummy Variable Model

Variable	Coefficient	Std. Error	T-ratio	Probability
Intercept	1.289*	0.21	6.18	0.00000
Time	-0.763*	0.17	-4.45	0.00001
GDP	0.138	0.13	1.06	0.288
log Inflation	-0.918	0.13	1.58	0.114
Financial Evaluations	0.461*	0.72	6.44	0.00000
Financial Uncertainty	-0.174	0.37	-0.05	0.963
Lithuania	0.205*	0.45	4.55	0.000
Czech Republic	0.156*	0.46	3.36	0.000
Poland	0.144*	0.49	2.92	0.003
Albania	-0.220*	0.74	-2.97	0.003
Russia	-0.345*	0.28	-12.55	0.000
Slovakia	-0.942*	0.34	-2.76	0.006
D1994	-0.120*	0.42	-2.84	0.005

Adjusted R-squared 0.76
Durbin Watson Statistic 2.02
Log likelihood 41.41
*$p < .01$

Economic Variables The economic variables are used to test the Policy Output approach to democratic consolidation. I expected that economic factors would have a strong influence upon mass democratic support in Central and Eastern Europe. Like the previous tests, financial perceptions and time are statistically significant, even after country dummy variables are introduced. Once again, the significance of citizens' financial evaluations and the insignificance of the economic conditions suggest that citizens are not judging the regime according to the state of the economy; rather, they use their own personal well-being as a measure of regime performance. Thus, policymakers should take measures to assure the population that individual well-being is protected in light of plummeting outputs.

Again, the variable for time is negative and statistically significant. This finding supports the hypothesis that there is a decline in satisfaction with democracy over time as euphoria, evidenced by high satisfaction levels at the time of transition, dissipates. The implication for policymakers is that they should make use of the honeymoon period to implement economic reforms that may produce unfavorable evaluations in the short run. This, of course, assumes that economic reforms have long-term benefits for the post-Communist economies.

The results regarding the economic indicators support the Policy Output approach to democratic support. The perceptions of financial well-being affect the level of satisfaction with the regime. Given Przeworski's model of support, it is not surprising that policy outputs, particularly economic well-being, influence regime support. The financial evaluations act as a measure of regime performance. In general, these findings support Przeworski's (1991) model of economic effects on democratic consolidation.

Country Control Variables Although these control variables are introduced to correct for unique variation of the cross sections, the findings have implications in terms of the Culturalist approach to democratic support. The most similar systems design assumes no difference across the states in the system, i.e., that there would be no internal 'cultural' effect upon regime satisfaction. The Culturalist approach argues that stable democracy is a product of the values and norms of particular societies. In other words, democracy is most successful in societies in which the political culture is congruent to the institutions. The results of the country control variables suggest an interesting pattern in regards to the cultural argument. In Table 3.3, we see that the country dummies for Lithuania, the Czech Republic, and Poland all have a positive effect on democratic satisfaction. The coefficients are statistically significant at or beyond the .003 level. The cross-sectional analysis for 1994 gives the first indication that something other than economic factors is influencing democratic support in these countries (see Figure 3.1 and 3.2). The level of democratic satisfaction for all three countries is higher than the predicted level.

The other three country dummy variables included in the model (Albania, Russia, and Slovakia) have a negative effect on democratic satisfaction. It is interesting that the countries that positively affect democratic satisfaction (Lithuania, Czech Republic, and Poland) have all had some kind of democratic history/experience. Figure 3.3 displays the regression line for the full model and the regression lines with the individual country effects.[3]

Figure 3.3: Predicted Level of Democratic Satisfaction Over Time

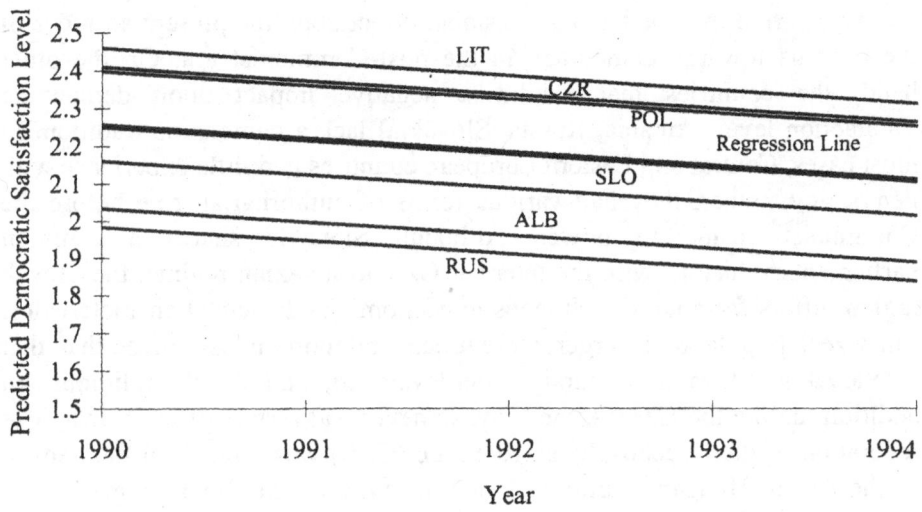

The three countries (Lithuania, Czech Republic, and Poland) with higher democratic satisfaction levels all experienced democracy and independence in the interwar period prior to being incorporated into the Soviet sphere of influence. Lithuania, for example, experienced a democratic regime from 1919 to 1926 prior to the dictatorships of Augustinas Voldemaras (1926-29) and Antanas Smetona (1929-39). Following the dictatorships, Lithuania assumed the status of a Soviet Socialist Republic in 1940. Poland, like Lithuania, was independent from the end of WW I until 1926. Subsequently, Poland was ruled by dictator Jozef Pilsudski until German occupation in 1939. However, Poland, under Communist rule, retained civic and religious institutions. The existence of Solidarity and the influence of the Catholic Church enabled Poland to develop a limited type of civil society. These 'civic' influences translate into democratic political values, i.e., positive support for democracy. Czechoslovakia's democratic experience extended across the entire interwar period from 1918-1938. During this time period,

Banks argues that 'Czechoslovakia was the most politically mature and democratically governed of the new states of Eastern Europe' (Banks, 1994-1995).

The history of democracy in these states may be influencing the regime support of the new democracies. The political culture developed in the interwar period may be having a residual effect upon the present attitudes of the citizens towards democracy in the post-Communist era. On the other hand, the countries that exhibit a negative impact upon democratic satisfaction level (Albania, Russia, Slovakia) lack a democratic tradition. In most cases, Central and Eastern European countries had little experience with democracy; rather, they had various forms of authoritarian rule before the Communists came to power. Although Slovakia shares a common parliamentary history with the interwar Czechoslovakian regime, the Slovak region differs from the Czech lands in economic and societal characteristics. The Czech population is larger, more urban, and more industrialized than that in Slovakia. Slovakia is rural, underdeveloped, and deeply religious. In addition, unlike the Czechs, the Slovaks never had a state of their own. The federation of the Czecho-Slovak Republic (CSR) was a result of the demise of the Austro-Hungarian Empire following WW I. The Slovak region has a long history of foreign domination. It can be argued that the Slovak political values are both currently and historically different than those of the Czechs. Butorova, Butorova, and Rosova argue that the Slovaks 'had no opportunity to acquire elementary democratic habits ... [and] people were increasingly inclined to submit passively to the authoritarian regime' (Butorova, Butorova, and Rosova, 1991). In addition, both Albania and Russia have long histories of authoritarian rule with no experience in democratic governance to draw upon.

These findings suggest that there is, indeed, variation across the system of formerly Communist states. A pattern in terms of the levels of democratic satisfaction emerges that indicates that economic influences are not the sole factors in explaining regime support. Rather, it may be that states with previous democratic experience have some type of residual democratic political culture that produces a higher democratic satisfaction level. Conversely, states with a prolonged history of authoritarianism (Russia and Albania) and/or foreign domination (Slovakia) have negative effects on satisfaction level independent of economic influences. These cases that have an additional impact (beyond the economic factors) upon democratic support deserve further investigation. Case study analysis is used to explore these differences in support.

Conclusions

In general, the Policy Outputs approach has been supported. The 1994 cross-sectional results reveal a strong positive relationship between the level of economic reform and popular support for democracy. This finding leads to the conclusion that the more transformed the economy is toward the market the greater the support for democracy. The implication of this finding is that the quicker the economy transforms the more likely the consolidation process will continue. Thus, radical economic reform is the optimal package for countries that have recently undergone transition. States that do not implement radical reform may lose popular support for the market reforms and, ultimately, stagnate economically and backslide into authoritarianism. The results of the 1994 cross-sectional analysis are also provocative in terms of the relationship between the market and democracy. The general implication is that the market is necessary for democratic consolidation. The Modernization School argues that socio-economic development is a requisite to democracy, but it falls short of suggesting that the market is the means to this development. My findings, however, directly link the market to democratic support.

Economic evaluations also have an influence upon mass support for democracy in Central and Eastern Europe. The political implications of the effects of economic evaluations in both the LSDV model and the 1994 cross section are telling. States with particularly unfavorable financial evaluations run the risk of losing mass support for democracy. In terms of policy strategies, states should not only adopt radical reform policies rather than gradual reform, but also use political means to convince the populace that their financial well-being is improving and that the means to improvement is, in fact, greater reform. Indeed, over time, economic restructuring that leads to favorable financial evaluations demonstrates governmental effectiveness and promotes consolidation. Therefore, the economic environment in the new democracies is critical for regime consolidation. However, it appears that this is only part of the story.

Evidence of individual country effects suggests that there are cultural influences upon regime support. Interestingly, states with some past democratic experience appear to have a greater affinity toward the democratic regime, while some states that lack this background have lower support levels than the economic model would predict. Thus, cultural variations may make a difference in terms of levels of support.

A synthesis of both the Policy Outputs and the Culturalist approach is necessary to understand fully the consolidation process in Central and Eastern Europe. In other words, the empirical analysis of the economic effects on mass support should be supplemented with country case studies to assess the role of political culture on the consolidation process.

Notes

1. The sample countries for each time point are as follows: 1) 1990: Poland, Czechoslovakia, Bulgaria (N=3), 2) 1991: Poland, Hungary, Czechoslovakia, Albania, Bulgaria, Romania, Russia, Estonia, Latvia, Lithuania (N=10), 3) 1992: Poland, Hungary, Czech Republic, Slovakia, Albania, Macedonia, Slovenia, Bulgaria, Moldova, Romania, Russia, Estonia, Latvia, Lithuania, Ukraine, Belarus, Armenia, Georgia (N=18), 4) 1993: Poland, Hungary, Czech Republic, Slovakia, Albania, Macedonia, Slovenia, Bulgaria, Romania, Russia, Estonia, Latvia, Lithuania, Ukraine, Belarus, Armenia (N=16), 5) 1994: Poland, Hungary, Czech Republic, Slovakia, Albania, Macedonia, Slovenia, Bulgaria, Romania, Russia, Estonia, Latvia, Lithuania, Ukraine, Belarus, Armenia, Georgia (N=17).
2. Biased estimates could result if the predicted y must fall within some range. The truncated linear regression specifies the upper and lower bounds for the predicted y. The truncated y=y* if y* falls in some range and y is observed otherwise. Thus, the truncated regression bounds the predicted y* to the range of the observed y and the variable coefficients are adjusted to these limits. Truncated regression is discussed in depth in G.S. Maddala's Limited and Qualitative Dependent Variables in Economics, Cambridge University Press (1983) and the January 1984 issue of the Journal of Economics.
3. The regression lines for Figure 3.3 show the democratic satisfaction levels over time (1990 to 1994), holding all other independent variables at their means.

PART II
CASE STUDIES

4 Introduction to Case Studies

Introduction

The empirical findings presented in Chapter Three indicate that economic reform, financial evaluations, and a set of specific countries have a positive effect on democratic support. I find no relationship between economic conditions and democratic support. These findings suggest that citizens' perceptions of financial well-being and the level of economic restructuring are more important that the actual state of the economy in determining the level of democratic support. The individual country effects are intriguing and demand further explanation of the consolidation process. The significant effects of particular country control variables suggest that there is variation across the post-Communist countries. Although the economic indicators have a strong effect on democratic support, additional internal factors also play a role in explaining democratic support. What are those factors? Why do particular countries have higher levels of mass support for democracy than predicted by the single model? What similarities exist in those countries that can explain this deviation? Also, why do some states have lower democratic support than what their economic conditions would indicate?

Analysis of country cases can reveal not only additional information but also further theoretical possibilities for explaining differences across countries. The Policy Outputs approach assumes that the economic factors are the primary explanations of democratic support. In addition, it assumes, given the sample of post-Communist states, that there will be little difference across the states. However, the LSDV results indicate that there are differences across these countries. The country dummy variables lead us to explore the fuller explanation of democratic support. A complementary theoretical explanation for democratic support is the compatibility or incompatibility of a society's political values and norms with its political system.

Political culture as an analytical device 'seeks to identify and define as precisely as possible the salient features of the orientation of a given nation (or group within a nation) to politics as expressed in its values and/or actions over an extended period of time' (Skilling, 1979, 118). This characterization of political culture carries two distinct implications in terms of analysis. The first approach is that political culture is the 'subjective orientation' of a nation. In other words, the political culture is found in the values and beliefs of the citizens. The second approach encompasses 'objective phenomena' by extending the definition of political culture to the actual behavior patterns found in a group or nation. This variation in usage of the term makes it difficult to identify the political culture of a country. In addition, the choice of methods affects the conclusions one draws from analysis. The use of political culture as a rigorous analytical framework should examine both the subjective values and beliefs of the citizenry and the objective historical experiences of a given nation.

The political culture of any given society can either assist or impede the democratic consolidation process. States with values congruent to democracy will more easily consolidate than states in which the values are not conducive to democratic institutions. I argue that the specific political cultures of the states are driving the individual country results. *Political culture* is something that is difficult to quantify. Thus, while the statistical model assists in determining the economic effects on democratic support and in pointing out the differences across the system, it falls short of a full explanation. However, a more complete explanation can be offered by systematic analyses of the country case studies. An examination of states' political cultures provides elucidation into the level of democratic support. The hope is that one can uncover the societal and political factors that foster or hinder popular democratic support in the face of a bleak economic environment. And, perhaps, policy prescriptions for states in transition can be made that will nurture the democratic consolidation process.

Research Design

The research design for the country case studies partially mirrors that used in the general statistical model presented in Chapter Three. The theoretical propositions concerning the relationship between the economic factors and democratic support are examined for each individual country case under consideration. Utilizing the same theoretical propositions in the case studies as those tested in the statistical models makes for a more rigorous empirical analysis of each country. Yin asserts that this is the preferred strategy for the organization of the case study as well as for defining alternate explanations (1994, 104). By allowing the theoretical orientation to guide the analysis, the case study focuses upon the features of primary interest. Thus, the first part of each case study looks at the economic conditions for each country and compares those conditions to the average for the sample of Central and Eastern Europe states. This comparison allows for the relative economic standing of each country under examination to be assessed. In addition, each hypothesized relationship between the economic factors and democratic support is examined.

This case study design uses the analytic technique of pattern matching. Pattern matching logic compares an empirically based pattern with a predicted one (Trochim, 1986; Yin, 1994, 104). The model presented in Chapter Three serves as the predicted pattern for all the Central and Eastern European states in the sample, and each individual country case will be matched against this general predicted pattern. This enables one to observe deviance as well as conformity to the predicted pattern. Since the case studies are explanatory in nature, the patterns will be related to both the dependent variable (democratic support) and the independent variables (economic factors).

The technique of pattern matching involves the logic of replication. Yin argues that the use of replication in multiple case studies 'is to consider multiple cases as one would multiple experiments' (45). The case studies utilize theoretical replication of both the economic propositions and the role of political culture upon democratic support. Each case study examines:

- the level of democratic support in comparison to the average democratic support for all the Central and Eastern European countries,
- the economic indicators in comparison to the average for the Central and Eastern European countries,
- hypothesized relationships between the economic variables and democratic support,
- the political culture of each country in terms of historical evidence and available survey data,
- prospects for democracy.

Criteria for Choosing Cases

Of the 18 country cases used in the LSDV model in Chapter Three, six cases (Lithuania, the Czech Republic, Poland, Slovakia, Albania, Russia) have an independent effect on citizens' satisfaction with democracy beyond the other general conditions in the model. Lithuania, the Czech Republic, and Poland have a higher level of democratic satisfaction than otherwise predicted. Conversely, the remaining three cases (Albania, Slovakia, Russia) have lower than predicted levels of regime satisfaction. This suggests that forces other than economic conditions and the perceptions of those conditions are affecting the support for democracy in these six specific cases.

The choice of country cases flows from both the research design and the types of questions being asked. The purpose of the case studies is to search for cultural explanations of mass democratic support with specific cultural experiences. Are there social and/or historical patterns across these states? What additional factors, or lack thereof, are influencing regime support in these new democracies? The technique of pattern matching is useful in sifting out general explanations of both negative and positive directional effects. Thus, the choice of country cases should include not only those cases in which there is a positive effect but also those with a negative effect upon democracy.

The cases are chosen in order to examine the diversity of results. The results may be classified into a threefold typology: those cases that positively affect democratic support, those that negatively affect democratic support, and those that conform to the general model. The cases investigated here represent the categories that deviate from the general model. In other words, the cases are chosen from the six countries that significantly affect the level of democratic support. The underlying logic of replication is to demonstrate that those contrasting results, found in the statistical model, are produced for predictable reasons (Yin, 1994, 46). Thus, two cases are chosen to examine positive deviation from the general model (Lithuania and the Czech Republic) and two cases are chosen from those that have a negative effect upon democratic support (Slovakia and Russia). These cases have the greatest significant effect upon mass support for democracy.

Theoretically, I expect that the cases that positively affect democratic support (Lithuania and the Czech Republic) have a political culture that is conducive to democracy. Although all of the former Communist states experienced decades of authoritarian rule and this undoubtedly has had an effect upon the population, the citizenry may be more democratically oriented due to a past democratic or liberal experience. In addition, the cases that negatively affect democratic support (Russia and Slovakia) may have authoritarian characteristics as an integral part of their political development. Thus, I expect a pattern in terms of political culture to emerge that helps in explaining the present democratic support.

Chapter Five and Chapter Seven examine the Czech Republic and Lithuania, respectively, and attempt to uncover preexisting democratic political cultures in these countries that may explain the positive influence on mass democratic support. Similarly, Chapter Six and Chapter Eight investigate Slovakia and Russia, respectively, and seek explication of the negative influence on democratic support. All four case studies rely heavily upon historical evidence of political development to determine the nature of the political culture. Available survey data are utilized to supplement the historical analyses.

5 The Czech Republic

Introduction

My empirical findings indicate that cultural factors in the Czech Republic have a positive effect on support for democracy while such factors have a negative effect in Slovakia. In other words, the Czech Republic has more popular support and Slovakia has less popular support for democracy than predicted by the economic model. This finding is intriguing given the shared history of both states under independent Czechoslovakia. The shared political experience of the Czechs and the Slovaks makes for some overlap in analysis and presents a challenge in terms of theoretical considerations. Nevertheless, both states are treated as separate country cases. This chapter introduces the format to be followed in each case study. It examines: the level of democratic support and the economic indicators in the Czech Republic in relation to the other Central and Eastern European states, the hypothesized relationships between economic factors and democratic support, the role of political culture in the support for democracy, and the prospects for democratic consolidation.

Democratic Support

Since level of popular democratic support is of foremost interest, it is useful to begin with an examination of the data for the Czech Republic in respect to the rest of Central and Eastern Europe.[1] An exploration of the data reveals that the level of democratic support in the Czech Republic is, on the whole, higher than the mean support level in Central and Eastern Europe (Figure 5.1; Table 5.1). Both Table 5.1 and Figure 5.1 demonstrate a sharp decline in democratic satisfaction in the Czech Republic from January to October, 1990. January 1990 marks the peak of democratic satisfaction in Czechoslovakia. This makes sense in light of the fact that the survey so closely followed the November 1989 'Velvet Revolution'. This high point epitomizes the euphoria following the fall of Communism. In addition, the drastic drop

Table 5.1   Democratic Satisfaction for the Czech Republic and Central and Eastern Europe

Year	Czech Republic	Average CEE	Difference Czech and CEE
January 1990	3.21	—	—
October 1990	2.25	2.40	-0.15
1991	2.15	2.26	-0.11
1992	2.31	2.12	0.19
1993	2.40	2.09	0.31
1994	2.33	1.97	0.36

Notes: Entries are the country means on a scale of 1 (not at all satisfied) to 4 (very satisfied).
CEE = Central and Eastern Europe.
Sources: Central and Eastern European Barometer (item 1) 1-5. Survey data for other Central and Eastern European states for January 1990 are not available.

Figure 5.1:   Democratic Satisfaction for the Czech Republic and Central and Eastern Europe

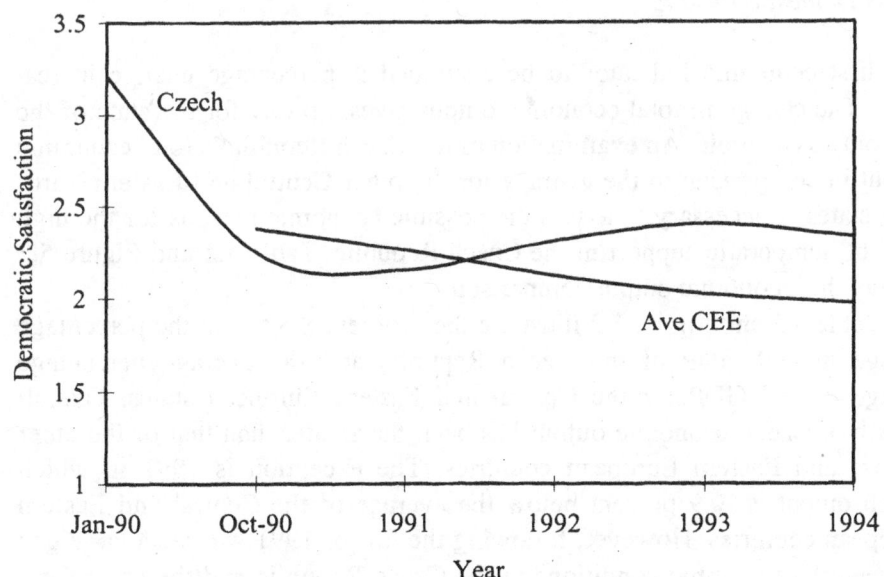

64 *The Economy and Political Culture in New Democracies*

from January to October of that year demonstrates just how short-lived the 'honeymoon period' was in Czechoslovakia. Interestingly, the low democratic satisfaction levels in the October 1990 and the 1991 surveys for Czechoslovakia are lower than the average satisfaction level for the Central and Eastern European states. This may be explained by the quick implementation of economic reforms following the Velvet Revolution. However, the satisfaction level increases after 1991 and is higher than the average CEE satisfaction levels in 1992, 1993, and 1994. In terms of 'pattern matching', this rise in satisfaction level over time (although not to the level reached in January 1990) does not follow the relationship found in the generalized statistical model. The LSDV model predicts a decrease in democratic satisfaction over time. The satisfaction with democracy decreases from the time of transition. This is expected given that the euphoria wanes following political liberalization and the initiation of economic transformation. Examination of the economic indicators and the democratic satisfaction level may reveal additional information concerning this early dip followed by a later rise in democratic satisfaction.

Economic Conditions

Gross Domestic Product

The first economic indicator to be examined is percentage change in real GDP. The change in total economic output gives a proxy for the state of the economy as a whole. An examination of the Czech Republic's total economic output in comparison to the average for the other Central and Eastern European states is necessary to assess the possible economic reasons for the high level of democratic support in the Czech Republic. Table 5.2 and Figure 5.2 display this economic output comparison.

Table 5.2 and Figure 5.2 illustrate the difference between the percentage change in real GDP of the Czech Republic and the average percentage change in real GDP for the Central and Eastern European states. Overall growth in Czech economic output has been far greater than that of the other Central and Eastern European countries. The exception is 1991 in which Czech output is -0.9 percent below the average of the Central and Eastern European countries. However, following the low of 1991, we see a large gap between the economic conditions in the Czech Republic and the other Central and Eastern European states. This differential in economic output can be attributed to both the high level of economic development in the Czech lands prior to transition and the quick economic reforms implemented at the beginning of transition (1990-1991). In relation to the other Central and Eastern European countries, Czechoslovakia in 1990 had a much stronger economy in terms of industrial development and infrastructure.

Table 5.2 Percentage Change in Real GDP for the Czech Republic and Central and Eastern Europe

Year	Czech Republic	Average CEE	Difference Czech and CEE
1990	-0.4	-5.0	4.6
1991	-14.0	-13.2	-0.8
1992	-6.0	-17.4	11.4
1993	-1.0	-6.7	5.7
1994	3.0	-3.2	6.2

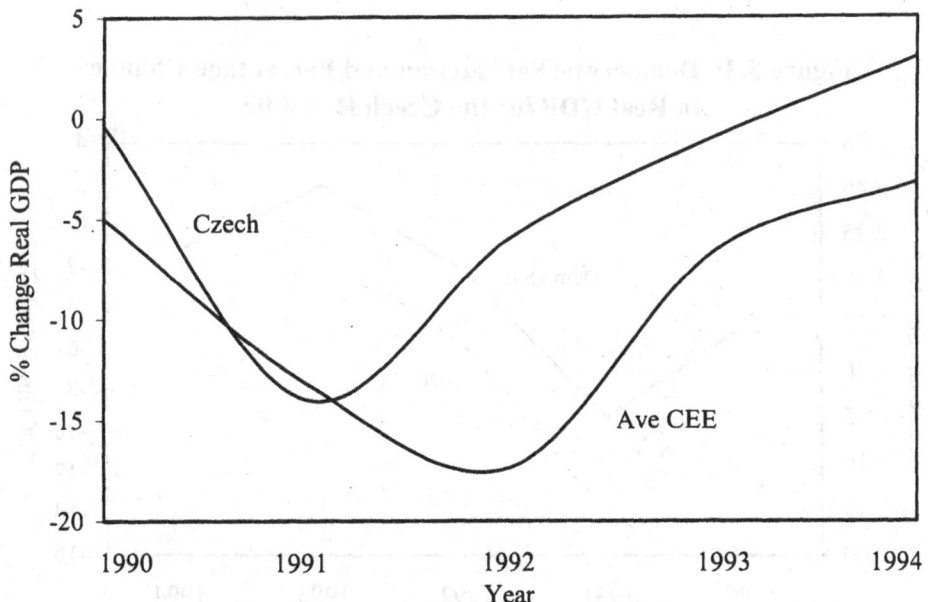

Figure 5.2: Percentage Change in Real GDP for the Czech Republic and Central and Eastern Europe

After November 1989 Czechoslovakia sought to construct functioning political institutions and engaged in constitution building rather than plunging directly into economic transformation. The year 1990 had relative political stability due to the reformist coalition of the Civic Forum (Czech) and Public Against Violence (Slovak). Having laid the foundations of democracy, the Czech-Slovak Federation embarked on radical economic reform in January 1991 (Åslund, 1994). The comprehensive economic reforms (including the lifting of price controls, currency stabilization, and privatization of small firms) account for the sharp decline in economic output in 1991. In other words, the 'shocks' of early 1991 produced the transition depression and laid the groundwork for the recovery evidenced in 1993 and 1994. Following 1991, we see the rebound effects of the shock treatment in the total economic output. This quick economic rebound put the Czech Republic's economic conditions in a better position relative to the other transition economies. In light of relatively better economic conditions, an examination of the hypothesized relationship between the economic conditions and democratic support is necessary.

H_1: If economic conditions improve, support for democracy will increase.

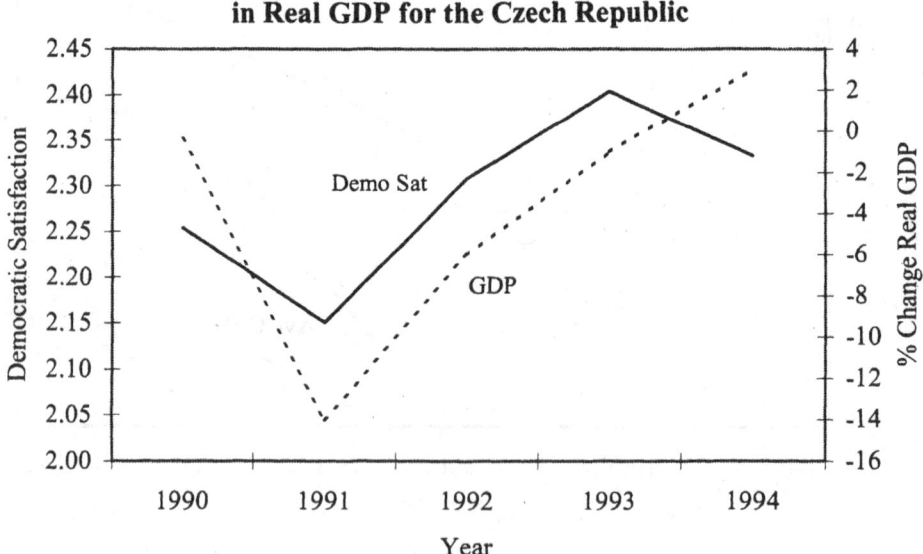

Figure 5.3: Democratic Satisfaction and Percentage Change in Real GDP for the Czech Republic

Figure 5.3 plots both the democratic satisfaction level and percentage change in real GDP for 1990-1994. The year 1991 is the low point for both satisfaction with democracy and economic output. The plot indicates a close positive relationship between percentage change in real GDP and democratic satisfaction for the Czech Republic. We see that following 1991, the Czech economy rebounds and in 1994 the Czech Republic experiences positive growth. The exception appears to be 1994, in which real GDP increases but democratic satisfaction declines slightly. On a whole, the relationship indicated by the general model is supported. Thus, Figure 5.3 clearly illustrates the strong positive relationship between economic output and democratic satisfaction level in the Czech Republic.

Inflation

Consumer prices, or inflation, is the second measure for economic conditions. Table 5.3 and Figure 5.4 provide a comparison of inflation for the Czech Republic and average inflation for the other Central and Eastern European states from 1990 to 1994.

Table 5.3 Inflation for the Czech Republic and Central and Eastern Europe

Year	Czech	Average CEE	log (CZE)	log(CEE)	Difference Czech and CEE
1990	18.4	76.7	2.91	4.34	-58.3
1991	52.0	186.5	3.95	5.23	-134.5
1992	13.0	922.0	2.57	6.83	-909.0
1993	18.0	274.4[a]	2.89	5.62	-256.4
1994	10.0	301.4[b]	2.30	5.71	-291.4

[a] Note: average inflation for Central and Eastern Europe has been calculated for 1993 without data for Ukraine and Armenia. Ukraine and Armenia are both extreme outliers in terms of the consumer price index with reported inflation for 1993 as 10,155 percent and 10,996 percent, respectively.
[b] For 1994, Georgia can also be considered an extreme inflationary case with a reported 7,380 percent; thus, it has been left out of the calculated average.

Figure 5.4: Inflation for the Czech Republic and Central and Eastern Europe

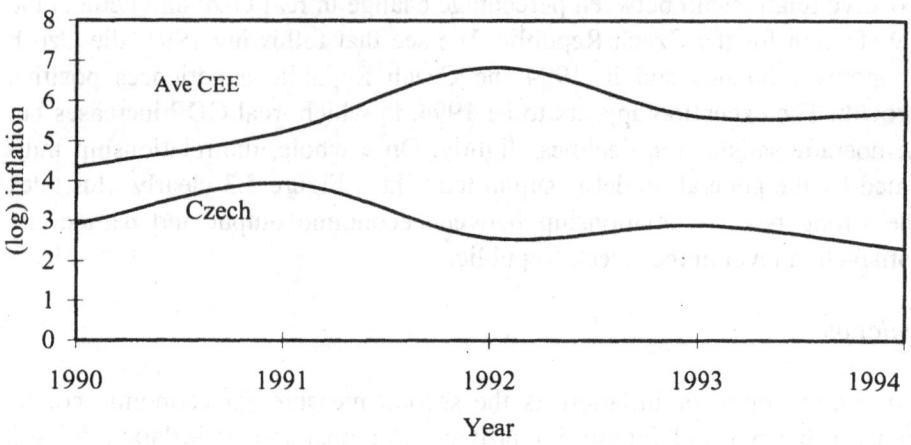

The second macroeconomic indicator, inflation, exhibits a pattern similar to percentage change in real GDP. Table 5.3 and Figure 5.4[2] demonstrate the relatively low levels of inflation for the Czech Republic from 1990 to 1994. Again, we can attribute the peak inflation of 52 percent (in 1991) to the economic reforms. This, however, is far below the average inflation for the other Central and Eastern European countries. And the reported 10 percent inflation for 1994 more closely approximates the inflation rate of Western Europe than that of the transitional economies. Thus, the Czech Republic has not suffered as much as the other states in terms of inflation.

Figure 5.5 plots inflation with democratic satisfaction level. Like percentage change in real GDP, inflation peaks in 1991. Following 1991 inflation decreases, the economic conditions improve, and democratic satisfaction increases. Again the exception of 1994 is evident. Inflation continues to decrease; however, democratic satisfaction also decreases. This slight dip, however, constitutes merely a .07 change in democratic satisfaction level. The level of satisfaction is still quite high in 1994. In fact, inflation in the Czech Republic has been quite low by regional standards. In addition, Figure 5.5 demonstrates strong support for the hypothesized relationship between inflation and democratic satisfaction. As inflation increases (1991) we clearly see a decrease in democratic satisfaction. Following the shock treatment of 1991, there is a sharp decrease in inflation coupled with an increase in democratic satisfaction.

Figure 5.5: Democratic Satisfaction and Inflation for the Czech Republic

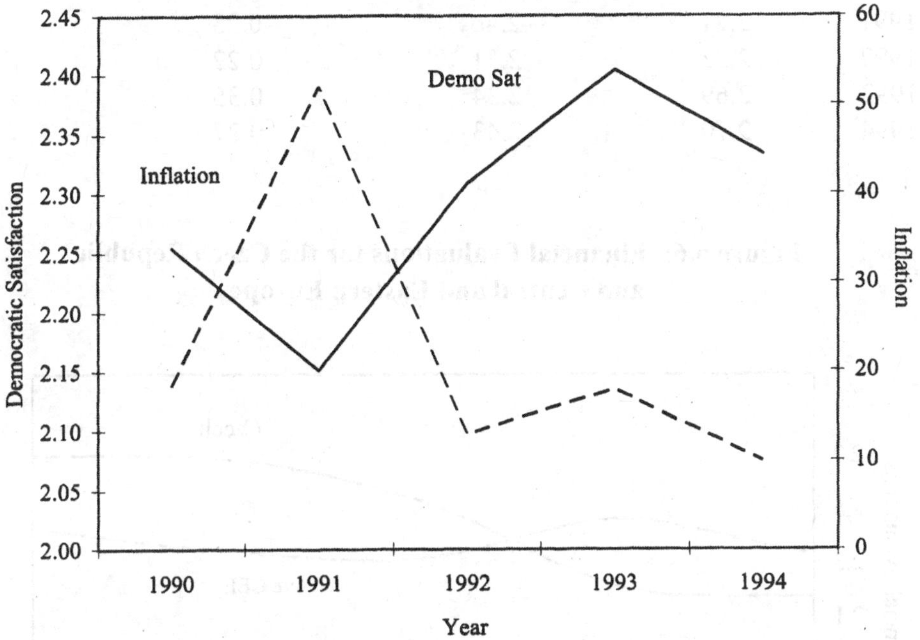

Financial Evaluations

Table 5.4 and Figure 5.6 provide a comparison of the Czech Republic's financial evaluations and the average score of financial evaluations of the Central and Eastern European countries. In both 1990 and 1991, Czech financial evaluations are below the average financial evaluations of Central and Eastern Europe. In 1990 economic restructuring had yet to be implemented in Czechoslovakia; thus, citizens' perceptions of their financial situation can be explained by the continued existence of centralized planning. In 1991 there is an improvement in financial evaluations; however, it is still below the average for the Central and Eastern European countries. Like GDP and inflation, this low score for Czechoslovakia in 1991 can be attributed to the effects of the shock therapy. Following 1991 Czech financial perceptions continue to increase as the economy rebounds.

Table 5.4 Financial Evaluations for the Czech Republic and Central and Eastern Europe

Year	Czech Republic	Average CEE	Difference Czech and CEE
1990	2.17	2.33	-0.16
1991	2.21	2.46	-0.25
1992	2.53	2.31	0.22
1993	2.69	2.34	0.35
1994	2.70	2.43	0.27

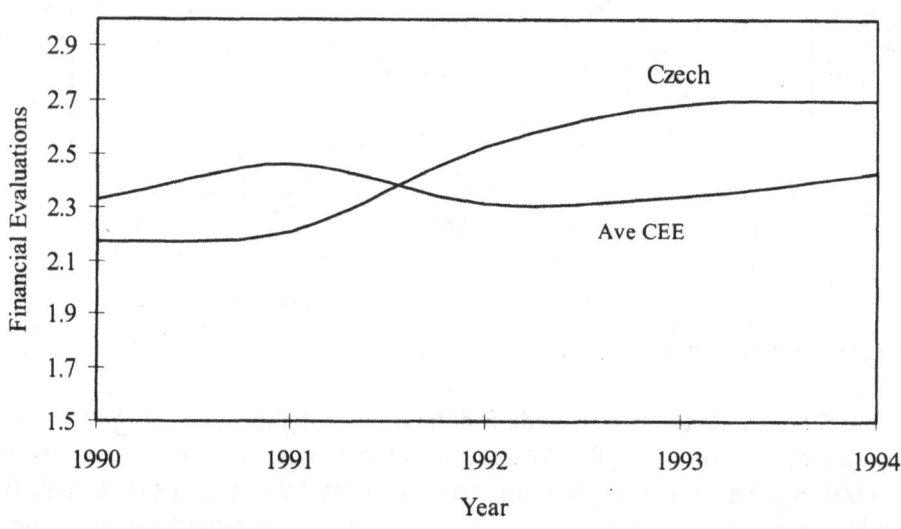

Figure 5.6: Financial Evaluations for the Czech Republic and Central and Eastern Europe

H2: *If financial evaluations improve, support for democracy will increase.*

Figure 5.7 plots the data for the financial evaluations and democratic satisfaction in the Czech Republic from 1990 to 1994. Although the increase in financial evaluations is small from 1990 to 1991 and 1993 to 1994, the evaluations do continue to improve over time. The positive relationship between financial evaluations and democratic satisfaction is clear.

All three of the economic indicators (percentage change in real GDP, inflation, and financial evaluations) reveal a strong relationship with popular democratic support in the Czech Republic. In addition, the generalized, hypothesized relationships are all supported. Thus, the Czech Republic fits nicely into the general theoretical model. The economic indicators for the Czech Republic tend to be higher than the average economic indicators for Central and Eastern Europe. The better conditions are a result of the relative strength of the economy entering transition as well as successful economic restructuring. One is led to conclude that the high level of support may be a function of the economic policy program.

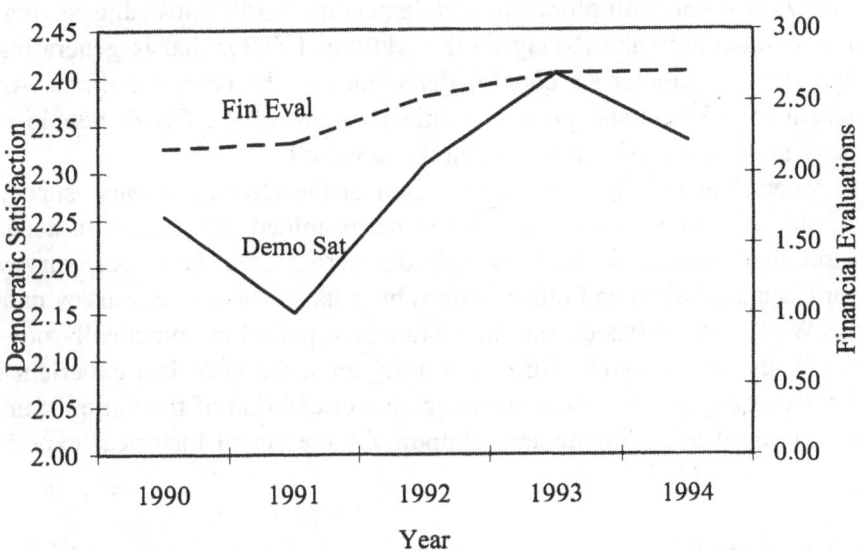

Figure 5.7: Democratic Satisfaction and Financial Evaluations for the Czech Republic

In this sense, the trends on the Czech Republic conform to the general cross-national pattern found in the empirical tests. But we must also recall from Chapter Three that the Czech Republic's overall level of democratic satisfaction is higher than predicted by its economic indicators, relative to the other seventeen nations analyzed. That difference, of course, cannot be seen in trends for the Czech Republic reported above. Thus, I explore here the characteristics of the Czech political culture as an additional element of the explanation. The high popular support or legitimacy of democracy may be a function of the political and social values and norms of the Czech citizenry. A democratic political culture may be demonstrated by examining the historical experience of the Czech people in light of the contemporary survey data.

Political Culture

The relatively consistent high level of democratic satisfaction since the fall of Communism in the Czech Republic comes as no surprise to certain specialists who have argued for years that pluralism is and has been the dominant characteristic of Czech political culture (Brown and Wightman, 1979; Paul, 1979; Skilling, 1977). The Czech historical record shows continuity of pluralistic political values prior to the Communist takeover in 1948. This past historical experience with pluralism and democratic institutions suggests that 'residual democratic values' may be the additional factor that is generating the high level of popular support for democracy in the present politics. An assessment of the past and present political culture of the Czech people is necessary to discern a continuity of pluralistic values.

In order to assess subjective orientation of the Czech citizenry, survey data of citizens' political attitudes should be examined. Moreover, an accurate assessment should account for attitudes across time. However, survey data for Czechoslovakia and other Eastern bloc states are scarce. Survey data prior to WW II as well as during the Communist period are practically nonexistent. Thus, this research will rely heavily upon the historical experience of the Czech people rather than the subjective orientation of the nation. Survey data is used as supplementary support for the actual historical experience.

Historical Evidence

In tracing the history of the Czech people we see the emergence of proto-democratic institutions under the Austro-Hungarian empire. This was followed by a fully functioning parliamentary democracy in the interwar period, authoritarian control by the Communists and the Soviet Union from 1948 to 1989 (with a brief rise in democratic values in 1968), and the reemergence of democracy since 1989. In other words, the historical experience of the Czech lands suggests relative continuity of pluralism.

Austro-Hungarian Control: 1867-1918 The state of Czechoslovakia was not constructed until after the first World War. Prior to 1918, the Czech lands (the Kingdom of Bohemia and the Margravate of Moravia) were controlled by the Austrian half of the dual monarchy. The year 1867 marked the formal division of the Austro-Hungarian empire that linked the Czechs with Vienna and the German sector (Leff, 1988). The Austrian influence on the Czech lands meant a major departure in the political development of the Czechs in comparison to the Slovaks, who were dominated by Hungary. This initial demarcation of rule set the Czechs and the Slovaks on different paths of modern political development. In fact, pronounced differences between the German-Czech and the Hungarian-Slovak relationships resulted in two distinct political cultures within Czechoslovakia. Differences between the Czechs and the Slovaks are a function of very distinct experiences under foreign rule. These differences include divergence in: levels of economic development, religious and cultural traditions and customs, and political experience. The dissimilarities in economic, cultural, and political development are manifest in the divergent attitudes toward democracy that characterize the present politics of the Czech Republic and Slovakia. (The Slovak experience is discussed in Chapter Six.)

Under Austrian rule, the Czechs could penetrate major social positions and higher education and ultimately achieve a high degree of political participation. Czech social advancement under German domination was made possible by the availability of Czech educational opportunities. Leff asserts that 'even though the system maintained a disproportionate number of German schools, the establishment of a Czech university as well as the network of officially sanctioned Czech elementary and secondary institutions afforded access to social advancement without the relinquishment of national identity' (1988, 17). In addition to the access to higher education, Czech opportunities were enhanced by the formal acceptance of the Czech language in 1880. The language directive of 1880 established a linguistic equality that allowed the Czechs social mobility (Hajda, 1964). Hadja cites evidence of this social mobility by a survey conducted on 94 outstanding 19th century Czechs. More than half had risen from the ranks of peasants, artisans, and tradesmen, indicating an open avenue for aspiring Czech intelligentsia (Hadja, 1964, 308). Leff and Hadja argue that educational opportunities and language acceptance not only furthered personal gains for Czechs but also fostered the development of autonomous institutional development. 'The network of universities, gymnasia, theaters, newspapers, magazines, publishing houses, bookstores, museums, orchestras, choral groups, artistic, scientific and professional clubs and associations – this network was the first institutional expression of wide-ranging, non-parochial cooperation among Czechs, the first element in their own, rather than the Hapsburg establishment' (Hadja, 1964, 309). This development of autonomous societal institutions marks the emergence of civil society in which Czech social structure became increasingly complex and differentiated.

A manifestation of this differentiation is demonstrated in the growth of anticlerical sentiment in Czech society, coupled with nationalist tendencies. Although Catholicism predominated, Czechs began '...to view the Roman Catholic hierarchy as a tool of Habsburg hegemony and grew steadily more secular in outlook' (Leff, 1988, 21). The secularism and progressivism of Czech intelligentsia were in sharp contrast to their more devout Slovak neighbors. Furthermore, this anticlericalism diversified the Czech political outlook.

The degree of political activity under the empire was reflective of the social and cultural growth in the Czech lands. Czech legislative participation comprised primarily by the Young Czechs from 1870 to 1907, apart from an eight-year boycott during the 1870s. After an expansion of the electorate in 1907, Czech partisanship began to differentiate. 'The Agrarians, the Social Democrats, the National Socialists, and the Catholics all emerged as parliamentary entities' (Leff, 1988, 24). Leff asserts that the 'Czechs had established a continuing and not insignificant leverage on policy making, an impact virtually denied the neighboring Slovaks' (1988, 24). In other words, the Czechs faced fewer obstacles to political participation than the Slovaks. This early parliamentary experience taught the Czechs how political transactions are conducted. Consequently, the Czechs had a working knowledge of parliamentary coalition-building and had gained experience with competing national interests through prewar party differentiation. This experience served as a blueprint for constructing the parliamentary democracy of the First Republic.

The First Republic: 1918-1938 The educational, economic, social, and political opportunities the Czechs received under Austrian rule created conditions that were conducive to both democratization and independence. The seed of pluralism that was planted prior to WW I flowered in the interwar period. In contrast to Slovakia and other Central and Eastern European states created following the War, the Czech lands had higher levels of industrialization, urbanization, and literacy. Wolchik (1991, 3) details this comparison of the Czech lands and their neighbors.

Czech Levels of urbanization and the social structure, particularly in the lands, were more similar to those of the developed Western European countries than those of Czechoslovakia's Central and Eastern European neighbors. Whereas from 70 to 80 percent of the population in Albania, Bulgaria, Romania, and Yugoslavia remained dependent on agriculture in 1930, and from 52 to 59 percent in Poland and Hungary in 1930, for example, only 35 percent of the population earned a living in this sector in Czechoslovakia in that year; approximately equal numbers were engaged in industry. Czechoslovakia was also more urbanized than its neighbors. Approximately 48 percent of the population lived in cities of five thousand and over in 1930, compared to 15 percent in Albania, from 20 to 22 percent in Romania, Yugoslavia, and Bulgaria, 27 percent in Poland, and 36 percent in Hungary. Czechoslovakia also had higher levels of literacy than other states in the region. By 1930, for example, the illiteracy rate was only 4.1 percent of the total population age ten and over.

The democratic system that emerged in 1918 was supported and maintained by the existence of these social requisites. Unlike other newly created republics, Czechoslovakia remained democratic until the imposition of rule by the Nazis. Many credit this persistence of democracy in interwar Czechoslovakia to the economic and social conditions, the absence of a native nobility, and its previous pluralist experience (Beneš, 1973; Mamatey, 1973; Anderle, 1979; Wolchik, 1991). In addition to these favorable conditions, strong leaders (such as Tomáš Masaryk) facilitated democracy by strong commitment to the institutions and procedures of self-government (Korbel, 1977; Anderle, 1979).

The values held by Masaryk influenced not only the functioning of the government but also had a substantial effect upon the citizenry. The stability of the system is evidence of the emphasis placed on pluralism. The country's parliamentary system consisted of a multiplicity of parties elected through proportional representation that resulted in the necessity of coalition governments. Such an arrangement can threaten political stability. However, Czechoslovakia remained stable. The stability of the system also reflected the democratic values held by party leaders. Austrian rule had taught the Czechs the importance of participation and the necessity of compromise. This experience provided a conception of the way politics should be transacted. This was most clearly evidenced by the 'petka', the five parties that made up the majority of governments in the interwar period.[3] The petka mechanism ensured steady participation by the major parties and continuity of policy making. In addition, this political approach functioned as a method to incorporate diverse groups into the political system (Mamatey, 1973; Beneš, 1973; Anderle, 1979).

The democratic system of interwar Czechoslovakia was ended not by instability; rather, foreign actors dismantled the Czechoslovakian state. Nazi influence on the Sudeten Germans resulted in an increase of ethnic tensions in Czechoslovakia. Ultimately, Nazi Germany, as well as the policy of appeasement by the Western Allies, was responsible for the demise of democracy (Rothschild, 1974; Korbel, 1977; Wolchik, 1991). It is reasonable to argue that democracy would have been sustained in the absence of outside intrusion.

The Munich agreement of September 29, 1938, forfeited the Sudetenland to Hitler. Czechoslovakian leader Eduard Beneš capitulated to German forces, and no armed resistance was offered (Rothschild, 1974; Korbel, 1977). The cession of the Sudetenland was the first step in the dismantling of the independent Czechoslovakia. Following Nazi annexation, Slovak nationalists moved to create an independent Slovakia in October of 1938. In March 1939 Germany established a Protectorate of Bohemia and Moravia, and Beneš went into exile in London (Korbel, 1977). The Slovak state set up in 1939 modeled its political organization as well as its policies after the Nazis. The Czech lands suffered substantial economic losses under German occupation, while also being subjected to the systematic suspension of democratic freedoms.

Limited Pluralism: 1945-1948 Immediately following liberation in 1945, Czechoslovakia returned to what Wolchik terms 'modified pluralism'. Unlike other Central and Eastern European states following the end of the war, Czechoslovakia was not completely dominated by the Communist party. Rather, non-Communist groups were allowed participation. 'Czechs and Slovaks managed to retain some freedom of action and a political system in which non-Communist groups played a significant role longer than any other country in the region' (Wolchik, 1991, 17). The non-Communists included the prewar President Beneš.

Postwar party politics excluded parties that had collaborated with the Nazis as well as Slovak parties associated with the fascist Slovak state (Suda, 1980)[4]. Moreover, the Košice Government program required that all parties be part of the governing coalition (Suda, 1980). However, the Communist Party had certain advantages over the non-Communist groups following liberation. The Communists held key ministry positions, controlled the police, and amassed popular support through the redistribution of German lands and appeals to patriotism (Suda, 1980; Korbel, 1977). The Communist Party had over one million members in 1946, and it received the largest vote share

(37.9 percent) of any party in elections of the same year (Suda, 195-201; Korbel, 234-7).

Czechoslovakia's limited pluralism came to an end in 1948. The Communist-controlled police staged demonstrations and threatened democratic leaders. The May elections of 1948 consisted solely of candidates preapproved by the Communists, and the resignation of President Beneš in June signaled the end of any Communist/non-Communist coalition.

Communist Domination: 1948-1962 Soviet pressure, withdrawal from participation in the Marshall Plan, and the creation of the Cominform, the original Communist economic association, in 1947 facilitated the Communist takeover in 1948 (Wolchik, 1991). The democratic values that permeated the interwar period did not result in a moderate democratic socialist political structure in postwar Czechoslovakia. Rather, the Communist Party sought to destroy this value system through integration and assimilation into the 'new' political and social values. Efforts to reduce support for non-Communist leaders included propaganda campaigns and active recruitment of Communist Party membership. Because of the dissonance of the Communist political structure and the values held by the citizenry, the Communist Party sought to transform the society through a series of purges and terror (Korbel, 1977). Communist Party takeover of the government eliminated all opposition. As Wochik remarks, 'all political parties with any potential for challenging the communist order were neutralized' (1991, 22).

The Communists took further steps to alter the Czechoslovakian society and rid it of democratic elements. Not only was the multiparty system terminated but also aspects of civil society (such as voluntary associations, trade unions, student groups, and non-Communist organizations) were dissolved or incorporated into mass organizations under Communist control (Wolchik, 1991). The Communist Party also sought to change religious and social values through use of the media and education. Religious schools were closed, church property confiscated, and religious participation stifled in an effort to further the indoctrination of Marxist ideology. The educational system and the media came under tight Communist control. The Communist totalitarian hand stretched its fingers into all aspects of life. 'The arts and cultural life, as well as leisure-time activities, were affected by these efforts, as political leaders attempted to politicize all aspects of life' (Wolchik, 1991, 24).

Socialism with a Human Face: 1962-1968 The reform movement began in the early 1960s in Czechoslovakia and culminated in political liberalization in the 1968 'Prague Spring'. The movement toward political liberalization in 1968 was the result of both domestic economic problems and international factors. This movement can be differentiated from the 1956 liberalization efforts in Hungary and Poland in that it was initiated from above. The rebellions in Hungary and Poland were a result of mass discontent with economic conditions and de-Stalinization in the Soviet Union. Czechoslovakia's reawakening was delayed because of its relative economic success throughout the 1950s. The economic performance of Czechoslovakia translated into an absence of economic discontent and assured that there was less pressure for change before the 1960s.

By the 1960s Stalinist economic policies and central planning began to fail in Czechoslovakia. The resulting economic crisis led the Communist Party to establish a panel of economists to devise a plan for improving the situation. They called for economic liberalization, which was approved by the 13th Congress of the Communist Party in 1966 (Skilling, 1976; Wolchik, 1991). However, the implementation of these reforms was slow. This led economists to question whether economic reform could be successful without corresponding political reform (Skilling, 1976; Wolchik, 1991). The criticism leveled by economists sparked broader criticism of political orthodoxy by intellectuals. Concurrently, there was a reaffirmation of Khrushchev's denunciation of Stalinism. Khrushchev attacked both the existing central economic planning structure and Soviet foreign policy concerning the Eastern bloc satellite states. Khrushchev argued that the Stalinist model might not have been applicable to all of the Eastern European states and claimed that 'different roads to socialism' were permissible (Crouch, 1989).

The easing of external pressure from the Soviet Union coupled with the reformist tendencies of the political elite led to debate over the nature of socialism in Czechoslovakia. In addition, the leadership change from Antonín Novotný to Alexander Dubček in January 1968 signaled the beginning of participation beyond the elite level to the mass level (Skilling, 1976). Dubček supported both economic and political change and his leadership opened the way for greater participation in the political system. Discussion that had been limited to economic and political elites in the early 1960s was now reflected in the media and in the arts (Wolchik, 1991, 31). Wolchik contends that 'once censorship effectively ceased to exist in March 1968, the way was open for free expression of a kind unseen in Czechoslovakia since 1948' (Wolchik, 1991, 31).

Party intellectuals sought to change socialism in Czechoslovakia into a form that better matched its democratic heritage and level of economic development. The resulting 'socialism with a human face' was an attempt by the leadership to address past abuses of Stalinism and to ensure that there would be no further abuses. Moreover, the program's objectives included institutionalizing freedom of expression, granting other civil liberties to the citizens, redefining the role of the Communist Party, and reforming the economy (Wolchik, 1991, 32). In addition, the reforms included the opening of Czech cultural life and a certain autonomy for the arts. The leadership called for an increased role of other governmental and societal organizations. However, because this movement was top-down in nature, dominance of the Communist Party was to remain intact. That is, 'Dubček and other leaders were steadfast in maintaining that the leading role of the party was not to be abandoned; they also refuted the idea of establishing a true multiparty political system with an opposition outside the Communist Party' (Wolchik, 1991, 32). Thus, Communist leadership envisioned a limited pluralism under a socialist political system.

The loosening grip of the Communists and the intensified discussion and debate among intellectuals resulted in greater involvement of the citizens. The social forces unleashed were not to be satisfied within the framework of the limitations desired by the leaders. Mass organizations appeared, other political parties emerged, and official trade unions and student groups began behaving as interest groups. Communist Party leaders could not contain the pressure from below for greater democratization.

This did not result in a crackdown by Czechoslovakian Communist leaders; rather, 'the Dubček leadership attempted to increase the legitimacy of the system by allowing more genuine participation by ordinary citizens' (Wolchik, 1991, 33). However, Soviet Communists were alarmed at the opening of the political system and feared that the reform movement would sweep into other Communist states. 'In the end, it was the Dubček leadership's inability to reassure Czechoslovakia's external allies that brought the end of the experiment' (Wolchik, 1991, 34). Once again, external forces ended pluralism in Czechoslovakia.

Normalization: 1969-1985 Following the Soviet invasion of Czechoslovakia in August 1968, the Communist leadership strove to eliminate nearly all of the changes made during the reform era. Normalization of Czechoslovakia meant a reversal of the political, economic, and cultural openness of the 1960s. The policy of 'normalization' included the reasserted dominance of the Communist Party, reduction of influence of non-party groups, state control of the media, and personnel changes in the Party, mass organizations, and universities (Kusin, 1982). Dubček was ousted as leader of the Party in April 1969 and replaced by hard-liner Gustav Husák (Wolchik, 1990). In addition, Dubček's supporters were replaced with persons who had opposed reform. Personnel changes in universities and research institutes far outnumbered the political personnel changes. Kusin (1982) estimates that approximately half a million personnel changes took place in the centers of intellectual life during 1969-70. Wolchik claims that these changes had a much greater impact in the Czech lands than in Slovakia because in the Czech lands a 'larger number of party officials and intellectuals had been involved in the democratizing aspects of the reform' (1991, 36). The enormity of the personnel purges had long-term effects on Czechoslovakia in that it drained the leadership of expertise. In addition, the change in leadership signaled a change in policy. Like other Communist regimes, the Husák leadership resorted to a policy of coercion to gain compliance of the citizenry (Gitelman, 1970; Wolchik, 1991).

Coercive measures and the personnel purges led many intellectuals to retreat from the political realm (Ulč, 1979). However, the Communists were unable to free Czechoslovakia completely from organized opposition and dissent. The development of Charter 77 in 1977 demonstrated the continued desire for political change by a segment of society. The Charter largely consisted of intellectuals and those who took part in the 1968 reform effort. Although the Charter acted independently in its promotion of human rights practices, it posed no real political threat to the Communists in the late 1970s and early 1980s. However, the Charter served as a forerunner to the events of 1989. Charter activists emerged as the leaders of the Civic Forum (the pro-democracy opposition) during the 'Velvet Revolution'. Ultimately, the Charter's influence was one of keeping the spirit of reform alive and offering an alternative means of examining public issues.

Velvet Revolution: 1985-Present Initially, the Czechoslovakian government did not embrace Gorbachev's policy of openness or *glasnost* (Wolchik, 1989; Sorbell, 1988). Charter members publicly supported Gorbachev's policies and urged the Czechoslovakian leadership to adopt them (Wolchik, 1991). However, the Husák leadership, fearing a repeat of the events of 1968, restricted political debate. This resistance to change was demonstrated by the arrest of Charter members in January 1988 and subsequent arrests of Václav Havel and some demonstrators in January of 1989. However, the continued poor economic performance of Czechoslovakia coupled with Gorbachev's policy of *perestroika* pressured the Communist leadership to announce economic reform (Wolchik, 1991). The reforms proposed in 1987 resembled those discussed by economists in 1968.

Political reform did not begin until the November 1989 formation of the Civic Forum and demonstrations in Prague. Following the appointment of hard-liner Karel Urbánek as party leader, a nationwide strike commenced on November 28, and the government agreed to power-sharing concessions. The constitution was altered by deleting the provision specifying the Communist Party's domination, which allowed for the subsequent multiparty elections. Soon after, Husák resigned after swearing in the first non-Communist administration in 41 years (Banks, 1992, 199). In the following multiparty elections of June 8 and 9, the reformist umbrella group (the Civic Forum [Czech] and the Public Against Violence [Slovak]), won a clear majority of 170 of 300 seats in the Federal Assembly. Dissident leader Václav Havel was elected president on July 5, 1990.

Disputes between the Czechs and Slovaks began in 1991 over the extent of federal powers and whether Slovak should be deemed an official language of the republic. Both disputes were resolved; however, politically, the issue of separation of the nations had grown. The question was strongly linked to debate over economic policy and to the nature of the political structure. The Czech Civic Forum split into two parties: the Civic Democratic Party (ODS) and the Civic Movement (OH). The ODS, headed by the Czech Finance Minister Václav Klaus, favored rapid transition to the market and privatization of state enterprises. The OH, consisting of Prague Spring dissidents, was more centrist in outlook and advocated moderate economic reform. In addition, the Slovak counterpart to the Civic Forum, Public Against Violence (VPN), also split into two formations: the Civic Democratic Union-Public Against Violence (ODU-VPN) and the Movement for a Democratic Slovakia (HZDS). The HZDS, headed by Slovak Prime Minister Vladmír Mečiar, took on a nationalist leaning by promoting democracy for Slovakia. The Mečiar faction accused the ODU-VPN of not representing Slovak interests, and Klaus and Mečiar openly battled over the issue of the pace of economic reform. The radical reforms promoted by Klaus tended to hurt the Slovak regions more than the Czech lands. Bankruptcy of heavy industries in Slovakia increased the unemployment rate to 12 percent compared to the 4 percent in the Czech lands in 1991-92. Mečiar stressed slower reform in the interests of the Slovaks. Their battle also intensified over the federal issue, Klaus favoring a strong central government and Mečiar favoring a weak central government and stronger national governments. The Slovaks subsequently rejected the Czech plan for a strong central government, and the move was made toward separation. In the summer of 1992, both Klaus and Mečiar created almost identical separation plans. The dissolution, or Velvet Divorce, of the Czech and Slovak Federative Republic was passed on November 25, 1992 and went into effect January 1, 1993.

The new Czech Republic adopted a unitary state structure with a bicameral parliament and an executive branch consisting of a Council of Ministers headed by a Prime Minister and a President elected by the parliament. From 1994 to 1996 the Klaus coalition remained stable and radical economic transition was pursued. The most notable reforms were in the area of privatization using the voucher strategy. All adult citizens received share vouchers for state-owned industries. The success of this plan is evident in that 80 percent of industry was privatized by the end of 1994 and 90 percent by the end of 1995. Although the economic reform effort was hailed as a success, the election of 1996 produced a backlash against the consequences of rapid transition. The Czech Social Democratic Party (CSSD), former Communists, took second place in the parliamentary elections of May 31-June 1 1996. Its leftist platform argued that greater attention should be paid to the social problems caused by the economic transition.

The historical account of Czech political development clearly points to a tradition of pluralism and participation. Throughout Czech history it is evident that liberalization and democracy have been repeatedly stifled by external intervention. Participation in politics, experience with diverse representation and autonomous civic organizations, and high levels of education and economic development characterize the Czech experience. The democratic political culture periodically reemerged from under the totalitarian system whenever the regime's grip loosened. The positive experience with democracy in the interwar period has had a lasting effect upon the norms and values of the Czech citizenry.

Survey Data

Although the availability of survey data during the Communist period is limited, the following survey data tend to support a continuity of Czech pluralistic culture. The subjective perceptions of the Czech people concerning pluralism can be inferred from surveys available from the Institute of Public Opinion of the Czechoslovak Academy of Sciences. These surveys were conducted in December 1946, prior to the Communist takeover, and in October 1968, following Soviet intervention. Two questions are of particular interest in accessing the political values of the Czech citizenry: 1) when you contemplate the history of the Czech nation, which period do you consider to be the most glorious, a time of advance and development? and, 2) which personalities in our history do you esteem most? The second question is especially useful because it was asked at both time points, 1946 and 1968, and a comparison over time can be made to estimate the extent of continuity of values. In addition, these questions were asked of Slovaks in 1968. (Data for Slovak perceptions in 1946 are not available.) Slovak perceptions of history will be discussed in the Slovakia case study.

The first survey examines the question of Czechs' perception of their history.

Table 5.5 Czech Perceptions of History (October 1968)

Question: *When you contemplate the history of the Czech nation, which period do you consider the most glorious, a time of advance and development?*[5]

	Percentage Respondents
The First Republic (1918-1938)	39
The age of Hus (1369-1415)	36
The reign of King Charles IV (1346-1378)	31
The period after January 1968	21
The National Revival (19th century)	15
1945-1948	9
The reign of King George of Podebrady (1458-71)	5
The reign of King Premysl Otakar II (1253-1278)	5
Great Moravia (9th century)	3
The period after February 1948	3
The age of St. Wenceslas (10th century)	1
Other periods	7

The First Republic was viewed as the most glorious period in 1968 with 39 percent of the respondents. The First Republic was the Czechs' first experience with full-fledged democracy. The survey response indicates that the democratic structures that existed during this period were the Czechs' most preferred form of government. It is important to keep in mind that the 1968 survey occurred two months after the Soviet intervention. Brown and Wightman argue that this 'doubtless[ly] added to the emotional appeal of the First Republic' (1979, 166). However, in a pre-August survey of the Czech people, respondents were questioned on political pluralism in terms of ideas and parties. The questioned asked: should there be 'one political line for all' or should the many concepts and proposals of different parties and groups exist 'side by side'? The respondents overwhelmingly supported a pluralism of ideas and parties: 81 percent of total respondents (68 percent who were members of the Communist Party) favored many concepts; among non-Party members the support was 86 percent, and for those with higher education it reached 94 percent.[6]

The second set of questions that provides insight into the values and beliefs of the Czech citizenry deals with historic personalities. The questions asked the respondents to name the significant historical figures and those who are most esteemed. The following tables reveal the results of these surveys.

Table 5.6 Czech Evaluations of Historic Personalities (1946)

Name the three men in Czech history whom you consider the most significant.

	Percentage Respondents
T. G. Masaryk	74
Beneš	62
Hus	35
King Charles IV	20
Comenius	17
Jan Žižka	17
St. Wenceslas	17
K.H. Borovský	12
Cyril and Methodius	11
King George of Podebrady	7

Table 5.7 Czech Evaluations of Historic Personalities (1968)

Question: Which personalities in your history do you esteem most?

Percentage Respondents

T. G. Masaryk	81
Hus	40
King Charles IV	33
Comenius	28
Svoboda	22
Dubček	20
Palacký	13
Jan Žižka	10
King George of Podebrady	9
Beneš	7

The significance of this question is most clearly demonstrated in the choice of esteemed personalities who are symbolically important in terms of democracy. Tomáš Masaryk clearly represented the basic beliefs of the Czech people prior to the Communist takeover and again following the Prague Spring. Overwhelmingly, the results of both the 1946 and the 1968 surveys reveal the fondness for Masaryk, who, as the founder and first President of Czechoslovakia, served as a symbol of pluralist values as well as ethnic and religious toleration (Brown and Wightman, 1979, 172). The attachment of the Czech people to Masaryk following the First Republic led the Communists, in their attempt to alter the Czech political culture, to attack 'Masarykism' and to engage in continuous efforts to discredit him. It is noteworthy that no other personalities replaced Masaryk in the 1968 survey and that his popularity increased over time. This is particularly interesting in light of the Communist campaign to stifle the glorification of the Czech democratic past and Masaryk himself.

In general, the survey data support the notion of some degree of democratic political culture. The survey addressing the perception of history is less indicative of this support than the surveys of historic personalities. The consistent high support for Masaryk clearly demonstrates an esteem for a representative of democratic ideals.

Prospects for Democracy

The Czech Republic's functioning democratic institutions as well as the high level of popular support for the democratic regime increase the likelihood of continued consolidation. The support for democracy is explained not only by the success of its initial economic reforms and the consequent economic conditions but also by the prevalent democratic political culture. Based on its performance to date, it appears clear that the Czech Republic should continue its economic transformation and, collaterally, pursue EU membership. Interestingly, the split with Slovakia should make the remaining economic transition less arduous for the Czechs in that the Czech lands are more highly developed.

As in the past, external intervention exists as a possible threat to the consolidation of democracy in the Czech Republic. However, the likelihood of such a scenario has been reduced by the fact that Russia, the usual suspect, is concerned with its own political and economic troubles. Moreover, the Czech Republic's recent entrance into NATO offers protection from outside military threat. Internally, the Czech Republic is not threatened by extremist factions and exhibits a stable parliamentary system. Thus, again, it can be expected that the Czech Republic will continue toward full democratic consolidation with few economic or cultural obstacles standing in the way.

Notes

1. Data for January 1990, October 1990, and 1991 are for Czechoslovakia. Separate data for Slovakia were not collected until 1992.
2. Figure 5.4 plots the log of inflation for the Czech Republic and the average for Central and Eastern Europe. The log is used for graphical purposes because of the huge difference between the Czech Republic and the average for Central and Eastern Europe.
3. The petka consisted of the leadership of the Agrarians, the Social Democrats, the National Socialists, the Czechoslovak Populists, and the National Democrats. These party leaders played a pivotal role in the allocation of cabinet posts following independence. The core parties continued to regulate governmental politics throughout the interwar period, except between March 1926 and November 1929.
4. Six parties (four Czech and two Slovak) were acceptable immediately following the war: the Communist Party of Czechoslovakia, the National Socialist Party, the Czechoslovak People's Party, the Social Democratic Party, the Communist Party of Slovakia, and the Slovak Democratic Party. See Zdenek Suda, *Zealots and Rebels: A History of the Ruling Communist Party of Czechoslovakia*. Stanford, Hoover Institution Press, 1980, pp.178-84.
5. Respondents for the 1968 survey were allowed to answer up to two periods. Thus, the percentages total more than one hundred. Both the 1946 and the 1968 tables are repro-

duced from Archie Brown and Gordon Wightman's 'Czechoslovakia: Revival and Retreat' in Brown and Gray's *Political Culture and Political Change in Communist States*, 1979, pp. 164-165.

6   These results are cited in Brown and Wightman (170). See Jaroslaw Piekaliewicz, 'Public Political Opinion in Czechoslovakia in the Dubček Era' in E.J Czerwinski and Jaroslaw Piekaliewicz (eds.), *The Soviet Invasion of Czechoslovakia: Its Effects on Eastern Europe* (1972) p. 15.

6 Slovakia

Introduction

As with the Czech Republic, this case study examines both economic conditions and levels of democratic satisfaction. Comparisons between Slovakia and the average for all the Central and Eastern European states are provided, as are comparisons between Slovakia and the Czech Republic. Empirical findings for Slovakia differ from the Czech Republic in one essential aspect – the country effect upon democratic satisfaction (Table 3.3; Figure 3.3). The Czech Republic's high level of popular support can be attributed to the quick implementation of economic reforms and recovery as well as to the history of a democratic political culture. One might expect that Slovakia, having shared statehood with the Czechs (including common economic policies until 1993), would also demonstrate a high level of democratic support. However, this is not the case. Drawing distinctions between the political cultures of the Czechs and Slovaks is particularly important in understanding the difference between the two states in terms of democratic support.

Democratic Support

In the case of Slovakia, it is useful to examine the level of democratic support not only in respect to Central and Eastern Europe as a whole but also as compared to the Czech Republic in particular. Table 6.1 and Figure 6.1 display the democratic satisfaction level for Slovakia, the Czech Republic, and the average for all the countries of Central and Eastern Europe. Democratic satisfaction for Slovakia for 1992 to 1994 is below that of both the Czech lands and the mean for the Central and Eastern European states. There is a sharp contrast between the Czech Republic and Slovakia. The satisfaction level for the Czech Republic remains relatively constant from 1991 to 1994. Slovakia, on the other hand, starts out far below the Czech level beginning in 1992 and continues to decrease over time. The initial gap between the Czechs and the Slovaks in 1992 is interesting in that it demonstrates a distinct difference between the two groups prior to Slovak separation on January 1, 1993. In addition, although the Slovak democratic satisfaction level is close to the mean for the Central and Eastern European states, it is below the average. Given the shared statehood with the Czech lands, one would expect the democratic satisfaction level to be higher than average.

Table 6.1 Democratic Satisfaction for Slovakia, the Czech Republic, and Central and Eastern Europe

Year	Czech Republic	Slovakia	Ave. CEE	Difference Slovakia and Czech	Difference Slovakia and CEE
(Oct.)1990	3.21	–	–	–	–
(Jan.)1990	2.25	–	2.40	–	–
1991	2.15	–	2.26	–	–
1992	2.31	2.09	2.12	-0.22	-0.03
1993	2.40	2.00	2.09	-0.40	-0.09
1994	2.33	1.93	1.97	-0.40	-0.04

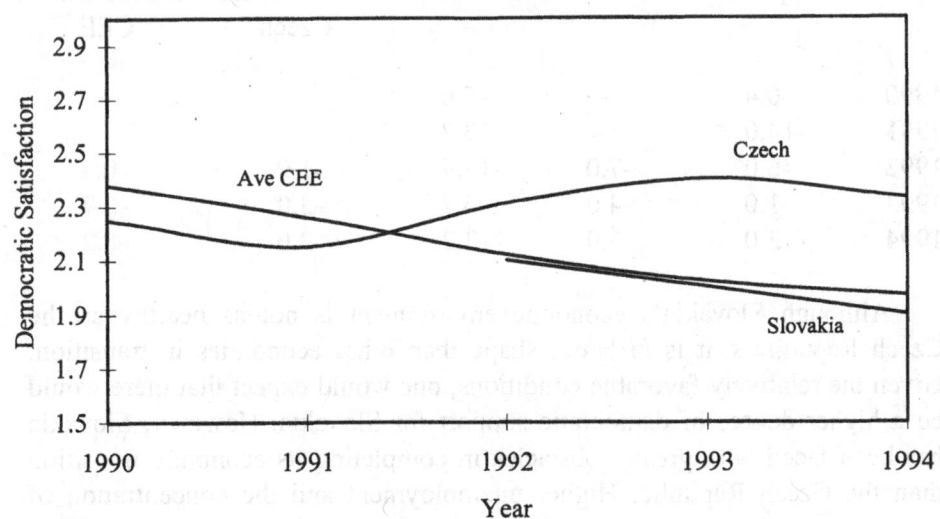

Figure 6.1: Democratic Satisfaction for Slovakia, the Czech Republic, and Central and Eastern Europe

Economic Indicators

An exploration of economic factors may provide some explanation for Slovakia's low levels of democratic support. It is advantageous to compare Slovakia's economic indicators with the average for all of Central and Eastern Europe as well as the Czech Republic. The comparison of the Czech Republic and Slovakia, particularly with respect to the financial evaluations, may furnish some interesting insights regarding the corresponding economic policies under shared statehood.

Gross Domestic Product

Table 6.2 and Figure 6.2 depict the economic output of Slovakia, the Czech Republic, and the average for Central and Eastern Europe. The economic output for Slovakia greatly resembles that of the Czech Republic. This is to be expected given the shared economic policies until the split. In addition, the Slovak economic conditions are well above the average for Central and Eastern Europe.

Table 6.2 Percentage Change in Real GDP for Slovakia, the Czech Republic, and Central and Eastern Europe

Year	Czech Republic	Slovakia	Average CEE	Difference Slovakia and Czech	Difference Slovakia and CEE
1990	-0.4	–	-5.0	–	–
1991	-14.0	–	-13.2	–	–
1992	-6.0	-7.0	-17.4	-1.0	-10.4
1993	-1.0	-4.0	-6.7	-3.0	-2.7
1994	3.0	5.0	-3.2	2.0	-8.2

Although Slovakia's economic environment is not as healthy as the Czech Republic's, it is in better shape than other economies in transition. Given the relatively favorable conditions, one would expect that there would be a higher degree of democratic support for Slovakia. However, Slovakia has been faced with greater obstacles in completing its economic transition than the Czech Republic. Higher unemployment and the concentration of heavy industry and outdated factories in the Slovak lands have made privatization more difficult.

H_1: If economic conditions improve, support for democracy will increase.

Figure: 6.2: Percentage Change in Real GDP for Slovakia, the Czech Republic, and Central and Eastern Europe

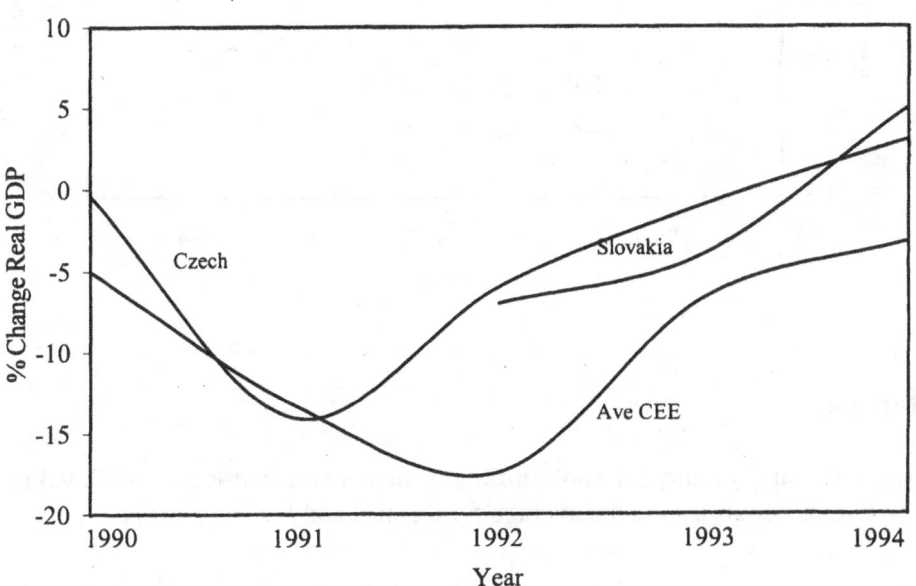

Figure 6.3 plots both the democratic satisfaction level and the percentage change in real GDP output for 1992-1994. The relationship is contrary to the proposed hypothesis — as GDP increases, democratic satisfaction decreases. In other words, the economy appears to be rebounding while popular support wanes. It may be that the populace is not yet feeling the effects of the positive growth.

Figure 6.3: Democratic Satisfaction and Percentage Change in Real GDP for Slovakia

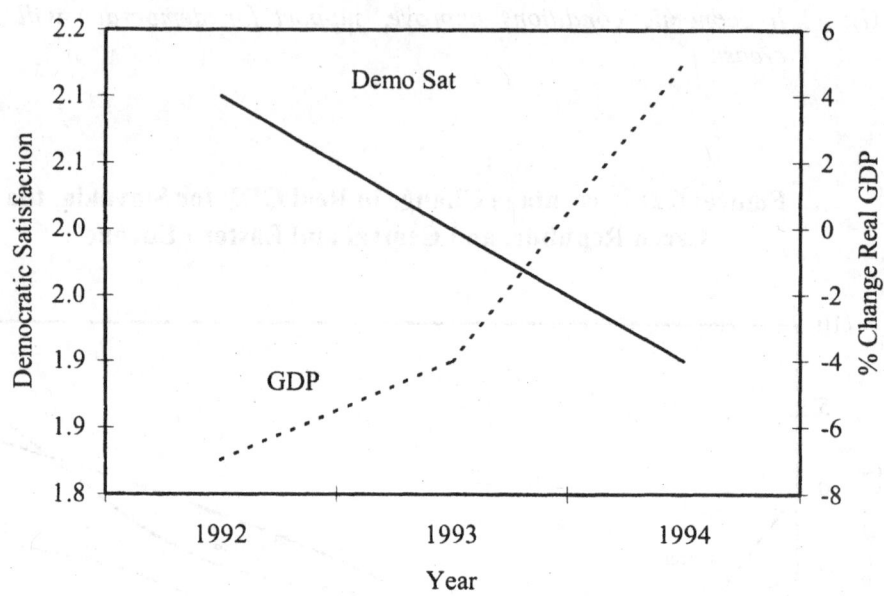

Inflation

Table 6.3 and Figure 6.4 show inflation, or consumer prices, for Slovakia, the Czech Republic, and the average for Central and Eastern Europe.

Table 6.3 Inflation for Slovakia, the Czech Republic, and Central and Eastern Europe

Year	CZE	log CZE	SLO	log SLO	Ave. CEE	log Ave. CEE	Diff SLO-CZE	Diff SLO-CEE
1990	18.4	2.91	–	–	76.7	4.34	–	–
1991	52.0	3.95	–	–	186.5	5.23	–	–
1992	13.0	2.57	9.0	2.20	922.0	6.83	-4.0	-913.0
1993	18.0	2.89	25.0	3.22	274.4	5.62	7.0	-250.6
1994	10.0	2.30	12.0	2.49	301.4	5.71	2.0	-290.6

Figure 6.4: Inflation for Slovakia, the Czech Republic, and Central and Eastern Europe

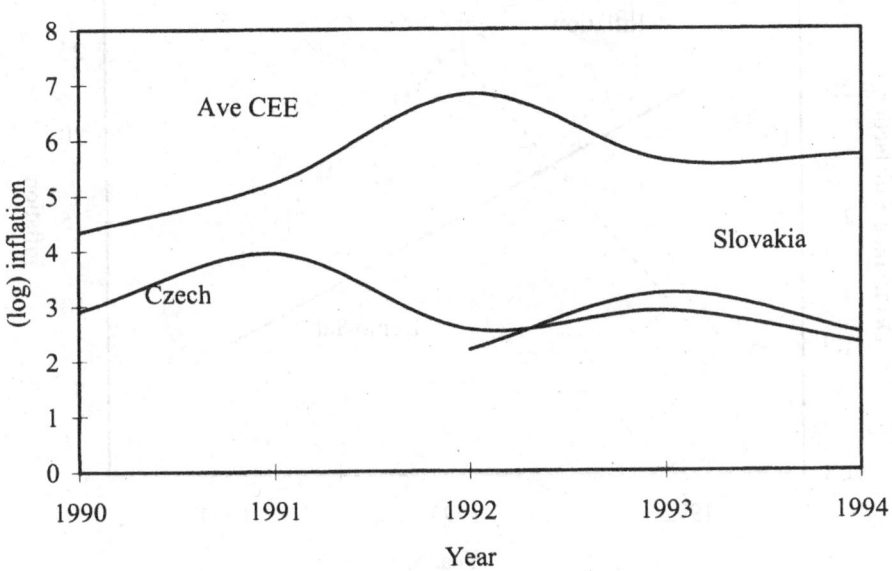

Like the Czech Republic, Slovakia's inflation has been extremely low in comparison to the hyperinflation experienced by most of Central and Eastern European transition economies. Inflation peaked in Slovakia in 1993 with a rate of 25 percent.[1] This low inflation rate signifies the success Slovakia has had with its economic policies.

In terms of objective economic conditions, Slovakia's macroeconomic environment more closely corresponds with that of the Czech Republic than with the average Central and Eastern European economies. This is to be expected given that the same economic policies were implemented in both areas from the beginning of the transition until 1993.

Figure 6.5 plots democratic satisfaction and inflation from 1992 to 1994.

94 *The Economy and Political Culture in New Democracies*

Figure 6.5: Democratic Satisfaction and Inflation for Slovakia

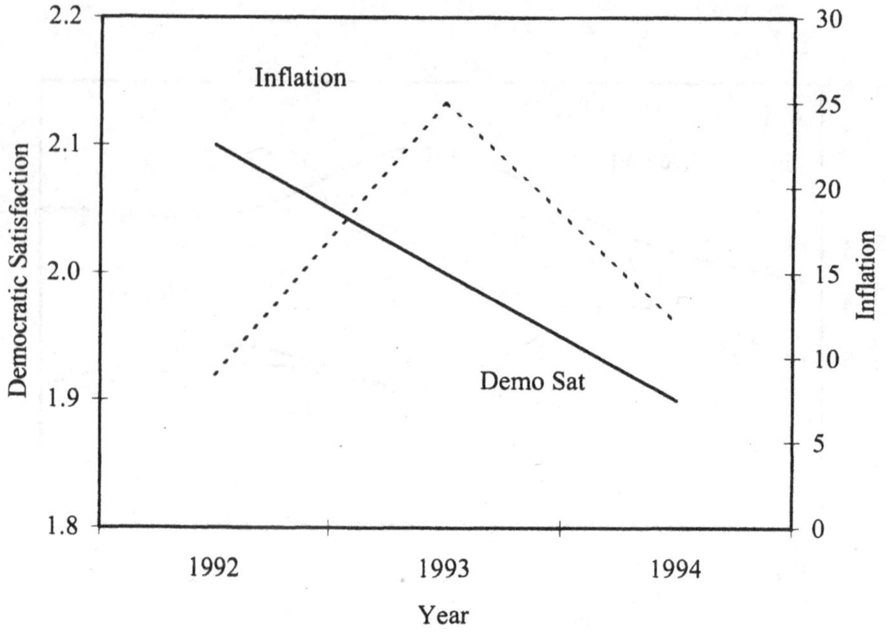

The hypothesized negative relationship is evident from 1992 to 1993; however, the relationship does not hold from 1993 to 1994, a period that reveals both a drop in inflation and a corresponding drop in democratic satisfaction. The financial evaluations may give us a clearer view of the citizens' perceptions of economic well-being.

Financial Evaluations

Table 6.4 displays citizen evaluations of the financial situation in Slovakia and the Czech Republic, and the average for all states in Central and Eastern Europe.

From Table 6.4 and Figure 6.6 we see that Slovakia deviates from the Czech Republic on how the financial situation is perceived. Slovakia more clearly approximates the mean of Central and Eastern Europe than that of the Czech Republic. The Czech Republic's perception of the financial situation is much higher than that of Slovakia. This is particularly interesting given the similar economic conditions of both countries. We would expect, particularly given the low inflation rate, that financial evaluations would be more optimistic than those displayed.

H_2:   If financial evaluations improve, democratic satisfaction will increase.

Table 6.4 Financial Evaluations for Slovakia, the Czech Republic, and Central and Eastern Europe

Year	Czech Republic	Slovakia	Average CEE	Difference Slovakia and Czech	Difference Slovakia and CEE
1990	2.17	—	2.33	—	—
1991	2.21	—	2.46	—	—
1992	2.53	2.29	2.31	-0.24	-0.02
1993	2.69	2.25	2.34	-0.44	-0.09
1994	2.70	2.47	2.43	-0.23	0.04

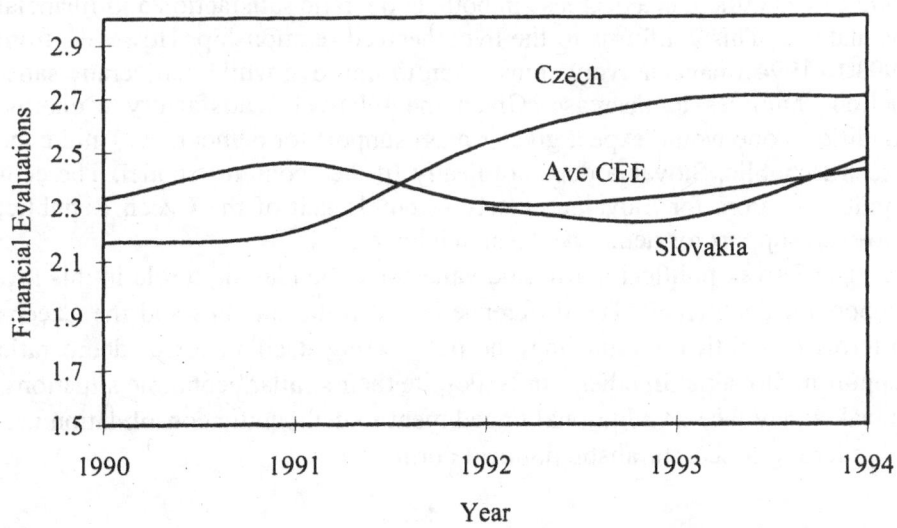

Figure 6.6: Financial Evaluations for Slovakia, the Czech Republic, and Central and Eastern Europe

96 The Economy and Political Culture in New Democracies

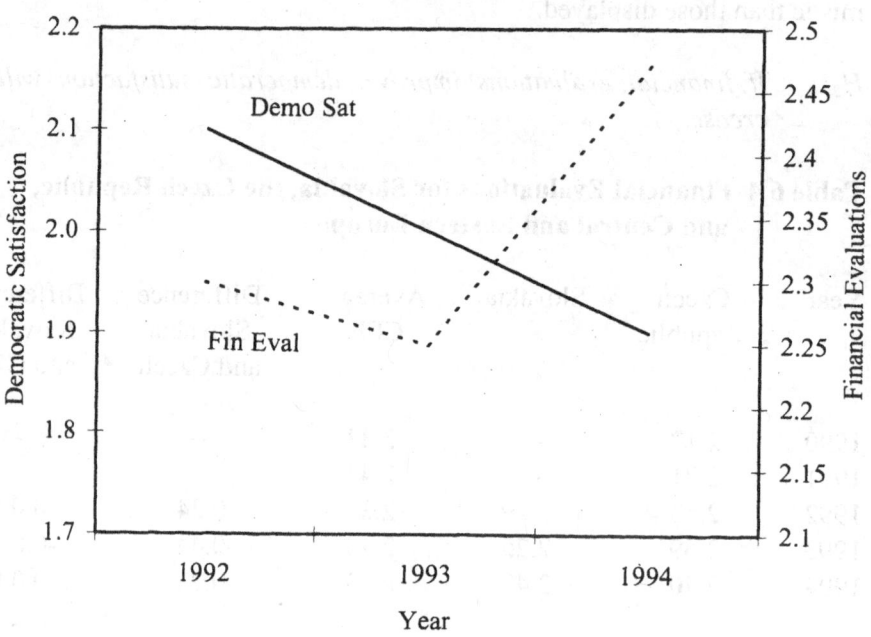

Figure 6.7: Democratic Satisfaction and Financial Evaluations for Slovakia

Figure 6.7 plots democratic satisfaction and financial evaluations. From 1992 to 1993, there is a decrease in both democratic satisfaction and financial evaluations. This conforms to the hypothesized relationship. However, from 1993 to 1994 financial evaluations begin to improve while democratic satisfaction continues to decrease. Given the relatively satisfactory economic conditions, one would expect greater mass support for democracy. Unlike the Czech Republic, Slovakia does not neatly fit the economic model. The economic indicators for Slovakia closely resemble that of the Czech Republic; however, support for democracy is much lower.

The Slovak political norms and values may be playing a role in this low support for democracy. The difference between the Slovaks and the Czechs in terms of political culture may be manifesting itself in lower democratic support in Slovakia. In other words, despite their similar economic situations, Slovakia may face an additional impediment to democratic consolidation i.e., an underdeveloped pluralistic political norm.

Political Culture

Much of the research on Czechoslovakia's political culture has explored the continuity of pluralism in the Czech political tradition and has relegated the Slovak political orientation to that of a 'sub-culture' within the dominant Czech framework (Skilling, 1977; Brown and Wightman, 1979). However, the Slovak political tradition was linked historically to Hungarian rule as well as to a shared experience with the Czech lands. As Seton-Watson (1965, 280) points out; it is important 'to realize the extreme difference of *milieu* between Slovaks and Czechs, the extent to which the Czechs had in the last century before the war repaired their own backwardness under the more enlightened rule of Austria, and above all the fact that the Czechs were free to go forward at a growing pace, while the Slovaks were falling behind in the race, if not actually beginning to go backwards.' In other words, it is possible to treat the Czech and Slovak cultures as distinct cultures. The analysis that follows examines the significant differences of these cultures in terms of political development.

Unlike the Czech Republic, Slovakia's political culture does not demonstrate a clear continuity of pluralistic political values. Rather, the Slovak historical experience has been one that can be characterized as a search for national identity. It is tempting to argue that the Slovaks were in some sense lacking political tradition – 'Slovak politics hardly existed "except in embryonic form"' (Paul, 1979, 138). However, in terms of Slovak democratic attitudes, it is more precise to say 'that the tradition of pluralism in Slovakia is not as pronounced, and is probably weaker, than in the Czech lands' (Paul, 1979, 138). A clear-cut, continuously democratic political culture is not evident for the Slovaks.

This ambiguous Slovak political culture, often manifesting itself in authoritarianism, may be one explanation for the negative democratic satisfaction that exists in the present political environment. Consequently, an assessment of the historical differences between Czech and Slovak social and economic development must be included in any attempt to explain the divergence that exists in the present levels of democratic support. Consistent with the methods used in my examination of the Czech Republic, the analysis of the historical development of Slovakia's political culture not only makes use of the objective historical experiences of the Slovaks but also incorporates the subjective values and beliefs of citizens as derived from available survey data.

Historical Evidence

The differences that characterize the Czech and Slovak political cultures can be traced to the distinct political experiences under the dual monarchy, variation in social and economic development, different perceptions of political access and representation during the First Republic, limited autonomy of Slovakia during WW II, and, ultimately, differences in status between Slovaks and Czechs during the 70 years these two nations were united as a single Czechoslovakian state.

Hungarian Rule: 896 (approximately)–1914 Slovak history is fundamentally differentiated from Czech history because of long-standing Hungarian dominance of the Slovak lands. Seton-Watson argues that 'Slovak history should be treated differently from that of Bohemia, for the simple reason that for one thousand years Slovakia had no separate history of her own, but formed a mere annex to that of Hungary' (Seton-Watson, 1955, 250). Slovakia existed in relative isolation from its neighbors to the north, east, and west due to geographical factors. The High Tatra Mountains to the north and the Carpathian Mountains to the east cut off contact with Poland and the Ukraine. Thus, naturally, Slovakia's external contacts were largely limited to the Magyars of the south, and, until the 19th century, the Slovak lands were considered to be 'northern Hungary' under Magyar domination.

The Slovaks were not the only minority group to fall under Magyar control; Croats, Serbs, Romanians, and Ruthenians were also dominated. Thus, a historical distinction can be made from what was considered Hungarian and what is Magyar. Nationalist sentiments of the Slovaks began in the 18th century and for the most part involved the issue of language.[2] Over time, the use of the Slovak language became a political, economic, and educational barrier to Slovak advancement within the Hungarian state.

The literary revival of the Slovak language in the 18th century was met with opposition in the 19th century by the Magyars, who took steps to exclude the use of any language other than Magyar as part of the 'Magyarization' of ethnic minorities. Seton-Watson details these measures:

> Already in 1830 Parliament had passed the first of a series of laws extending the sphere of the Magyar language; and Count Stephen Széchényi had won a unique position by his sensational offer of a year's income as preliminary endowment of a Hungarian Academy. In the same year Magyar was made obligatory for all advocates or holders of public office. In 1836 it was made, jointly with Latin, the language of the laws, and became optional for all official documents, and in courts of second instance. In 1839-1840 it became the offi-

cial language of the Government and the exclusive language of all registers and its knowledge was made obligatory for clergy of all denominations. At last, in 1843, it was declared the exclusive language of legislation, of the Government and of official business, and it was declared in principle to be also the exclusive language of public instruction, though the enforcement of this were left to a future parliament.

The suppression of the Slovak language had far-reaching consequences for education and political development. Moreover, the issue of language took on a religious aspect. The promotion of the Slovak language in the literary revival is attributed largely to the Jesuits and the Catholic clergy. The Lutheran Church chose, instead, to support the Magyar language as '...the truest guardian and protector of the liberty of our country, of Europe and of the Protestant cause'[3] (Seton-Watson, 1965, 260). Thus, the national awakening of the Slovaks stems from the issue of the Slovak language as well as the Catholicism of the people.

The suppression of the Slovak language took on national political significance in 1848 in the Slav Congress. The Congress, simultaneously addressing the Crown and the National Government at Pest, demanded 'the right to use the mother tongue in all public deliberations and in courts of law, Slovak schools and a university, a Slovak National Guard, Universal Suffrage and complete freedom of assembly, association and press' (Seton-Watson, 1965, 262). However, the demands were met with the execution of those promoting nationalist sentiments and general accusations that the Slovaks were promoting Panslavism. Increasingly, the Slovaks looked to Vienna and Francis Joseph for recognition as a distinct political nation. These appeals, however, were largely ignored.

The Austro-Hungarian Compromise of 1867, which established a new Dualist Hungary, brought about a renewed wave of Magyarization. Seton-Watson argues that 'the Ausgleich of 1867 opens a new era for all non-Magyar nationalities, who were handed over to the unrestricted political control of the now dominant Magyars' (Seton-Watson, 1965, 267). This new era regulated all non-Magyars by the 'Law of Equal Rights of the Nationalities', specifying that non-Magyar nationalities were entitled to their own language and culture within the Hungarian state. However, the intent and practice of the law was not to foster separate national entities within Hungary. Rather, the law was designed to promote greater assimilation of non-Magyars through 'a policy of mildness and concession' (Seton-Watson, 1965, 267). Moreover, the practice of the law, carried out largely by Koloman Tisza, reaffirmed Magyar as the official language of the State. Thus, the law of nationalities was what both Seton-Watson and Kirschbaum call a 'dead letter'.

Unlike the Czechs under Austrian rule, the Slovaks were unable to pursue any educational or political advancement due to the implemented Magyarization policies. Seton-Watson asserts that 'throughout the Dualist period the entire state school system was Magyarized...from 1875 to 1918 the Slovaks were entirely without secondary schools' (Seton-Watson, 1965, 268). In addition, during this same period, the Electoral Law of 1874, coupled with corrupt electoral practices, limited the amount of non-Magyar political participation in the Hungarian Parliament. In the face of continued Magyarization, the Slovaks failed to get any members elected to the Hungarian Diet throughout the 1870s and 1880s[4]. Politically, the Slovaks, mainly through the leadership of the Slovak National Party, adopted a policy of abstention and passivity (Seton-Watson, 1965, 270; Kirschbaum, 1995, 140).

The linguistic, educational, social, and political suppression of the Slovaks under the Magyars not only sparked the national awakening of the Slovaks but also pushed them toward the Czechs in their pursuit of national development. Moreover, the Czech attitude toward the Slovaks began to change in the early 1900s from one of paternalistic or benign interest to one of a Czechoslovak orientation. 'In 1915, Masaryk made the union of the Czechs and Slovaks an objective of Czech politics' (Kirschbaum, 1995, 149). Masaryk officially proclaimed this Czechoslovak alignment to the British Foreign Secretary in a memorandum that stated 'the Slovaks are Bohemians in spite of their using their dialect as their literary language' (Seton-Watson, 1943, 125).

The outbreak of WW I stifled any further political developments in Slovakia; however, progress toward statehood continued through the actions of Slovaks living abroad. In October of 1915, the Cleveland Agreement was signed by both American Czechs and Slovaks with the clear intention of forming a federal state made up of two independent nations (Kirschbaum, 1995, 150). This agreement specified 'in addition to universal, direct, and secret suffrage, that Slovakia would have its own Diet, government, and financial and political administration, and that Slovak would be the official language' (Kirschbaum, 1995, 150). However, by 1918, the Czech agenda had changed, and Masaryk signed the Pittsburgh Pact, which contained only a limited degree of linguistic and administrative autonomy for Slovakia under common statehood. The Slovak National Council issued a third document, the Declaration of the Slovak Nation, which proposed a political union with the Czechs.[5] This document took the Slovaks out of Hungary and formed a new union with the Czech nation (Kirschbaum, 1995, 152).

The First Czechoslovak Republic: 1918-1938 The formation of the Czechoslovak state immediately transferred the Slovaks from one political system into another. The Slovaks lacked the necessary political experience for the new republic, specifically in three areas: mass political parties, political leadership, and administration. In terms of political parties, 'although the Slovak National Party, the Slovak People's Party, and a branch of the Social Democratic Party had existed in Hungary, none was a mass party, certainly not in the modern sense of the word' (Kirschbaum, 1995, 155). They were largely elite parties, consisting of members of the intelligentsia, who had concentrated on the battle against Magyarization. The absence of an active political leadership left Slovakia without clearly defined goals for the future.[6] The administrative organization had been controlled by Budapest, and officials were landed nobility who returned to Hungary following the breakup of Austria-Hungary. In addition, the Slovaks lacked a political center for administration. Prague had become the center for the Czechs and eventually the center for the Czechoslovak nation. The new political structure itself added to the disappointment of the Slovak aspirations toward autonomy.

In addition to these political problems, the Slovaks faced the task of socio-economic development. Seton-Watson asserts 'If politically the Middle Ages did not end in Hungary until 1848, it might plausibly be argued that economically they continued till 1918' (1965, 280). The economic environment and the administrative organization strikingly resembled that of feudal society. Thus, the new statehood pushed the Slovaks into the painful process of industrialization. The traditional occupational structure of Slovakia is demonstrated in the following table adapted from Leff (1988).

Table 6.5 Occupational Structure in 1910 by Nationality

	Agriculture	Industry	Transport and Commerce	Professions and State Service
Czech Lands				
German	26.0	44.6	14.6	13.8
Czech	39.1	36.2	10.9	12.3
Slovakia				
Slovak	72.3	15.8	2.3	1.9
German	29.9	41.8	14.5	7.5
Magyar	52.5	21.9	8.7	9.1

Source: Compiled from data in L'Office de Statistique d'état, *Manuel statistique de la République tchécoslovaque, 1920* (Prague, 1922), pp. 19-22.

The Slovak population was most heavily represented in the agrarian sector and least represented in the professions and state service. Interestingly, the Czech profile more closely resembles the Germans than the Slovaks. This skewed occupational profile clearly illustrates the economic and social discrepancies between the Czech and Slovak populations.

The final hurdle for the Slovak integration into the new state was psychological in nature. Kirschbaum (1995, 157) describes this problem thusly:

> The Magyar social and political system had inculcated in the population an attitude of deference toward authority and respect for social rank. As a personal mechanism for the preservation of language and national identity, this attitude was not an unsuccessful way of handling external pressure; as a collective pattern of behavior, however, it bred passivity, resignation, suspicion, and almost always also opposition. These were not social characteristics that would facilitate a transition as radical as the one the Slovaks were about to undergo.

Thus, the Slovaks were called upon not only to form a new state but also a new political culture. The Czechs had adopted an ideology of Czechoslovakianism; however, the response by the Slovaks was nationalism. The ideology of Czechoslovakianism aimed to integrate the two nations into a single state. This aim was visibly manifest in the passage of the Language Law that stated:'The Czecho-Slovak language is the state (official) language of the Republic'. However, Temperley (1921, 470) argues that 'this clause of course represents a legal fiction, since there is no such thing as a Czecho-Slovak language, but two intimately related dialects, enjoying full parity in the administration, justice and education.' The Language Law was perceived as a threat to the Slovak language, and nationalism was a natural response given the history of oppression of the Slovak language and culture.

Under the Czechoslovak state, the Slovak lands benefited from many of the governmental policies, particularly in terms of administration, infrastructure, and social legislation. However, although the Slovak standard of living improved, economic policy determined that Slovakia would primarily continue to play an agricultural role. The policy of 'agrarian Slovakia', Kirschbaum argues, 'rather than establishing a beneficial division of labor ... created an economic dualism that disadvantaged Slovakia' (1995, 173).

Regardless of the economic disadvantage, Slovakia enjoyed parliamentary government with regular elections and political freedom. In addition, Slovakia made substantial progress in the area of education (Johnson, 1985; Korbel, 1977). Wolchik argues that 'the extension of educational opportunities in Slovak to the mass public and the new freedom of Slovak intellectuals to write and publish in Slovak without restrictions experienced under Hungarian rule led to a revival of Slovak culture during this period' (1991, 13).

The Republic also enabled Slovakia to deal effectively with the problems of modernization. Political parties were mobilized and were able to promote their interests. Slovak citizenry actively participated in politics. Ironically, it can be argued that this participation in the political process was geared toward combatting Czechoslovakianism and achieving Slovak autonomy (Kirschbaum, 1995, 175). During this time, the Slovak People's Party and the Slovak National Party continued to press for autonomy. The dissatisfaction of the Slovaks with Czechoslovakianism as well as their economic grievances were evidenced by the support for the Slovak People's Party in the 1925 elections. The Slovak People's Party, led by Father Andrej Hlinka, was the leading vote-getter among Slovaks and received 34.4 percent of the vote statewide, and 23 parliamentary seats. Thus, throughout the First Republic, the ideology of Czechoslovakianism never truly took hold in Slovakia, while the idea of an autonomous Slovak nation was never forgotten.

The Slovak Republic: 1939-1945 The growing power of the Nazi party coupled with the extremist nationalist views of Slovak leaders such as Vojtech Tuka and Josef Tiso (successive leaders of the Slovak People's Party following Hlinka's death in 1938) paved the way for the establishment of the Slovak state. Although the Slovak state was, for all practical purposes, a puppet government of the Reich, it did satisfy the nationalist desire for autonomy (Wolchik, 1991; Rothschild, 1974; Korbel, 1977). Kirschbaum asserts that the Slovak fascist state was an option that assured the nation's survival (1995, 186). The option of resistance invited overthrow and German occupation for Slovakia. Thus, the leaders of Slovakia were aware that in order to stay out of the war and achieve independence, they needed to allow Germany to determine policy[7].

Slovakia declared independence on March 14, 1939, and 'the Slovak Provincial Assembly ... transformed itself into a full-fledged Parliament and proceeded to approve a new government with Tiso as prime minister' (Kirschbaum, 1995, 190). Subsequently, the Slovak constitution was promulgated on July 21, 1939. It established a presidential system with Tiso as president and Tuka as prime minister. Slovakia, under the leadership of Tiso and as a result of the Treaty of Protection with Germany, successfully avoided the war for five years.

The differences between Czech and Slovak perceptions of the Slovak Republic are noteworthy. Suda asserts that 'understandably, the establishment of a Nazi satellite state in Slovakia was generally felt by the Czechs as treason, a stab in the back from the nearest of kin' (Suda, 1980, 119). Suda further argues that 'it was only at this point that the Czech public realized that the social and political value system of the First Republic had not been shared by the Slovaks, or had only been shared by a minority among them' (1980, 119). It can be argued that the Czechs did not realize the importance the Slovaks placed upon national autonomy. The Slovaks perceived the succession of Slovakia as an opportunity not only to rule themselves during the time of war but also to establish autonomy that would follow in the postwar period (Wolchik, 1991; Rothschild, 1974; Korbel, 1977; Hoensch, 1973; Jelinek, 1976; Thomson, 1953). However, the British recognition of the Czechoslovak government-in-exile in 1941 signaled that the future of the Slovak Republic was uncertain. By 1943 it was evident that the Allies would win the war, and Beneš announced that Slovakia 'as a state separated from the Czech lands ... will never be recognized by the victorious Allies' (Benes, 1944, 40-41).

Internal political conflict developed among Slovak politicians over the fate of Slovakia, and this ultimately culminated in the Slovak Uprising of 1944, which meant the end of the Slovak Republic. Ironically, it was the destruction of the Slovak state by the Slovaks that allowed them to join the victors and avoid military dictatorship under Beneš (Mikula, 1944, 126). The Slovaks who participated in the Uprising and the Slovak National Council (SNC) wished to restore Czechoslovakia on the principle of 'equal with equal'. This had been decided upon prior to the Uprising in the Christmas Agreement of 1943, a program of the SNC that stipulated a political structure on the basis of federation. However, the fascist Slovak state was not so easily forgotten by the Czechs.

1945-1948 The Slovak independence of 1939-1945 allowed Slovakia to mature politically and prove to itself that it was capable of self-government. The Slovaks felt that reunification with the Czech lands should be based upon equal representation rather than Czech dominance. However, the Czech response to the wayward Slovaks was not supportive of equal partnership; rather, it sought punishment for the Slovak nationalist political leaders.

Initially, negotiations for the new Czechoslovak Republic under the Košice governmental program granted a degree of autonomy to Slovak governmental bodies, as demanded by the Slovaks (Rychlik, 1995). However, the Košice program did not resolve the question of the division of jurisdiction between the central government and the Slovak bodies. That issue was settled in the Third Prague agreement of 1947, which mandated a strong central body and strictly limited Slovak status. As the election results of 1946 demonstrated, both the Czech political parties and the Czech and Slovak Communist parties supported strong centralism. However, the strong Communist support in the Czech lands (40.17 percent) was not evident in the Slovak lands, in which the outright winner was the Democratic Party (62 percent). The Slovak Communist Party supported centralism and limitation of Slovak powers until Slovakia gained a more equal economic standing and/or after the 'final victory of the working class' (Rychlik, 1995, 193). The trial and execution of Jozef Tiso in 1947 also helped to relegate the Slovaks to a secondary status. Ultimately, the Constitutional Committee, in the hands of the Communists, 'left the Slovak authorities with even less jurisdiction than the Third Prague Agreement had done' (Rychlik, 1995, 193).

1948-1968 The Communists adopted a campaign to crush the idea of Slovak nationalism. This was supported both by Communist ideology in general, which called for a merging of classless communist nations, and by a series of purges of Slovak nationalists, who were accused of supporting 'bourgeois nationalism'. Under Marxist-Leninist ideology, the working classes of all nations have the same interests. Thus, there is no need for separate nations – separation is a bourgeois solution to the problems created by ethnic and cultural differences (Kirschbaum, 1987, 133). The campaign against 'bourgeois nationalism' resulted in a series of trials, sentencing, and executions of Slovak Communist intellectuals who sought a place for Slovakia under the new political structure.[8]

Although the Communists sought to extinguish Slovak nationalism, the regime itself was not anti-Slovak (Rychlik, 1995, 193). Rychlik asserts that under Communist Czechoslovakia, 'Slovaks were present at all levels of the party and state apparatus, including the State Security Police, and persecuted their compatriots with equal cruelty'(1995, 194). In addition, the Communist policy of integrating the Slovak economy into that of the Czech lands had unintended consequences. The development of the 1950s effectively changed the Slovak agrarian economy into an industrialized economy. The consequence, however, was not greater integration of the Czechs and Slovaks. The necessity for the Slovak lands to undergo economic development further justified the asymmetrical political structure. Moreover, as Rychlik states, 'the notion that this would solve the Slovak problem was completely mistaken: the standard of living of entire sections of the Slovak population increased and subsequently Slovak self-confidence increased too' (1995, 194).

The relaxation following Stalin's death and Khrushchev's famous speech to the 20th Party Congress led to the rehabilitation of the so-called bourgeois nationalists. These political leaders, particularly Gustav Husák, raised the question of a federal state and greater autonomy for Slovakia. Kirschbaum (1987) argues that 'this rehabilitation in fact meant that the federal demand of 1944 by the 'povstalci' had been legitimate and the accusation of 'Slovak bourgeois nationalism' unjust' (135). Czech leadership in the early 1960s, under Antonín Novotný, who was well known for his anti-Slovak views, was able to suppress Slovak demands effectively. Alexander Dubček, First Secretary of the Czechoslovak Communist Party (CPS) and a Slovak, had 'allowed the CPS to become a vehicle of reform in Slovakia and he protected writers and intellectuals from Novotný's wrath' (Kirschbaum, 1987, 135). Dubček publicly raised the Slovak national issue in 1966 and 1967 by linking it to the 19th century reformer Ludovit Štúr. He stated: 'Štúr's ideas on the development of Slovakia were reborn in the Slovak Revolt ...[when] the national and international aspirations of Slovakia were clear – soldiers and partisans fought not only for the rights of the Slovak nation but also for the renewal of Czechoslovakia as a state of two equal nations, as a home of Czechs and Slovaks and built on nationally and socially just principles' (Shawcross, 1970, 124).

The replacement of Novotný with Dubček in 1968 allowed the Slovaks to press for federalism. Dubček became a symbol not only of liberalization for Czechs and Slovaks but also for the federalization of Czechoslovakia. In fact, the 'Prague Spring' launched the process for federalization at the constitutional level. This is not to say that liberalization was not important for the Slovaks. Piekalkiewicz (1972, 82) cites public opinion polls from July 1968 which indicate that 86 percent of Slovaks were in favor of broadening the measures for individual freedom. But for the Slovaks, the issue of federation was directly related to the issue of liberty.

On January 1, 1969, a new constitution for Czechoslovakia was implemented specifying a federal government. For the Slovaks, federalization stood as a remnant of the 'Prague Spring'. As Leff notes, 'federalization is the sole major institutional legacy of the Prague Spring' (1988, 243). But while constitutional federalism eliminated the asymmetrical political structure, the lack of federalism in the party structure meant that there were no significant changes in the governance of the state. The unitary party structure was not altered nor questioned. As Pithart (1995) states 'it is remarkable that the basic objection, namely that the leading role of the Party (guaranteed in the constitution and based on "democratic centralism") was incompatible with any conception of federation, was never raised, not even by the Slovak side' (207). Husák, a Slovak and proponent of federalism, replaced Dubček in 1970 and proceeded with normalization.

The federalization of the state did allow for representational gains by the Slovaks at the federal level. Leff points out that 'between 1969 and 1983, Slovaks received about one-third of the ministerial assignments, an advance to truly proportional representation at the top' (1988, 253). However, federation without liberalization proved to be an empty shell. Power continued to be in the hands of the Communists and 'the concept of federation degenerated during the period of so-called "normalization"'(Rychlik, 1995, 197).

In addition, Czech-Slovak relations worsened following the Prague Spring. Czech democrats suffered during the purges emanating from the normalization program in the 1970s. Slovaks were purged to a lesser extent than the Czechs, because their cause favoring federalism was considered more 'legitimate' than Czech liberalization. The difference in goals between the Czechs and Slovaks (in terms of democracy for the former and autonomy for the latter) was also reflected in the composition of the dissident movement of the 1970s and 1980s. Slovak dissidence played itself out in the form of religious expression rather than political expression. Leff notes that 'over the seven-year period surveyed, 1977-1984, fully 61 percent of the Slovak actions triggering government reprisals involved religious matters – especially unauthorized religious observances and unauthorized religious dissemination of religious materials' (1988, 265). Thus, opposition in Slovakia took on a national/cultural flavor rather than a political one.

Velvet Revolution and Velvet Divorce 1989-present Following the Communist abandonment of a monopoly of power in November 1989, the reformist Civic Forum and its Slovak counterpart, the Public Against Violence, obtained a clear majority in the June 1990 multiparty balloting. This umbrella group subsequently split into two Czech and two Slovak political parties. Divisions between the Czechs and the Slovaks became apparent in terms of economic policies and the construction of the federal system. Most of the Czechoslovakian heavy industry was located in Slovakia, and the economic transition has had greater adverse effects in the Slovak lands than in the Czech lands. In addition, the question of greater Slovak autonomy arose in the consideration of a new constitution. These issues led to the official separation of the two nations on January 1, 1993.[9]

The 1993 Slovak constitution stipulated a unitary state, a unicameral legislature, and an executive branch consisting of a president chosen by the

National Assembly. The president, in turn, appoints the prime minister. The Slovak constitution guarantees rights to ethnic minorities. This protection against discrimination is particularly important given the large Hungarian population.

Following the separation, Prime Minister Vladimir Mečiar failed to attend the inauguration of Czech President Vacláv Havel, thereby straining political relations with the Czech Republic. In addition, Mečiar was reproached for authoritarian inclinations. As Arthur S. Banks states 'internally, the Mečiar government came under increasing criticism for its alleged dictatorial tendencies and its reluctance to tackle the entrenched position of former Communists in the state bureaucracy' (1993, 737). In addition, former Communist Mical Kovác was elected president in February 1993. Mečiar led a minority government until his ouster by a vote of no-confidence in March 1994. Jozef Moravcík, from the Democratic Union of Slovakia (DUS), replaced Mečiar and headed up a center-left coalition. The Moravcík government attempted to push forward with privatization efforts by implementing the voucher share system. In addition, President Kovác openly attacked Mečiar and announced on Czech television that Mečiar 'could be considered a danger for Slovakia' (Banks, 1994, 779). Mečiar, however, soon returned to power following the September 30-October 1 elections.

Mečiar's electoral victory meant a return to greater authoritarianism in Slovakia. Banks states that 'Mečiar's return to power in December 1994 at the head of a coalition representing the forces of populism (HZDS), nationalism (SNS), and socialism (KRS) signaled a reversion to governmental attitudes inherited from the Communist era, including underlying hostility to economic liberalization notwithstanding the public commitment to an eventual market economy' (1995, 842). This red-brown coalition changed privatization policy from the voucher system to a system of direct divestment by tender, which opponents criticized as being not in the best interest of the Slovak people but rather in the interest of a state bureaucracy dominated by former Communists. Tensions increased between the prime minister and the president during 1995 as the prime minister not only moved to increase the power of the government but also called for the president's resignation. Mečiar successfully switched control of the Slovak Security Service (SIS) from the president to the government and 'the National Council voted to strip the president of his duties as commander in chief and to transfer them to the government' (Banks, 1995, 843). This conflict between Mečiar and Kovác ultimately culminated in an all-out battle surrounding the kidnapping of Kovác's son on August 31, 1995. Kovác alleges that the SIS, acting under

Mečiar's order, was responsible for the crime. The affair remains controversial with accusations of a cover-up by Mečiar opponents.

Tension between the government and the Hungarian minority has also increased. The nationalist tendencies of Mečiar and the passage of a new language law in November 1995 have strained relations. The language law stipulates that Slovak is the only official language and that education in Hungarian-dominated schools must be bilingual. 'In opposing the measure, Hungarian leaders were increasingly subjected to physical intimidation in 1996, some of it appearing to be officially sanctioned' (Banks, Day, Muller, 1997, 749).

The authoritarian tendencies of Mečiar's government have been noted by both the EU (in which Slovakia has applied for membership) and the US State Department. The State Department issued a report in March 1996 citing human rights abuses by the Slovakian government. Alleged violations included intimidation of political opposition, abuse of police powers, and government hampering of the media.

Historically, Slovakia has been a nation in search of an identity and a state. Nationalism and the drive toward autonomy have dominated the Slovak political agenda. This emphasis has, over time, been more important to the Slovaks than the establishment and continuation of democracy. Slovak political culture is distinct from the more liberal, pluralistic culture of the Czechs. The Slovak experience and political development under the repressive Magyars has resulted in a political culture tolerant of authoritarianism. The long sought after statehood achieved in 1993 has, in all likelihood, slowed the democratic consolidation process. Less than pluralistic values are expressed not only in the level of democratic support by the citizenry but also in the post-Communist politics and workings of the Mečiar government.

Survey Data

The historical account demonstrates continued Slovak nationalist aspirations. In addition, the Slovak historical experience and traditions diverge from that of the Czechs. This difference is manifest in two distinct political cultures. While the Czech political culture is one dominated by pluralistic political values, the Slovak political culture has been characterized by a search for national identity, specifically in terms of language, and further development of its society, economics, and culture.

An examination of the subjective perceptions of the Slovaks, in comparison to the Czechs, reinforces the differences between the two nationalities. Surveys of Slovaks exist for 1968. Like the Czech surveys, these surveys are derived from the Institute of Public Opinion of the Czechoslovak Academy of Sciences. The two questions used in assessing the political values of the Slovak citizenry are: 1) when you contemplate the history of the Slovak nation, which period do you consider to be the most glorious, a time of advance and development? and, 2) which period do you consider to be the least glorious, the most unfortunate time for the Slovak nation? The results of these survey questions are reported in Tables 6.6 and 6.7.

Table 6.6 Slovak Perceptions of History: Question One (October 1968)

Question: When you contemplate the history of the Slovak nation, which periods do you consider to be the most glorious, a time of advance and development?

Time Period	Percentage of Respondents
The Age of Štúr [in particular, the 1840s]	36
The period after January 1968	36
The Slovak National Uprising [1944]	26
The First Republic [1918-1938]	17
The period after February 1948	16
1945-1948	13
The Slovak state [1939-1945]	13
Great Moravia [9th century]	3
Other periods	3

The top two places for the most glorious time period were the Age of Štúr and the period after January 1968 (Prague Spring). The Age of Štúr represents the time of national awakening in the Slovak lands under the leadership of Ludovit Štúr. This was not mentioned under the Czech responses given the different leadership of the 19th century. However, 15 percent of Czech respondents answered 'national revival', which broadly corresponds to the Slovak Age of Štúr response.

What is most striking about these results is the divergent perceptions between Czechs and Slovaks in regard to the First Republic. More than twice as many Czechs responded that the First Republic was the most glorious period in history than the Slovaks (see Table 5.5). In addition, 16 percent of the

Slovak respondents answered that the most glorious period was the period after February 1948. This demonstrates a much larger degree of support for the Communists than was characteristic of the Czechs. (Only 3 percent of the Czechs identified the period after February 1948 as the most glorious period in their history.) In addition, 13 percent of Slovaks answered that the Slovak State was the most glorious period. Brown and Wightman take this 'to reflect the extent of separatism among the Slovaks, a desire on the part of over one-eighth of the population for a complete break with the Czechs'(1979, 168). However, in terms of separatism, Brown and Wightman note that a much larger percentage answered that the Slovak state was the least glorious period (Table 6.7) (169).

Table 6.7 Slovak Perceptions of History: Question Two (October 1968)

Question: And which period do you consider to be the least glorious, the most unfortunate time for the Slovak nation?

Time Period	Percentage of Respondents
The Slovak State	44
Austro-Hungarian Empire	38
The 1950s	31
August 1968	25
The First Republic [1918-1938]	5
The collapse of Great Moravia	2
Foreign invasions	1

Both the Czechs and the Slovaks view the period of WW II as the most unfortunate period in their history. However, the percentage of Czech responses that identify the German Protectorate of Bohemia and Movaria as the least glorious is much higher, at 59 percent (See Table 5.5), than the Slovak 44 percent. The period of Magyar domination takes second place as the most unfortunate period in history. There seems to be some agreement between the Czechs and Slovaks in terms of recent history. Both groups express dissatisfaction concerning the Communist regime of the 1950s and the Soviet intervention of 1968.

Table 6.8 Slovak Evaluations of Historic Personalities (October 1968)

Question: Which personalities in our history do you esteem most?

Personalities	Percentage of Respondents
Štúr	62
Dubček	56
Štefánik	42
T. G. Masaryk	31
Svoboda	17
Comenius	9
Gottwald	8
Hviezdoslav	6
Hus	6
Husák	6

The Slovak personality preferences diverge significantly from the Czech perceptions (Table 5.7). The Slovak rankings seem to surround the issue of nationality, whereas the Czech rankings seem to represent pluralism. Štúr, as the top choice of leaders, indicates a glorification of the national awakening in Slovakia. Thus, for the Slovaks, the development of an independent Slovak language and culture is a priority. The second choice of Dubček also indicates nationalist tendency. Although Dubček is a recognized symbol of liberalization, for the Slovaks he represented an opportunity to gain greater Slovak autonomy. The difference between the Czech and Slovak ranking of Masaryk is especially interesting. Eighty-one percent of the Czechs ranked Masaryk as the most esteemed historic leader. In contrast, Masaryk ranked fourth on the Slovak list as he was chosen by only 31 percent of the respondents. This too suggests that the Slovaks place less of an emphasis on pluralism than the Czechs.

Prospects for Democracy

In terms of democratic consolidation, the Slovaks face an additional obstacle due to their political culture. Their attitudes and values must be modified to incorporate more pluralistic values. Political culture results from historical experience and the nature of a country's political development; however, it is malleable. With sustained economic well-being the attitudes and beliefs of the citizenry can become more congruent with democratic institutions. However, the initial post-Communist government seemed reluctant to pursue radical economic reforms. Therefore, the slow pace of privatization needs to be addressed, and a return to the voucher share system, so successful in the Czech case, might assist in that effort.

The former Mečiar government demonstrated authoritarian tendencies, directly threatening further democratic consolidation in Slovakia. The increasing restrictions on minority rights as well as governmental human rights abuses is evidence of backsliding. However, the September 1998 legislative balloting resulted in a coalition government headed by the Slovak Democratic Coalition (SDK). New Prime Minister Mikuláš Dzurinda has promised to improve relations with the Hungarian minority as well as to implement greater economic reforms. The 1999 constitutional amendment for the direct election of presidents further checks the government from amassing power. These recent developments indicate that Slovakia may be headed towards a more democratic polity.

Notes

1   Figure 6.4 plots the log of inflation for Slovakia, the Czech Republic, and average Central and Eastern Europe. This is done due to the difficulty of displaying both the extreme average CEE inflation scores and the low scores for both Slovakia and the Czech Republic.
2   Slovak national identity first asserted itself through the Slovak language in the literary revival of the 18th century. The first attempt at utilizing Slovak as a literary language occurred in 1783 with the publication of Joseph Bajza's novel *The Adventures of the Young Man René*. This was followed, in 1887, by an essay on Slavonic philosophy and the first Slovak Grammar by Anton Bernolák, who founded the Slovak Literary Society in 1792. For further discussion see R.W. Seton-Watson's *History of the Czechs and Slovaks* pp. 257-260.
3   This statement was made by Count Charles Zay in 1840 as he addressed the General Assembly of the Lutheran Church.
4   Seven Slovaks were elected to the Hungarian Diet in 1906 and three in 1910.
5   All three documents were quite imprecise in their specifications and the union of the Czechs and Slovaks was uncertain from inception.
6   The only stated Slovak goals were contained in the Cleveland Agreement and the Pittsburgh Pact.
7   Slovakia participated in the Third Reich's policies toward the Jewish population. As early as January 1939, the Slovak government began to limit Jewish participation in Slovak life (Kirschbaum, 1995, 196). This type of legislation culminated in the deportation of Jews that began on March 25, 1942. Ultimately, the deportation resulted in 'the evacuation of what was a total of 57,628 men, women, and children, which represented two-thirds of the Jewish population in Slovakia' (Kamenec, 1992).

8   In addition to the execution of Tiso, Vlado Clementis, Minister of Foreign Affairs was executed in 1952. Gustáv Husák and Ladislav Novomenský received long sentences for the 'betrayal of the Slovak National Uprising' (Rychlik, 1995, 193).
9   For more details on the events precipitating the 'Velvet Divorce' see Chapter Five.

7 Lithuania

Introduction

This chapter examines: the level of democratic support in Lithuania as compared to the average level of support in Central and Eastern Europe, the economic conditions in Lithuania as compared to the average economic conditions in Central and Eastern Europe, the hypothesized relationships between economic factors and democratic support in Lithuania, the political culture of Lithuania, and the prospects for democracy in Lithuania. According to the statistical results of the LSDV model (Table 3.3; Figure 3.3), the coefficient for the Lithuania dummy variable has a positive effect on the level of democratic satisfaction. This positive effect indicates that economic factors are not the only factors influencing the level of democratic support. As demonstrated in this chapter, political culture also plays a role in the prospects for democratic consolidation in Lithuania.

Democratic Support

Table 7.1 and Figure 7.1 show that democratic support is consistently higher in Lithuania than the average for the Central and Eastern European countries for 1991-1994. Although democratic support in Lithuania decreases from 1991-1994, it maintains a higher level of support than the mean. The decrease in support over time is expected. Support is likely to wane from the time of political transition. However, the lowest point in Lithuanian democratic support, 2.21 (1994), is a relatively high level of regime support. In fact, Lithuania has the highest level of support of any of the Central and Eastern European countries in 1994. As discussed below, this consistently high satisfaction with democracy may be attributed to the economic environment.

Table 7.1 Democratic Satisfaction for Lithuania and Central and Eastern Europe

Year	Lithuania	Average CEE	Difference Lithuania and Average CEE
1990	–	2.40	–
1991	2.60	2.26	0.34
1992	2.51	2.12	0.39
1993	2.26	2.09	0.17
1994	2.21	1.97	0.24

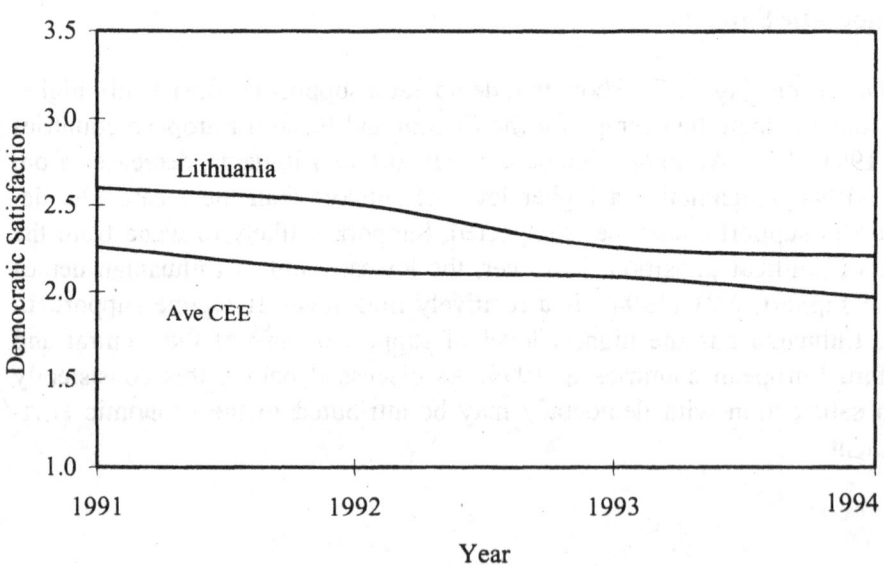

Figure 7.1: Democratic Satisfaction for Lithuania and Central and Eastern Europe

Economic Indicators

Gross Domestic Product

The percentage change in real GDP serves as a primary indicator of the state of the economy as a whole. The economies in transition all experienced dramatic decreases in their economic output for the time period under consideration. Table 7.2 and Figure 7.2 display the percentage change in real GDP for Lithuania and the average percentage change GDP for Central and Eastern Europe.

Table 7.2 Percentage Change in Real GDP for Lithuania and Central and Eastern Europe

Year	Lithuania	Average CEE	Difference Lithuania and Average CEE
1990	–	-5.0	–
1991	-13.0	-13.2	0.2
1992	-38.0	-17.4	-20.6
1993	-24.0	-6.7	-17.3
1994	2.0	-3.2	5.2

Lithuania's economic output drops significantly from the time of independence through 1993. This decline is expected because the Lithuanian economy was intertwined with the Soviet economy. Prior to independence, Lithuania was just one segment in the centralized structure of the Soviet economy. The principle of specialization within the command economy made Lithuania dependent upon the Soviet Union. Lithuania specialized in industrial production, exporting primarily to other Soviet republics (80.5 percent; 43.9 percent to Russia). Furthermore, Lithuania imported 89.1 percent of its goods and supplies (47.3 percent from Russia) (Vardys and Sedaitis, 1997, 67). In addition, Lithuania was almost completely dependent on Russia and other Soviet Republics for its natural resources. Vardys and Sedaitis (1997) estimate that Lithuania had to import 80 percent of its natural resources, including energy, from Russia (67). When Lithuania declared independence in March 1990, following the legislative balloting in which the Lithuanian Movement for Restructuring (*Lietuvos Persitvarkymo Sajūdis*) won a majority over the Communist Party, Gorbachev responded with an economic blockade. Ensuing problems with the Soviet Union as well as subsequent economic reforms explain the tremendous drop in economic output.

Figure 7.2: Percentage Change in Real GDP for Lithuania and Central and Eastern Europe

[Figure: Line graph showing % Change Real GDP from 1991 to 1994. Ave CEE line starts around -14 in 1991, dips to about -17 in 1992, and rises to about -3 in 1994. Lithuania line starts around -14 in 1991, drops to about -37 in 1992, and rises to about +2 in 1994.]

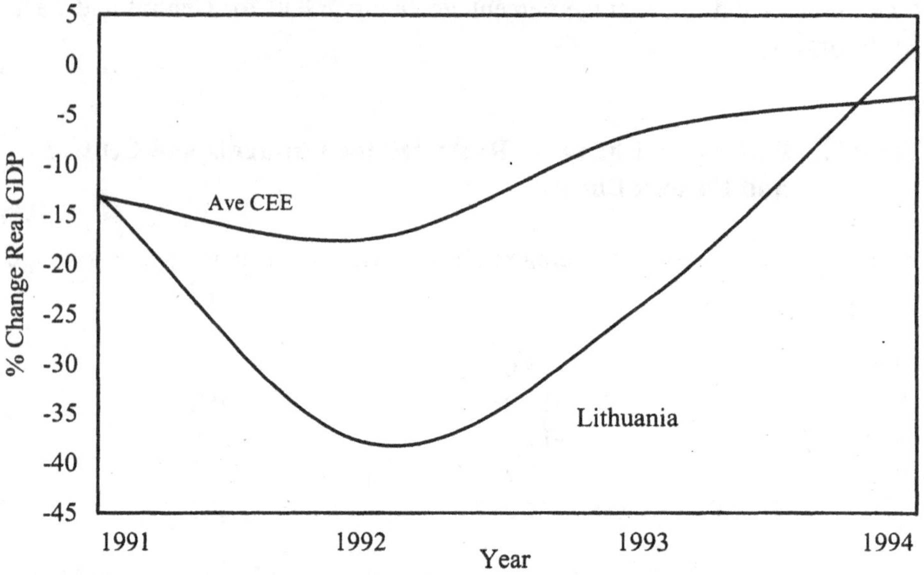

Although Lithuania's decrease in economic output is greater than the average for Central and Eastern Europe, Lithuania entered transition with a relatively high level of industrialization. Thus, the economic situation prior to independence was more favorable than it was for most of the former Soviet bloc states.[1] The negative growth for 1991 can be explained by the Soviet economic sanctions. The further decrease of GDP in 1992 was a result of the economic restructuring. The economy began to rebound in 1993 and Lithuania experienced positive growth in 1994.

I expect that economic conditions affect the level of democratic satisfaction. Pattern matching for the following hypothesis is exhibited in Figure 7.3.

H_1:   *If economic conditions improve, support for democracy will increase.*

Figure 7.3: Democratic Satisfaction and Percentage Change in Real GDP for Lithuania

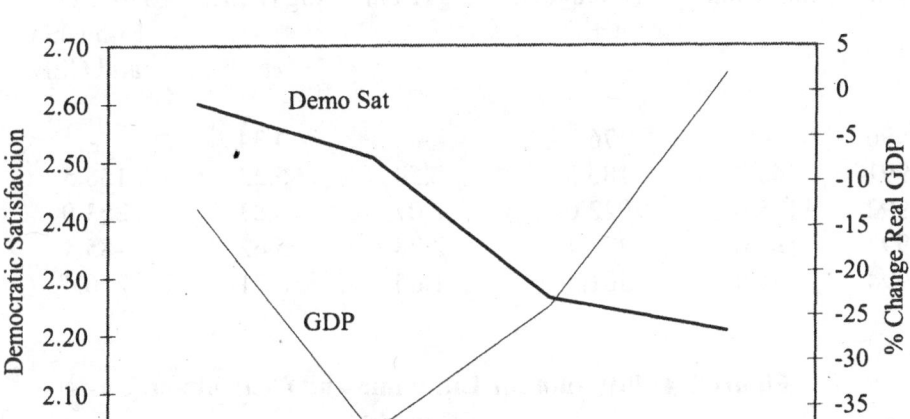

Figure 7.3 plots both democratic satisfaction and percentage change in real GDP. The proposed relationship is partially supported. As GDP decreased from 1991 to 1992, democratic satisfaction decreased. However, democratic satisfaction continued to decrease throughout the entire period even as the economic output began to recover. Yet, as mentioned earlier, the level of democratic satisfaction remains relatively high despite this decrease over time. Given the severe drop in GDP, I would have expected a greater decrease in democratic satisfaction.

Inflation

The second indicator of economic conditions is consumer prices or inflation. Table 7.3 and Figure 7.4 compare inflation for Lithuania to the average for Central and Eastern Europe.

Table 7.3 Inflation for Lithuania and Central and Eastern Europe

Year	Lithuania	Average CEE	log (LIT)	log (CEE)	Difference Lithuania and CEE
1990	–	76.7	–	4.34	–
1991	345.0	186.5	2.54	5.23	158.5
1992	1175.0	922.0	3.07	6.83	253.0
1993	189.0	274.4	2.28	5.62	-85.4
1994	45.0	301.4	1.65	5.71	-256.4

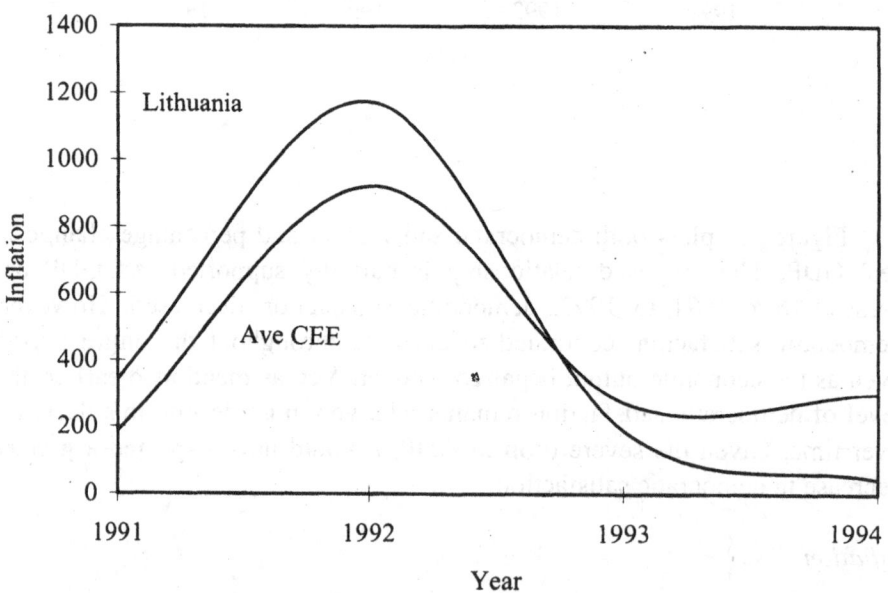

Figure 7.4: Inflation for Lithuania and Central and Eastern Europe

Inflation for Lithuania is higher than the average for Central and Eastern Europe for 1991 and 1992. However, inflation dramatically decreases from 1992 to 1993. Inflation further decreases in 1994 to a more manageable 45 percent. The initial increases are due to the elimination of price controls in early 1991. The latter decrease demonstrates the success of the economic policies. Figure 7.5 plots inflation and democratic satisfaction for Lithuania from 1991 to 1994. The expected inverse relationship is evident from 1991 to 1992; however, it does not hold for 1992-1994. Democratic satisfaction continues to decrease as inflation decreases. These findings are similar to the relationship found with gross domestic product.

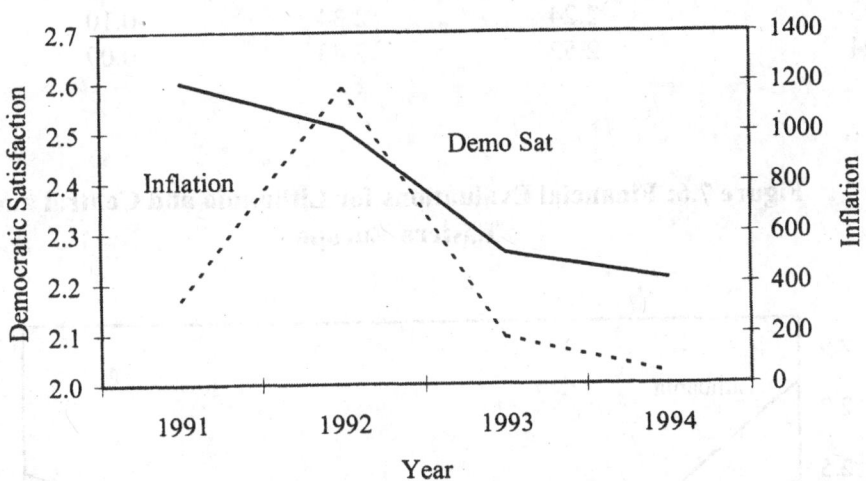

Figure 7.5: Inflation and Democratic Satisfaction for Lithuania

The proposed positive relationship between economic conditions and democratic satisfaction is hardly supported in the case of Lithuania. The statistical results presented in Chapter Three suggest that financial evaluations of the citizenry are a more important indicator of democratic support than the actual economic conditions. The following section examines the extent to which this holds true for Lithuania.

Financial Evaluations

Table 7.4 and Figure 7.6 compare financial evaluations for Lithuania to the average for Central and Eastern Europe.

Table 7.4 Financial Evaluations for Lithuania and Central and Eastern Europe

Year	Lithuania	Average CEE	Difference Lithuania and Average CEE
1990	–	2.33	–
1991	2.79	2.46	0.33
1992	2.16	2.31	-0.15
1993	2.24	2.34	-0.10
1994	2.52	2.43	0.09

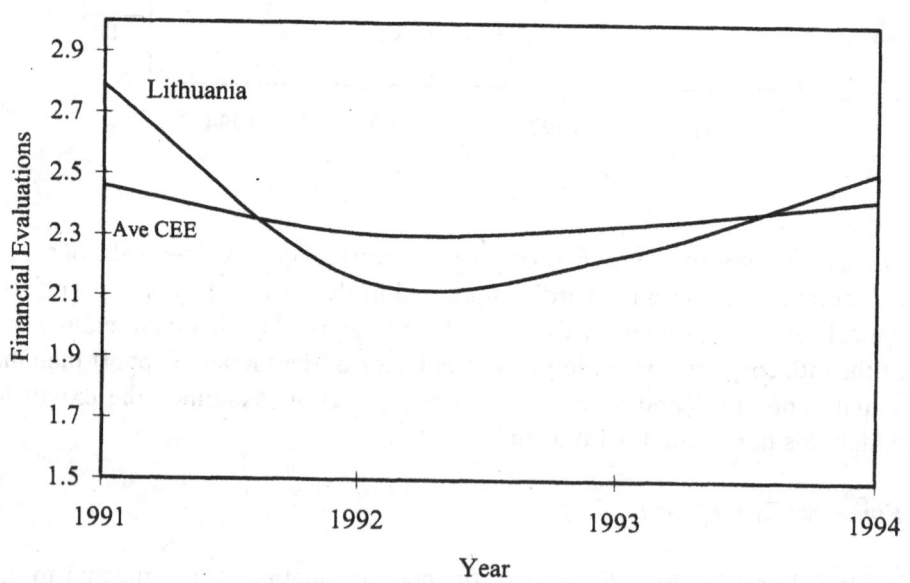

Figure 7.6: Financial Evaluations for Lithuania and Central and Eastern Europe

The financial evaluations for Lithuania in 1991 are very optimistic – much higher than the average for the CEE states. They drop considerably in

1992 and reflect the poor conditions for that year. This drop in evaluations signifies the end of the honeymoon period. However, financial evaluations improve in 1993 and 1994. The financial evaluations display a pattern similar to both GDP and inflation. The pattern is one of an initial decrease from 1991 to 1992, followed by improvement from 1992-1994.

Figure 7.7 plots democratic satisfaction and financial evaluations for Lithuania. Figure 7.7 assesses the following hypothesis:

H_2: *If financial evaluations improve, support for democracy will increase.*

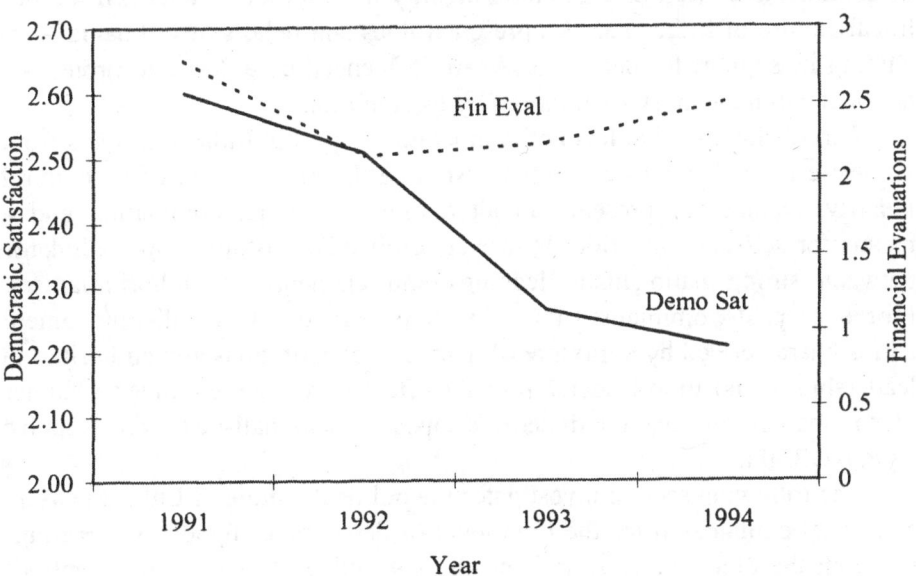

Figure 7.7: Democratic Satisfaction and Financial Evaluations for Lithuania

Again, the hypothesized relationship is only partially supported by the data. From 1991 to 1992 both financial evaluations and democratic satisfaction decrease. However, from 1992 to 1994, financial evaluations increase while democratic satisfaction continues to decrease.

The data for Lithuania suggest that something more than economic factors is influencing democratic support. The evidence does not consistently support the hypothesized relationships. Democratic support decreases over time; however, the regime support is still relatively high in relationship to the other Central and Eastern European countries. Investigation into political culture and current politics is necessary to assess the democratic support levels in Lithuania.

Political Culture

Unlike the Czech Republic (discussed in Chapter Five), it is not commonly argued that Lithuania has a long history of pluralistic values. Rather, Lithuania's history contains some elements of democracy (such as multiple parties in the 19th century) and episodic periods of independence. Strongly nationalist sentiments as well as a Catholic identity have long characterized the political culture of Lithuania. The present values and beliefs of Lithuania – including its support for democracy – are influenced by a desire to protect its national culture against assimilation by foreign rule.

I argue that the high level of democratic support in Lithuania stems from its desire for independence from Russia and the preservation of its cultural identity. Democracy presents an alternative to foreign domination and a means for self-determination. However, Lithuanian history shows a linkage between strong nationalistic leanings and elements of authoritarianism. Moreover, post-Communist Lithuania is a product of a nationalist movement and is characterized by a mixture of democratic institutions and authoritarian leadership. Opposition leadership of the late 1980s emerged under a banner of nationalism and has continued its appeal to nationalism to gain support from the Right.

The following section investigates the political culture of Lithuania as an additional explanation for the high level of democratic support. By examining both the objective (history) and the subjective (survey) components of political culture, a better understanding of the political dynamics of the new democratic regime is achieved.

Historical Evidence

Throughout its history, Lithuania has been plagued by unwanted external influences from Poland, Russia, and Germany. Lithuania's geopolitical position is conducive to foreign domination. As the southernmost Baltic state, it lies at a crossroads between Western Europe and Russia. The Lithuanian lands are an extension of the Eastern European Plain, making invasion from the east (Berlin) and the west (Moscow) quite easy. This unfortunate geopolitical position has added to the struggle for national survival, not just in the sense of avoiding foreign rule, but also in terms of maintaining a distinct cultural identity.

Medieval Lithuania (1230-1795) Lithuania first became a unified nation in 1230 under the leadership of the Grand Duke Mindaugas. The medieval Lithuanian state was composed of a minority of Lithuanians and a majority of Russians and Byelorussians. The pagan religion of Lithuania led invaders from the West to attempt to Christianize and to rule the Lithuanian lands. Latvia had been Christianized in 1186 by Western merchants and missionaries who created a military organization, the Order of the Brothers of the Sword, to protect and to promote their missionary efforts. However, the Order's attempt to establish Christianity in Lithuania ended in military defeat in 1236. The Order was later aided by the Knights of the Cross, German military-missionaries. The Knights of the Cross sought to Christianize the pagan Prussians as well as western Lithuania; however, they were continuously foiled in their efforts (Vardys and Sedaitis, 1997, 7-10).

A prolonged conflict took place between the Knights of the Cross and the Lithuanian people. In an attempt to settle the conflict, Grand Duke Mindaugas of Lithuania converted to Christianity and, subsequently, became the first and only King of Lithuania in 1253. Lithuanian nobility rejected Christianization and ten years later assassinated Mindaugas and reverted to paganism (Vardys and Sedaitis, 1997; 10; Iwaskiw, 1996, 177-8; Halecki, 1952, 79-81; Jusaitis, 1918, 12-14). At that time, Lithuania remained the only pagan European nation. Thus, the Knights of the Cross redoubled their efforts at Christianization. Lithuania sought to defend itself from the Knights as well as to expand eastward into Russian lands.[2] In order to prevent the Teutonic Knights from assuming control of Lithuania, Grand Duke Jogaila (Jagiello in Polish) agreed to marry Polish Queen Jadwiga and accept the Polish crown in 1386. However, the acceptance of the crown meant not only the Christianization of Lithuania, but also the joining of Lithuania to Poland. Unlike other Christian states, 'Lithuania did not become an independent Church province under Rome'; rather, it was placed under the jurisdiction of the Polish Church (Vardys and Sedaitis, 1997, 12). Because Church leadership came from Poland, the Polish language and culture were readily disseminated. In fact, 'The Polish or Polonized priests ... were endeavoring to locate themselves in Lithuania, but were not taking the trouble to learn the Lithuanian language but simply scorned it' (Jusaitis, 1918, 30).

Much debate exists among Lithuanian scholars regarding the impact that Christianization had on Lithuania's national culture. Some argue that Christianization and the joining of Lithuania to Poland led to a national decline. Thus, Jurginis maintains that 'the Catholic Church ruined the state founded by the Lithuanians'. Moreover, he argues that the Catholic nobility and feudal lords quickly became 'Polonized' while the national cultural identity was left to the peasantry (qtd in Vardys and Sedaitis, 1997, 13). Conversely, Zenonas Ivinskis argues that if Christianization had been successful under Mindaugas, Western culture 'would have reached Lithuania much sooner' and a distinct Lithuanian culture would have been protected (qtd in Vardys and Sedaitis, 1997, 13)[3]. This argument is particularly valid in terms of language development. The fact that Lithuania's written language was not developed until the mid-16th century indicates a cultural lag behind its European counterparts. Because most draftsmen of alphabets were Christian clerics, the Lithuanian resistance to Christianity discouraged linguistic development.[4] And, as Lieven (1993, 48) points out, 'amazingly enough, by the sixteenth century, there were six officially recognized languages in the Polish-Lithuanian Kingdom, including Polish, Latin, "Ruthene" (Ukrainian-Byelorussian), German, Armenian, and Hebrew – but not Lithuanian'. This suggests strong outside cultural influences and explains the ease of Polonization of the Lithuanian nobility.

The Protestant Reformation helped Lithuanian cultural development (Vardys and Sedaitis, 1997, 15-16). Protestant influences, came from the converted Prussian state. Prussia's Grand Duke Albrecht of Hohenzollern promoted Lutheranism to his Lithuanian neighbors and specifically targeted members of the clergy. Ironically, Teutonic Prussia became a primary patron of Lithuanian culture. Vardys and Sedaitis (1997, 15-16) note this advocacy:

> In 1544 Duke Albrecht established a university in Königsberg that trained Lithuanians for pastoral work. Over the next three centuries, the formerly anti-Lithuanian Teutonic Prussia became the main source of native Lithuanian literature and a haven from russification policies from the East. Until the middle of the nineteenth century, Prussia supported many unassimilated Lithuanian inhabitants and Lutheran parishes.

In fact, the first published book in the Lithuanian language, written by Martynas Mažvydas in 1547, was a translation of the Lutheran catechism.

Catholic authorities responded to the Lutheran influence by establishing a Jesuit university in Vilnius in 1570 (Vardys and Sedaitis, 1997, 16-17; Jusaitis, 1918, 65-68).

Initially, dynastic union with Poland did not alter the administrative structure of the Lithuanian state. The Lithuanian Code of Law (known as the Lithuanian Statute) and the administrative system functioned independently from Poland. The Grand Duke was elected separately each time there was a succession to the Polish crown. However, this changed in 1569 when Zygmunt II August (Sigismindus Secundus) issued an edict stating that the Grand Duchy of Lithuania and the Kingdom of Poland would become a single state. Thus, the Polish political structure, consisting of local diets made up of landed nobility, prevailed over Lithuanian administration. However, linguistic differences, local customs, and traditions persisted (Verdys and Sedaitis, 1997, 15).

This period in Lithuanian history is particularly interesting because of the nation's paradoxical goals and their consequences. Lithuania's purpose for uniting with Poland was to protect itself from foreign attack (particularly by Moscow). This was sufficiently achieved for 250 years. However, the union resulted in diminished Lithuanian autonomy and halted cultural development. Lieven (1993) argues that, in the long term, this resulted in a 'massive Lithuanian inferiority complex and a sense of cultural vulnerability *vis-i-vis* the Poles' (48).

Lithuania under the Russian Empire (1795-1918) Polish domination of Lithuania ended with the annexation of Lithuania by Catherine II of Russia in 1795. The partitioning of Poland at the end of the 18th century signaled a change in the development of Lithuanian culture. Lithuania was emancipated politically and culturally as a result of the Polish-Russian conflict. Polish insurrections in 1831 and 1863 were brutally repressed and spurred the Czarist regime to separate the Poles from the Lithuanians.[5] The policy of separation offered the Lithuanians an opportunity to detach culturally from the Poles. At the same time, however, Czarist Russia aimed at assimilating the Lithuanians into Russian culture and Orthodoxy (Vardys and Sedaitis, 1997, 16; Iwaskiw, 1996, 178-79).

Russia pursued anti-Catholic policies against both the Poles and the Lithuanians. The university at Vilnius was closed, as were Catholic Churches and monasteries, and theological study was moved to St. Petersburg. Russia attempted to quicken assimilation by prohibiting Lithuanian language schools and the printing of Lithuanian books that used the Latin alphabet.

Furthermore, the Russians sought to deepen the divide between the Lithuanian peasantry and the Polonized landowners. For example, following the serf emancipation of 1861, the Czar granted much more land to Lithuanian peasants than to Russian peasants at the expense of the Polish landlords (Vardys and Sedaitis, 1997, 16-17).

The generous land reform of 1861 and the earlier liberation of peasants under Prussian control in the Uznemune province (southwest region) allowed the peasants a measure of well-being and opportunities for education. Although the spread of education and the development of a secular intelligentsia was much greater in Latvia and Estonia, new Lithuanian professional and urban intelligentsia nonetheless emerged (Vardys and Sedaitis, 1997, 18).[6] From 1883, as Jusaitis (1918, 79) points out, 'Lithuanian literature ... spread with unbounded force through Lithuania. As time went on new poets, writers of fiction, scientific writers, and other writers appeared'. Lithuanians, educated in Russian universities, formed an intelligentsia that was atheist and socialist. The Church also played a critical role in the development of a national culture, aiding in the education of Lithuanian peasants by smuggling Lithuanian-Latin texts from East Prussia. The Church also allowed Lithuanian peasants to enter the clergy, giving wider access to education. Increased educational opportunity and urbanization led to a cultural awakening, which in the 1880s saw the development of multiple parties and the root of a clerical/anti-clerical cleavage. By the 1905 Russian revolution, two extremes existed in Lithuanian politics, the pro-Socialist Left and the Catholic Right (Vardys and Sedaitis, 1997, 18-19).

Although Lithuania had fewer industrialized workers than Latvia or Estonia, the first political party to be founded was the Lithuanian Socialist Party (1896). It was followed by the Lithuanian Christian Democrats in 1904.[7] The revolution of 1905 was nonviolent in Lithuania and served as the impetus for Lithuanian demands for autonomy. All political groups were represented at the Vilnius conference, which called for national autonomy within a federal Russian state and the right to use Lithuanian language in local government and schools (Vardys and Sedaitis, 1997, 19-20; Senn, 1959, 9-10; Jusaitis, 1918, 79-80). The Russian army quickly suppressed nationalism; however, freedom to publish in Lithuanian-Latin was granted.

Independence (1918-1940) The onset of WW I led to the German occupation of Lithuania in 1915. A large group of Lithuanians fled to Russia where they formed political organizations and, in 1917, with the start of the March Revolution, established the Lithuanian National Council in St. Petersburg.

The Council subsequently elected a representative congress to serve as a government-in-exile.[8] However, the congress demanded full independence for Lithuania and in April 1918 the Bolshevik government shut down the Council (Vardys and Sedaitis, 1997, 20-21; Senn, 1959, 24-25).

In Lithuania, the German occupiers allowed the formation of a Lithuanian Council (Vardys and Sedaitis, 1997, 21; Senn, 1959, 25-26). However, the Germans pressured the Lithuanians to accept an alliance with Germany. In response, the Council 'demanded independence, favored a democratic government with a freely elected parliament, and stated that if Germany would recognize Lithuania, Lithuania would establish closer relations with Germany' (Vardys and Sedaitis, 1997, 21). The Brest Litovsk treaty placed the Baltic region under German control; however, when it became clear that the Germans would lose the war, Germany gave full control to the 'embryonic Lithuanian state' (Senn, 1959, 46).

Although Lithuania was now free to form a government, it faced threats from both Russia and Poland. The Bolsheviks invaded Lithuania in November 1918 and took control of Vilnius in December (Lieven, 1993, 58). The Lithuanian Communist Party, however, proved too weak to maintain Communist control, and the Bolsheviks were driven out in 1919. Immediately following the Bolsheviks' withdrawal, the Poles captured Vilnuis.[9] Led by Josef Pilsudski, the Poles hoped to reunite Lithuania with Poland.

Parliamentary Democracy The democratic ideals put forth by Woodrow Wison and the League of Nations were highly influential in the aftermath of WW I, and democratic constitutions were adopted by the Baltic states. Lithuania, basing its democracy on that of the Weimar Republic, emphasized the legislature over the executive. And, like the Weimar, Lithuania experienced political instability. A multiparty system with pure proportional representation was necessary to address the deep ideological cleavage in Lithuanian society; however, it produced weak governments and ultimately undercut the democratic process. Lithuanian democracy lasted only seven years, and during that time it produced a total of eleven governments (Vardys and Sedaitis, 1997, 33-34).

The Catholic Church played a strong role in the parliamentary politics of the interwar period. Although the Catholic-oriented parties (such as the Christian Democrats) were independent political organizations, the Church successfully influenced public policy.[10] In addition, the Church strongly supported democracy and opposed the ensuing authoritarian regime. Strong Catholic identity also enabled Lithuanians to overcome class divisions. The commitment to Catholicism led to a stable bloc of political parties representing socially and economically diverse groups. This rightist, authoritarian Christian Democratic bloc competed with the Left bloc consisting of the Peasant People's Party and the Social Democratic Party.[11] Similar interests between the blocs on economic and social issues led to cooperation from 1920 to 1926. The breakdown of this cooperation, stemming largely from religious issues, directly contributed to the growth of the radical Right. The Populist-Social Democratic coalition took power in 1926 and was supported by ethnic minorities. The Nationalists, with the aid of military forces and the Catholic Church, staged a coup d'état in December 1926. Initially, the Nationalists ruled in coalition with the Christian Democrats until a new constitution providing for a strong presidency was promulgated in 1927 (Vardys and Sedaitis, 1997, 33-35).

Antanas Smetona was elected president and ruled with the support of the military, and his regime was not unlike other fascist regimes of the period.[12] However, although Lithuania was subject to a dictatorship and a virtual one-party rule, Smetona was less brutal than some of his fascist counterparts and less radical in his promotion of nationalism; he also eschewed racial ideology. In addition, both the universities and the courts retained independence. Several attempts were made by the outlawed Social Democrats and Christian Democrats to oust Smetona. However, it was external forces that ultimately brought down the regime (Lieven, 1993, 67).

Following the non-aggression pact between Germany and the Soviet Union in 1939[13], Stalin stationed Red Army troops in Lithuania. Soviet forces fully occupied Lithuania in the summer of 1940, and on August 3, 1940, the Soviet Union annexed Lithuania, which became a Soviet constituent republic (Iwaskiw, 1996, 180-181).

Social and Economic Development Lithuania achieved independence in 1919 with a legacy of industrial underdevelopment. Since the Czars had not promoted industry in Lithuania, the break with Russia did not cause substantial economic problems. The Lithuanian economy subsequently matured into a mixed capitalist system with state ownership and state participation in industry. In fact, the state owned over 60 percent of common stock capital during Smetona's presidency. State investment in the economy eased the economic woes of the depression and allowed Lithuania to avoid foreign debt. However, industrial development and, by extension, urbanization were slow due to lack of natural resources and technology (Vardys and Sedaitis, 1997, 41).

Agricultural reforms undertaken in 1922 served as the foundation for Lithuanian interwar prosperity by redistributing land to the peasantry and establishing medium-sized farms. Politically, the reforms helped the new democracy gain legitimacy; socially, they created a middle class. In addition, the state encouraged the formation of cooperatives, particularly in the production of meat and dairy products, which subsequently became Lithuania's largest exports (Vardys and Sedaitis, 40).

Interwar Lithuania saw great advances in education. In 1928 primary education became compulsory, and the illiteracy rate fell dramatically in a brief time. Vardys and Sedaitis make note of this remarkable feat: 'comparatively few developing countries ever manage to reduce illiteracy from 44 to 12 percent in seventeen years' (1997, 42). New secondary, agricultural, and technological schools were built. Moreover, several specialized colleges were created, and a university was founded in Kaunas.

Educational opportunities became widespread, and this was undoubtably linked to the rapid expansion of independent mass organizations. In fact, 'Social and religious organizations ... grew in number to the hundreds of thousands' (Vardys and Sedaitis, 1997, 42). In other words, civil society emerged in Lithuania during this period. Vardys and Sedaitis (1997, 42) argue that these positive social and economic advancements permanently affected the political culture of Lithuania.

> In Gorbachev's age of glasnost, the life, politics, and achievements of independence emerged as the rightful legacy of Lithuanian citizens. Old leaders and institutions that had been denounced by the Soviets were fondly remembered and idealized. The experience of national independence had become a permanent part of Lithuania's political culture. It survived a ruthless half-century of Soviet violence and manipulation and could not be eradicated from the national memory.

Soviet Lithuania As previously noted, the Soviet Union entered Lithuania soon after signing the Molotov-Ribbentrop Pact. Stalin quickly sought to Sovietize Lithuania by nationalizing financial institutions and subjecting Lithuania to Soviet laws. He ordered a replacement of Lithuanian managerial and governmental personnel with Russian officials. As Misiunas and Taagepera (1993, 25) report, '11 of 12 mayors of principal cities, 19 of the 23 mayors of towns, and 175 out of 261 county heads were replaced'. These changes caused economic displacement and social unrest. The outbreak of WW II and Nazi occupation in 1941 interrupted Soviet rule in the region. Initially, the occupation brought relief to the Lithuanians, who expected to regain self-rule. However, the Germans subsequently embarked on their policy of wholesale annihilation of the Jewish population and attempted to use the Lithuanians in the military campaign against the Russians. The Lithuanians resisted, attempted to form a provisional government, and declared independence. The Nazis dismissed these efforts; however, Lithuanian resistance was widespread. Ultimately, the resistance efforts led to deaths, arrests, and deportations (Vardys and Sedaitis, 1997, 54-58).

The Soviets recaptured Lithuania in 1944, and its boundaries were extended as a result of the acquisition of German territory. However, the population was greatly depleted.[14] The Communist leaders were faced with an area that had been devastated by war, had lost much of its educated class, and was in need of wholesale economic restructuring. In addition, the Communist Party was extremely weak in Lithuania; the bulk of its members were Russian, and 'In 1947, only 18.4 percent of its membership was Lithuanian' (Vardys and Sedaitis, 1997, 61).

As part of Lithuania's integration into the Soviet empire, the Russian language was taught in schools and became the language of administration, public communication, and all economic institutions. However, the Lithuanian Communist leader, Antanas Sniečkus, gained a reputation during his long rule as a protector of intellectuals and Lithuanian national culture. Although Sniečkus maintained a hard-line approach during the Stalin years, he 'would often circumvent Moscow for nationalist reasons' (Lieven, 1993, 63). It was Sniečkus who insisted that Lithuanians learn their native language in addition to Russian. Furthermore, Sniečkus is 'mostly remembered for dissuading Moscow from pursuing economic expansion in Lithuania and so minimizing environmental devastation and the influx of a very large Russian immigration, as occurred in the other Baltic states' (Lieven, 1993, 64).

The economic restructuring of Lithuania included the nationalization of industry and collectivization of agriculture, the latter being accomplished by the land reform in 1949 despite Sniečkus' protests that Lithuania was not prepared to collectivize. As a result, agricultural output drastically dropped so that 'it took longer than a decade for Lithuanian output levels to recover' (Lieven, 1993, 65). However, following Stalin's death, Lithuania refocused its agricultural emphasis toward meat and dairy products; productivity consequently increased. In addition, Lithuania underwent large-scale industrialization.[15] The Soviet plan of an integrated economy and the principle of specialization made industrialized Lithuania dependent upon Russia for its natural resources and its markets. Although Lithuania had to import most of its natural resources, its industrial and agricultural success allowed the

Lithuanians to enjoy a higher standard of living than the other Soviet republics. As industrialization increased, urbanization and growth of the professions also took place. The price that Lithuania paid for industrialization was an influx of Russian immigrants as well as industrial pollution (Vardys and Sedaitis, 1997, 64-71).

Lithuania was also subject to restrictive Soviet cultural policies. From the time of Stalin, the Soviets, in their effort to create the 'new Soviet man', looked to eliminate the national identity of the Lithuanians and assimilate them into Russian culture. The goal was to eliminate national loyalties and suppress the Catholic Church. All cultural achievements of the Lithuanians in the arts and literature were purged. Ninety percent of Church property was confiscated and religious education was outlawed. However, the task of resocialization proved difficult for the Soviets because of the early development of resistance followed by a widespread dissent movement (Vardys and Sedaitis, 1997, 72-72; Vardys, 1978, 47-51).

Resistance and Dissent Movement In order to protect their culture, traditions, and values, Lithuanians participated in two types of struggles: violent and nonviolent. This resistance, Vardys and Sedaitis argue, 'deeply influenced the evolution of Lithuanian political culture and kept alive the spirit of national survival' (1997, 80). From 1944 to 1952 Lithuanians fought an armed struggle against Soviet rule. Known as the partisans, or the 'forest brothers', the Lithuanian insurrectionists rejected the legitimacy of Soviet rule and considered it to be temporary. Numbering approximately 30,000 at their peak in 1947, the armed men lived in the forests of Lithuania and fought using guerrilla tactics. The civil society of the independence period provided for wide social cohesion in Lithuania that supported the insurgency. The goal of the partisans was to be rid of the Soviets and establish an independent democratic regime. Thus, in addition to their military organization, the partisans also developed a political organization known as the Supreme Committee for the Reconstruction of Lithuania (1946), which was later reorganized into Lithuania's Movement of Freedom Fighters (1949). The Movement's activities were two-fold: obstructionist and protective. The partisans attempted to obstruct the Soviet regime and the collectivization process. They also protected Lithuanian civilians from the Soviet military, documented Soviet crimes, and published underground newspapers. The Soviet secret police (NKVD) infiltrated the partisans and used extreme measures against its members (torture was commonplace). Partisan retaliation resulted in severe Soviet response and the massacre of thousands of Lithuanians.[16] Although the partisan movement was destroyed and the goal of independence was not achieved, the historical legacy of the movement branded its members as heroes and resistance to the regime continued (Vardys and Sedaitis, 1997, 80-84).

The dissent movement throughout the 1960s and 1970s concentrated on religious rights, human rights, nationalism, and self-determination. The dissenters sought peaceful means for change and kept the national culture alive within the Soviet system. This movement was extensive, and membership cut across class lines. The role of Catholic dissenters was critical. In 1972, they began publishing the *Chronicle of the Catholic Church of Lithuania*, which became the 'voice of Lithuania'. This publication not only discussed national and religious issues for Lithuanians, but also notified the West of the state of Soviet rule in Lithuania. Dissenters were well organized, and cooperation among groups was widespread. In addition to the dissent movement, the Lithuanian intelligentsia resisted Soviet cultural policies; writers and artists kept the national culture alive under the Communists and the members of the Lithuanian Artists Association became political subversives. However, the creative intellectuals generally worked within the system for survival and did not fight for independence (Vardys and Sedaitis, 1997, 84-97).

Sajūdis Movement, Independence, and Present Politics (1988-1997) The emergence of Lithuania as an independent state in 1991 was the result of the nationalist independence movement that emerged in the late 1980s under Gorbachev's reformism. The movement was based on the belief that the Soviet Union had illegally annexed Lithuania and that Lithuania had a right to self-determination. Three primary actors shaped both the independence movement and present politics – Sajūdis, the Lithuanian Communist Party, and Moscow. The interactions among these actors demonstrated the extent of Lithuanian nationalism and the desire for an alternative to rule from Moscow. Thus, the events of the last decade clearly illustrate a political culture based on nationalism and an alienation from Soviet rule. Ironically, it was Gorbachev's revolution from above that served as the impetus for the Lithuanian nationalist movement (Vardys and Sedaitis, 1997, 97-101).

Gorbachev's glasnost and perestroika were slow to be accepted in Lithuania. At first, Lithuanians had doubts as to the meaning of the proposed reforms. Communist leader Petras Griškevičius, who succeeded Sniečkus in 1974, was more conservative than Gorbachev and considered the reforms revolutionary. However, by 1988 a plethora of new groups outside of the Communist Party had emerged, and civil society had begun to appear from under the Soviet monolith. Sajūdis became an umbrella group for the new associations in 1988. Modeled after the People's Front of Estonian intellectuals, Sajūdis consisted of both Communists and non-Communists. Initially, it promoted individual rights and the expression of Lithuanian culture; however, within a year it called for independence and secession from the Soviet Union. By the end of 1988 political parties developed. Many Sajūdis members joined the Lithuanian Democratic Party, a breakaway faction of the Lithuanian Communist Party that was nationalist with a left-of-center social platform. Parties that had existed in earlier periods of Lithuanian history also reemerged, including the Christian Democratic Party, the Social Democratic Party, and the Nationalist Party (Vardys and Sedaitis, 1997, 101-110).

In the summer of 1988, Sajūdis gained strength and became radicalized by an extremist dissent group, The Lithuanian Freedom League (LFL). Although the group had no access to the media, it organized mass meetings and demonstrations, and its popular support grew (Vardys and Sedaitis, 1997).[17] Throughout 1988 and 1989 the broadly based nationalist movement initiated by Sajūdis led the drive for independence within the Communist system; as Misiunas and Taagepera (1993, 322) note, 'the key term in the operative political lexicon of the opposition was "sovereignty"'. However, the Lithuanian Communist Party advocated a gradual move toward economic and political reform.

The Communists were defeated in the March 1990 elections with Sajūdis winning a majority of seats in the Lithuanian Supreme Soviet. This victory replaced Communist Chairman Algirdas Brazauskas with Vytautas Landsbergis, who appointed Danutė Prunskienė, a Sajūdis-endorsed Communist, as Chairman of the Council of Ministers (Prime Minister). Following the announcement of the electoral results, Landsbergis rejected the Molotov-Ribbentrop Pact and the 1940 annexation of Lithuania by the Soviets and declared Lithuanian independence (Banks, Day, Muller, 1997, 502).

Moscow responded to this declaration with the implementation of an economic blockade, which, due to Lithuania's economic dependence on the Soviet Union, crippled Lithuania. Following negotiations with Moscow, a moratorium on independence was declared on June 29. Frustrated with the delay in independence, Landsbergis ended the moratorium on January 2, 1991. Within a week, 'Prime Minister Prunskienė resigned ... following widespread opposition to price increases she had authorized' (Banks, Day, Muller, 1997, 502). Internal discontent, stemming from economic reforms, was exacerbated by worsening relations with the Soviets. On January 11, 1991, the Soviets moved troops into Vilnius and occupied government buildings. Subsequent Soviet-Lithuanian clashes resulted in hundreds of injuries and the death of 14 Lithuanians. Lithuanians responded on February 9 by holding a national poll in which 90.47 percent of the respondents answered yes to independence. Clashes continued until Moscow's recognition of Lithuanian independence on September 6, 1991 (Banks, Day, Muller, 502).

After finally achieving full recognition as an independent state, the Lithuanian government was faced with the arduous task of reconstructing the economy. The first half of 1992 saw parliamentary paralysis on the issue of economic reform. The economy was 'in deep crisis', and criticism was leveled at the government's policies from both the Left and the Right (Vardys and Sedaitis, 1997, 201). The former Communists placed the blame on the shock reforms implemented by the reformist leadership. Meanwhile, liberal deputies criticized the government for not pursuing austerity measures and continuing 'socialist' policies of full employment and welfare support. Thus, the economic transition became the focal point of Lithuanian politics.

As part of the restructuring effort, Lithuania entered into trade relations with Russia to gain access to energy supplies. The agreement provided for an exchange of energy resources (oil, gas, and nuclear) for Lithuanian agricultural and manufactured goods. However, Russia, facing its own economic difficulties, increased the price of energy resources in 1992 (Vardys and Sedaities, 1997, 201)[18]. Moreover, the freeing of price controls created a shortage of consumer goods throughout 1992, and a coupon system was introduced to address shortage problems. In addition, privatization of state-owned enterprises began with the implementation of a voucher system. The privatization of enterprises and housing proved to be a success; however, the reorganization of agriculture was disastrous. Agricultural reforms passed by parliament in 1991 were vague and contradictory. The quick pace of the radical land reform resulted in displaced farmers, land being abandoned or left fallow because of uncertainty of ownership, and a shortage of farming equipment. The collectivized farming system was effectively dismantled but it was not replaced with a viable alternative. The short-term economic costs of the reforms were great, and the issue of the appropriate approach to economic reform split the legislature between the right-of-center Sajūdis and the left-of-center Lithuanian Democratic Labor Party (discussed below).

Landsbergis attempted to break the gridlock on economic reform by increasing his executive power through a referendum on May 23, 1992. Banks states, 'while nearly 70 percent of the votes cast were affirmative, a participation rate less than half of the electorate doomed the proposal, which, branded as excessively authoritarian, contributed to the Sajūdis electoral debacle late in the year' (1993, 494). Landsbergis's move toward authoritarianism, coupled with poor economic conditions and widespread shortages, led to the electoral success of the Lithuanian Democratic Labor Party (LDDP) in the legislative balloting on October 27 and November 15, 1992. The LDDP, led by former Communist Brazauskas and formed from a faction of the Lithuanian Communist Party in 1990, campaigned on a platform of gradual economic reform. The extent of the backlash against Sajūdis is demonstrated by the lack of electoral support – it won less than 20 percent of the vote. The election of the former Communists in 1992 shocked many; the *Wall Street Journal* stated 'Lithuania, the first republic to break away from the Soviet Union, also became the first in which former Communists have scored a political comeback in a popular parliamentary vote' (1992, 1). The return of former Communists to power in Central and Eastern Europe has since been referred to as the 'Lithuanian syndrome'.

The swing from the nationalist Right to the former Communists did not signal a return to Communism; rather, it demonstrated the disappointment in Sajūdis. Economic crisis, Landsbergis's authoritarian tendencies, and lack of political experience resulted in their defeat. Following the election, the LDDP sought to assure the populace that it did not intend to return to Soviet-style governing. The LDDP claimed to be a social democratic party rather than 'socialist'. It continued policies to strengthen Lithuanian independence, upheld the negotiated Soviet troop withdrawal, and agreed not to reverse Lithuania's free-market reforms. However, support for the former Communists waned, and Lithuania once again shifted toward the Right.

The 1996 parliamentary balloting ousted the former Communists in favor of the nationalist Sajūdis, now operating under the name of Homeland Union (TS). Unlike the 1992 elections, the backlash against the incumbents was not due to economic crisis, but rather to corruption. As in other post-Communist states (particularly Russia), economic transition enriched political elites while the majority of the populace suffered. This economic disparity led to distrust of both elites and the new institutions. Prior to the 1996 elections, former Communist Prime Minister Šleževičius, accused of being involved in a banking scandal, was forced to resign by presidential decree. This scandal epitomized the corruption and abuse of power by political elites and severely damaged the LDDP. While the LDDP was on a decline due to financial scandal and internal dissension, Sajūdis was on the rise, having reorganized as a functioning political party (TS). Prior to its defeat in 1992, Sajūdis had refused to organize. As a result, the bloc had splintered, and Sajūdis had been weakened as a political force. However, the electoral defeat and the experience of parliamentary politics led Landbergis to form the TS as a right-of-center party. The TS-led government coalition subsequently endorsed greater economic reform as well as policies addressing corruption.

The present politics of Lithuania clearly demonstrates the influence of nationalism, especially as related to the desire to separate from Russia. Lithuania never accepted the legitimacy of Soviet rule. This is evidenced by the early insurrectionists of the 1940s and 1950s and, more recently, by the widespread support for the independence movement. This nationalism, however, is not clearly linked to democratic values. Rather, it has had a tendency to manifest itself in forms of 'soft' authoritarianism. This was seen in the interwar period with the Smetona regime and in the post-Communist era with the actions of Landbergis. Tendencies toward authoritarianism are seen not only with Landbergis' attempt to expand executive power, but also in the general disregard for the rule of law. The post-Communist era is fraught with examples of both the former Communists and the reformists ignoring constitutional provisions.[19] Both blocs have abused parliamentary procedures regarding voting and quorums, thereby displaying a lack of experience with the workings of democracy. In addition, the lack of centrist parties has plagued current politics, leaving the voters with only a choice between extremes. Hence, the electoral outcomes demonstrate wide swings from Right to Left. However, the recent TS-led government has sought to broaden its political and ideological base by forming a coalition with both the Lithuanian Christian Democratic Party (LKDP) and the Lithuanian Center Union (LCS).

Having achieved independence, Lithuania must redefine its national cultural identity and adapt its traditions to the new democratic institutions. The permanent constitution adopted in 1992 was a result of compromise and consensus across the parliamentary parties. It was an attempt to reconcile Lithuanian traditions with democratic principles. This is most clearly seen in regard to religious freedom. The constitution 'on the one hand ... declares that "freedom of thought, religion and conscience shall not be restrained," but on the other it specifies that the state "shall recognize those churches and religious organizations which are traditional in Lithuania while other churches and religious organizations [shall be recognized] if they have support in society and if their teaching as well as their rituals do not contradict law and morality" ' (Vardys and Sedaitis, 1997, 206-7).

The history of political development in Lithuania plainly shows the Lithuanian desire for self-determination. However, it does not demonstrate overt democratic political values. Democracy is supported as an alternative to foreign rule rather than as something that should be valued in and of itself.

Survey Data

Survey data examining the extent of Lithuanian alienation from the Soviet regime are available. Miller (1993) investigates support for the Soviet system in 1990 by looking at the level of alienation in the Soviet republics of Russia, Ukraine, and Lithuania. He uses the New Soviet Citizen Survey (NSCS) conducted in 1990 and argues that the extent of political legitimacy can be assessed by exploring the attitudes of citizens toward leadership, the Communist Party, the Supreme Soviet, the military, a system of multiple political parties, and freedom to demonstrate. I expect that the Lithuanian responses will demonstrate a high degree of alienation from the Soviet regime. Table 7.5, which is located on page 140, presents the responses to the seven support-alienation items. The asterisk indicates that a particular response reflects a lack of support.

The survey data indicate that Lithuanians, on the whole, reject the Soviet system. In fact, for each alienation item over 50 percent of the respondents are alienated from the various Soviet institutions. In addition, the majority of respondents support a system with multiple parties and prefer freedom to demonstrate over an orderly society. Given the historical and more recent relationship between Lithuanians and the Soviet leadership, it is not surprising that over 85 percent of Lithuanians believe that Soviet leaders don't care, and that over three-quarters of the respondents rate the CPSU and the Soviet military negatively.

Although this survey indicates a high level of alienation from the Soviet system, it does not suggest an equally strong commitment to democratic values. Fifty-five percent of respondents believe that multiple parties are good for the system; however, over 12 percent disagreed with multiple parties and over 10 percent responded 'don't know'. This 22 percent represents a large segment of the population that does not support multiple parties. In addition, although 51.9 percent of respondents disagree that 'an orderly society is more important than freedom to demonstrate', almost 22 percent of the respondents agree with this statement. Although democratic values are not as prevalent as feelings of alienation from the Soviet political system, the overwhelming alienation from the Soviet regime may be enough to lend the new democracy legitimacy. I expect that Lithuanian attitudes toward multiple parties as well as preferences toward order are likely to become more democratic with experience.

Table 7.5 Lithuanian Response to Systems Support/Alienation Items (1990)

	Lithuania
Trust Soviet Leaders	
Always or Most of the Time	13.7
Only some of the time*	50.9
Never*	31.9
DK	3.5
Leaders Don't Care	
Agree*	85.4
Pro/Con	9.6
Disagree	2.2
DK	2.8
Rating of CPSU	
Negative*	79.3
Neutral	10.6
Positive	7.7
DK	2.4
Rating of the Supreme Soviet	
Negative*	63.2
Neutral	23.1
Positive	8.5
DK	5.2
Rating of the Military	
Negative*	78.5
Neutral	10.1
Positive	9.4
DK	2.0
Multiple Political Parties Good for the System	
Agree*	55.0
Pro/Con	22.0
Disagree	12.4
DK	10.6
Orderly Society More Important than Freedom to Demonstrate	
Agree	21.6
Pro/Con	17.0
Disagree*	51.9
DK	9.6

Prospects for Democracy

Consolidation of democracy and installation of a market economy are likely for Lithuania. Its democratic institutions are functioning,[20] and the government is committed to economic transition. The high level of mass support and the success of present economic policies assure completion of the consolidation process, provided the populace supports democracy not only as an alternative to foreign rule, but also as the best alternative for governing. Economic success can convince Lithuanians that both the market and democracy benefit the country.

The current (1998) center-right coalition (Homeland Union [TS], Lithuanian Christian Democratic Party [LKDP], Lithuanian Center Union [LCS]) is pursuing quick entrance into the European Union by accelerating modernizing policies. Widespread support for EU entrance exists across political parties. As Banks, Day, and Muller note, 'prior to the [1996] election, all-party support had been forthcoming in June for parliamentary ratification of the 1995 association treaty with the EU, coupled with the adoption of a constitutional amendment legalizing the sale of nonagricultural land to foreigners (the previous ban on such sales was incompatible with the treaty terms)' (1997, 503).

In addition to pursuing closer ties with Western Europe, the current government continues the privatization policy implemented in 1995. This economic policy established a State Privatization Agency and based privatization on cash sales. The initial privatization policy (based on a voucher system) of 1992 was successful in privatizing 85 percent of the state-owned enterprises by 1995. Such success is critical to the completion of the market economy. In addition, the Lithuania government should concentrate its efforts on agricultural reform. The disastrous land reform of the early 1990s has made agricultural production slump. The decollectivized farms need to be privatized and formed into small, efficient, and competitive farms.

Politically, the shift from authoritarianism to democracy in Lithuania will take time. Although Lithuania lacks a political center, it is devoid of ethnic conflict and has an active civil society. Ethnic conflict, such as has emerged in other former Soviet republics, has not been a problem for Lithuania, largely because its population is over eighty percent Lithuanian. In addition, the constitution has included minority protections and granted citizenship to the Russian minority. Thus, ethnic problems have been avoided. Moreover, the momentum of the independence movement spurred the creation of active social groups. In 1994, Lithuania had over 700 social groups registered. This emergence of civil society is vital to the consolidation process and provides durability to the regime.

Notes

1. Lithuania's standard of living was greater than that of Russia in 1989. US Census Bureau and *Statesman's Year Book* report for 1989 that Lithuanian enterprises paid wages 2 percent higher than the Soviet average and Lithuania's per capita income of 2,757.95 rubles was 9 percent above the Soviet average for the same year.
2. It was during the reign of Grand Duke Gedimias (1275-1341) that the Jewish community of Vilnius first emerged. Gedimias, in an attempt to manipulate the politics of Christianization, invited Western merchants, craftsmen, and scholars to resettle in Lithuania. In Lithuania, the Jews enjoyed social and religious rights denied to them in the West (Vardys and Sedaitis, 1997).
3. A similar position is taken by Jusaitis. 'Nearly all the literature of the European nations, with the exception of the Greeks and Latins, began after the adoption of Christianity. Lithuania was the last European nation to accept Christianity' (Jusaitis, 1918, 65).
4. Since Lithuania had no written language prior to the 16th century, the official language used at the Lithuanian court of the Grand Duchy was 'Chancellory Slavonic'. (This is very similar to present day Byelorussian). For more extensive treatment of the issue of language see Anatol Lieven's *The Baltic Revolution* (1993).
5. The Lithuanian provinces of Vilnius and Kaunas participated in the revolts of 1831 and 1863 (Vardys and Sedaitis, 1997, 16; Iwaskiw, 1996, 178).
6. Serfs in Latvia and Estonia were liberated in 1807 without land. In addition, German nobles in these regions contributed to a quicker development of commercial agriculture. Thus, both Estonia and Latvia enjoyed greater prosperity and literacy among the populace in the 19th century than did Lithuania.
7. The Lithuanian Christian Democrats did not publish a party platform until 1904; however, they had started two underground publications prior to this: *Survey* (1890-96) and *Guardian of the Homeland* (1896-1904) (Vardys and Sedaitis, 1997, 19).
8. Groups elected to the congress on May 27, 1917 were: Socialist Populist Party (90), Christian Democrats (41), Social Democrats (39), Catholic Nationalists (32), Santara Party (30), and National Progress Party (20). Lithuanian Bolsheviks were also elected, but they withdrew from the Congress (Vardys and Sedaitis, 1997, 20).
9. Historically, Vilnius has been a cosmopolitan city. At the time of the Polish invasion, the Vilnius population was largely Polish and Jewish. Lithuanians were a minority estimated to be between 13 and 20 percent of the population.
10. Catholic parties were able to thwart attempts by the Social Democrats and the Populists to separate Church and state. In addition, the Church was able to use its influence to eliminate civil marriage and divorce. The Church also received funding from the state and made religious education compulsory (Vardys and Sedaitis, 1997, 34).
11. The Christian Democratic bloc consisted of the Christian Democratic Party, the Farmers Alliance, and the Labor Federation, which represented the interests of professional, agricultural, and workers' groups (Vardys and Sedaitis, 1997, 34).
12. By 1926, Mussolini had control of Italy and Pilsudski was in control of Poland.
13. The non-aggression pact is known as the Molotov-Ribbentrop Pact, which has never been considered legitimate by the Lithuanians.

Lithuania 143

14 Estimates of the loss of civilian population under the German occupation range from 300,000-500,000 . Additional population losses came from Soviet deportations and arrests. Also, the German population was repatriated to Germany accounting for the loss of an additional 52,000 people. For more information see: Misiunas and Taagepera (1993), *The Baltic States: Years of Dependence, 1940-1980*, pp. 275-326, and Dov Levin, 'Lithuania,' *Encyclopedia of the Holocaust*, vol. 3, ed. Israel Gutman (New York and London: MacMillan, 1990), pp. 895-899.
15 Gosplan reported in 1989 that industrial production had increased 84 percent since 1940. And, by 1990 industrial production accounted for 52 percent of the national product (Vardys and Sedaitis, 1997, 66).
16 Soviet sources estimate the loss of life was 20,000 for each side. Other sources indicate up to 30,000 (Vardys and Sedaitis, 1997, 84).
17 The LFL held an illegal demonstration in Vilinius on September 28, 1988, to mark the anniversary of the Molotov-Ribbentrop Pact. The demonstration ended in violence. Public outrage was directed toward Moscow, and support for both the LFL and the Movement for Restructuring increased (Vardys and Sedaitis, 1997, 111).
18 Russia insisted on hard currency payments for energy resources causing energy shortages in Lithuania where hard currency was scare (Vardys and Sedaitis, 1997, 201-201).
19 Some examples include: 1) the removal of Prunskienė in 1991 – the rightist majority bypassed the two-thirds vote needed for removal by changing the requirement to a simple majority, 2) the election of deputy speakers in 1992 – the LDDP ignored the constitutional provision for one deputy speaker and elected two, 3) suppression of freedom of the press – the LDDP decreed five days before the 1992 presidential elections that the media was restricted from publishing discrediting information about the candidates.
20 Lithuania has passed Huntington's "two turnover" requirement for democratic consolidation. There has been a peaceful transfer of power in the three democratic elections held thus far (1990 - Sajūdis; 1992 - LDDP; 1996 - Homeland Union). In addition, the constitution adopted in 1992 granted sovereignty to the parliament.

8 Russia

Introduction

This chapter explores the level of democratic support in Russia, the hypothesized relationships between economic factors and democratic support, and Russian political culture and its role in the contemporary level of support for the democratic regime. Like Slovakia, the empirical findings for Russia indicate a negative influence on support for democracy (Table 3.3; Figure 3.3). This is to be expected given Russia's enormous economic woes. Moreover, it can be anticipated that a history of authoritarianism and the legacy of the Communist regime constitute an ancillary hindrance to democratic support.

Democratic Support

The level of democratic support in Russia from 1991 to 1994 is much lower than the mean of Central and Eastern European countries taken as a whole (Table 8.1; Figure 8.1).

Table 8.1 Democratic Satisfaction for Russia and Central and Eastern Europe

Year	Russia	Average CEE	Difference Russia and Average CEE
1990	–	2.40	–
1991	1.87	2.26	-0.39
1992	1.75	2.12	-0.37
1993	1.83	2.09	-0.26
1994	1.59	1.97	-0.38

Figure 8.1: Democratic Satisfaction for Russia and Central and Eastern Europe

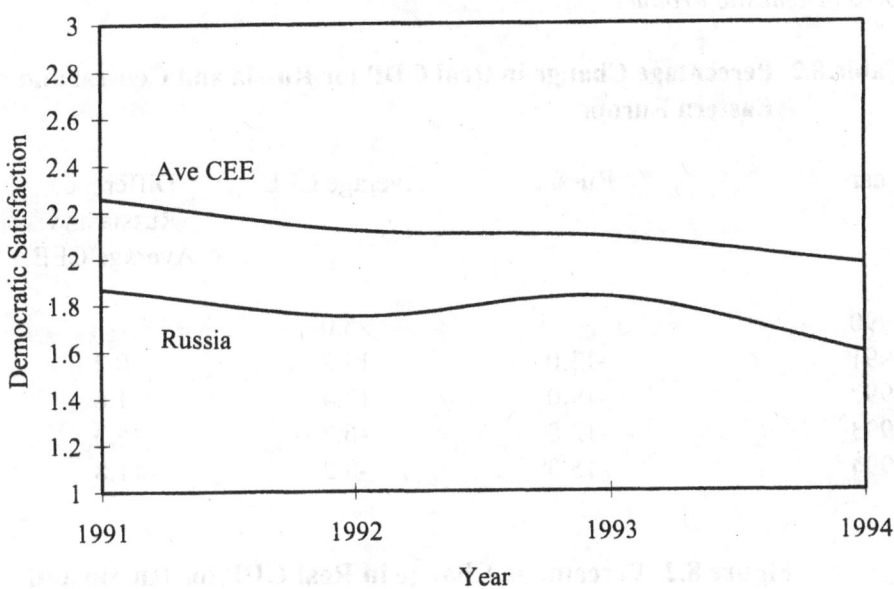

Democratic satisfaction is low at the beginning of the political and economic transitions of 1991. It remains relatively constant from 1991 to 1993, then drops very low in 1994. Figure 8.1 plots democratic satisfaction for Russia and the average for Central and Eastern Europe. Russia's level of support remains below the average throughout the period from 1991 to 1994. Unlike Czechoslovakia, Russia began transition with a relatively low level of democratic satisfaction. It appears that Russia did not experience the 'honeymoon period' that Czechoslovakia enjoyed; rather, Russians were skeptical of democracy from the beginning of transition.

Economic Conditions

The low levels of democratic support in Russia may be explained by objective economic conditions and by perceptions of those conditions. The empirical model indicates that countries with low regime support are those in which

146 *The Economy and Political Culture in New Democracies*

the economy is particularly weak. Thus, pattern matching of the hypothesized relationships is useful to determine how well Russia fits the model.

Gross Domestic Product

Table 8.2 Percentage Change in Real GDP for Russia and Central and Eastern Europe

Year	Russia	Average CEE	Difference Russia and Average CEE
1990	–	-5.0	-
1991	-13.0	-13.2	0.2
1992	-19.0	-17.4	-1.6
1993	-12.0	-6.7	-5.3
1994	-15.0	-3.2	-11.8

Figure 8.2: Percentage Change in Real GDP for Russia and Central and Eastern Europe

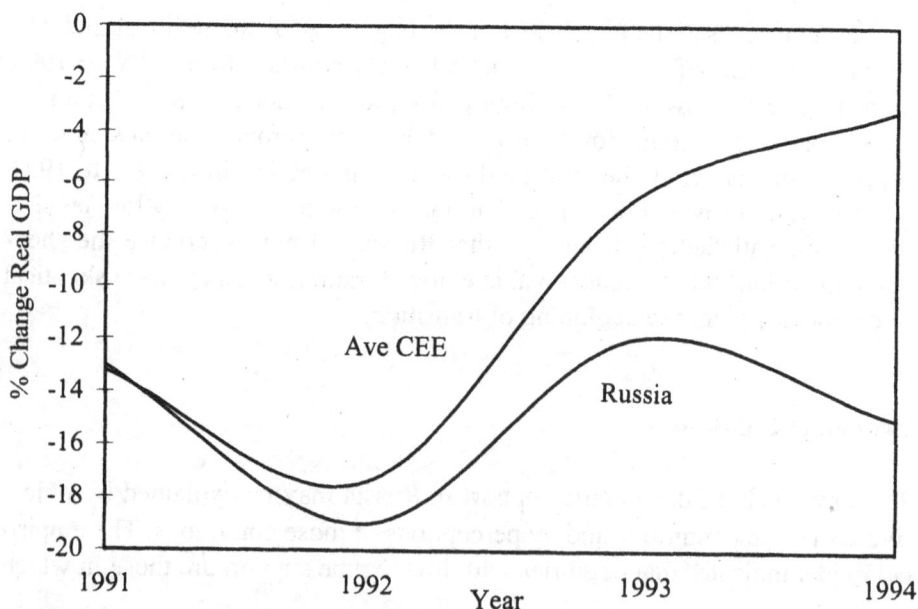

As Table 8.2 and Figure 8.2 indicate, the percentage decreases in real GDP for Russia were quite high and, by 1994, had not begun to rebound. Russia is experiencing prolonged economic hardship. The average percentage change in real GDP for Central and Eastern Europe shows an increase after 1992, while Russia continues to slump in terms of economic output. The size and extent of the Russian economy pose greater difficulty in transition than other Central and Eastern European economies. The restructuring of the central ministries and the complications in privatizing heavy industry make for protracted low economic output, which we would expect to translate into low democratic satisfaction levels.

H_1: If economic conditions improve, support for democracy will increase.

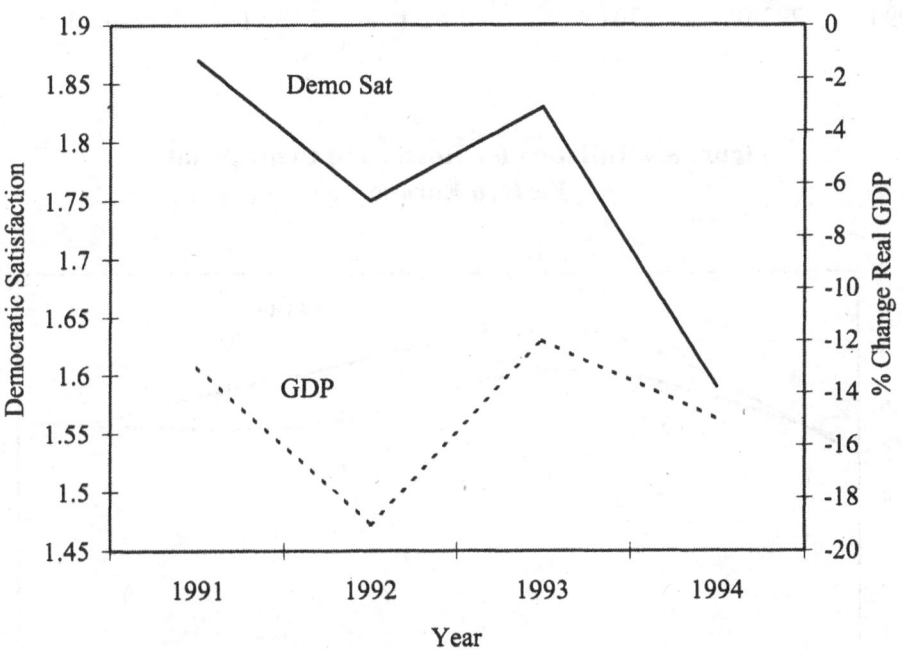

Figure 8.3: Democratic Satisfaction and Percentage Change in Real GDP for Russia

148 The Economy and Political Culture in New Democracies

Figure 8.3 plots the percentage change in real GDP and democratic satisfaction. It appears that the relationship between GDP and democratic satisfaction is positive. For each time point from 1991 to 1994, GDP and democratic satisfaction increase and decrease simultaneously. On a whole, this positive relationship supports the basic theoretical proposition.

Inflation

Table 8.3 Inflation for Russia and Central and Eastern Europe

Year	Russia	Average CEE	log (RUS)	log (CEE)	Difference Russia and CEE
1990	–	76.7	–	4.34	–
1991	144.0	186.5	4.97	5.23	-42.5
1992	2318.0	922.0	7.75	6.83	1396.0
1993	841.0	274.4	6.74	5.62	566.6
1994	203.0	301.4	5.31	5.71	-98.4

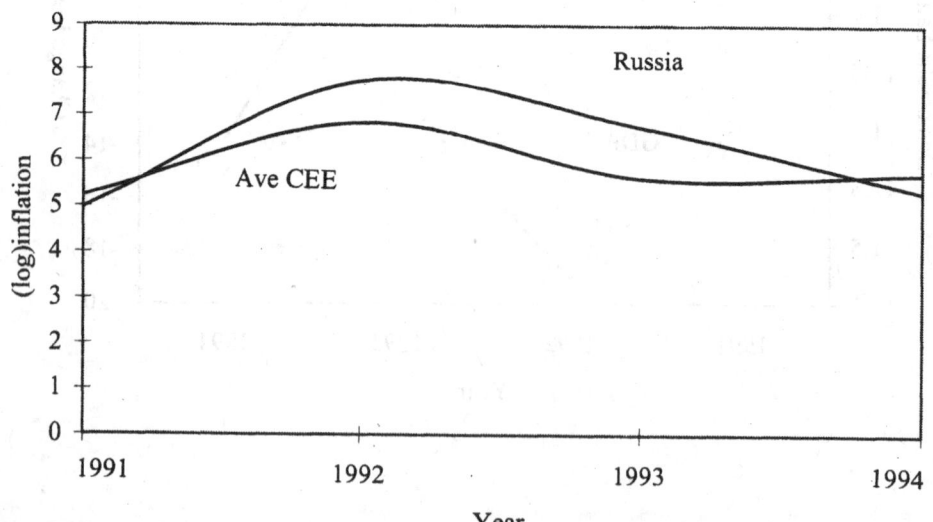

Figure 8.4 Inflation for Russia and Central and Eastern Europe

As Table 8.3 and Figure 8.4 show, inflation in Russia is higher than that of the average for the CEE countries. Before Russia can proceed with further economic transformation, it must get inflation under control. Russia should introduce greater budget constraints, increase interest rates, and close inefficient industry by implementing bankruptcy legislation.

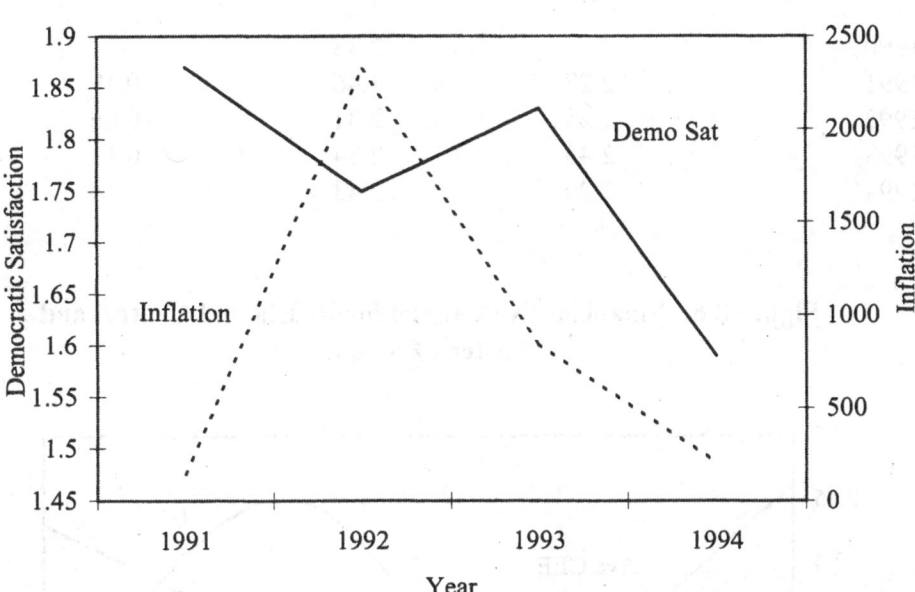

Figure 8.5: Democratic Satisfaction and Inflation for Russia

Figure 8.5 examines the relationship between democratic satisfaction and inflation. The hypothesized negative relationship seems to hold from 1991 to 1993. As inflation increased from 1991 to 1992, democratic satisfaction dropped and as inflation began to decline in 1992, democratic satisfaction increased. However, support for democracy took a sharp dip from 1993 to 1994. In general, the relationship is atypical.

Financial Evaluations

Table 8.4 and Figure 8.6 compare Russian financial evaluations to the average financial evaluations for Central and Eastern Europe. Interestingly, Russian perceptions are not that far off the average and, in fact, exceeded it in

1993. We would expect Russian evaluations to be lower than the average given that economic conditions for Russia were worse than the overall mean.

Table 8.4 Financial Evaluations for Russia and Central and Eastern Europe

Year	Russia	Average CEE	Diff. Russia and Average CEE
1990	–	2.33	–
1991	2.27	2.46	-0.19
1992	2.25	2.31	-0.06
1993	2.45	2.34	0.11
1994	2.29	2.43	-0.14

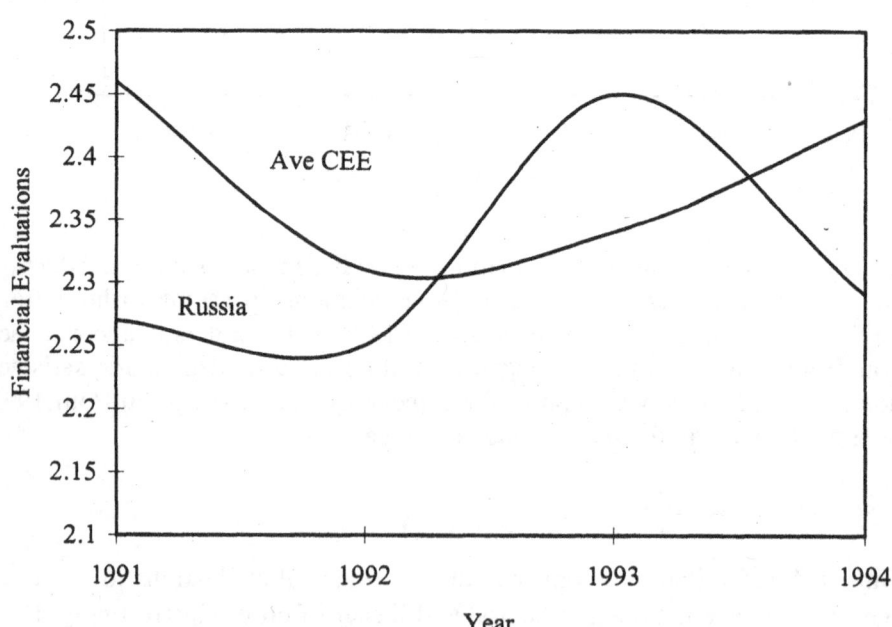

Figure 8.6: Financial Evaluations for Russia and Central and Eastern Europe

Russian citizens seem to be more optimistic in their financial evaluations than expected. Figure 8.7 looks at the relationship between democratic satisfaction and financial evaluations.

H_2: *If financial evaluations improve, democratic satisfaction will increase.*

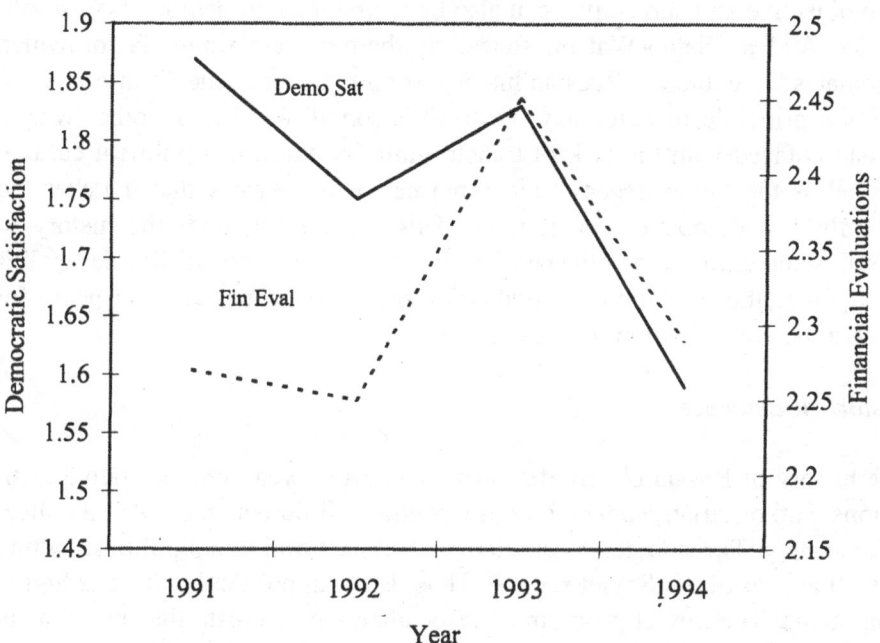

Figure 8.7: Democratic Satisfaction and Financial Evaluations for Russia

Figure 8.7 depicts a relatively positive relationship between democratic satisfaction and financial evaluations. In fact, as found in the cross-national analysis, perceptions of financial situation are, in Russia as elsewhere, a better predictor of democratic satisfaction than are actual economic conditions.

The fit of democratic satisfaction in Russia to the quantitative predicators is mixed. But, we must still bear in mind that satisfaction with democracy in Russia has been considerably lower than would have been expected, compared to other post-Communist countries, even given the poor Russian economic record.

Political Culture

The future of Russian democracy is threatened not only by the enormous economic problems of market transition but also by a long history of authoritarianism. Political culture, as demonstrated in the Czech case, can be an advantage to the continuance of democracy if underlying values and norms are congruent to democratic institutions. However, political culture, both objective and subjective, can also be a hindrance to democratic consolidation. And as Seton-Watson states, 'if there is one single factor which dominates the course of Russian history, at any rate since the Tatar conquest, it is the principle of autocracy' (Seton-Watson, 1967, 10). In other words, Russia is faced with the task of transforming its traditional political culture, as well as the Soviet legacy, into a normative framework that matches the nation's new democratic institutions. This section examines the history of Russia's autocratic rule with specific reference to 'traditional' Russian political culture, the evolution of totalitarianism, and the present prospects for democratic consolidation in Russia.

Historical Evidence

The history of Russia clearly displays a pattern of weak representative institutions, authoritarian leaders, a highly centralized bureaucracy, and a collectivist society. These factors characterized Russia's traditional political culture as well as that of the Soviet regime. Thus, Russian political culture is highly continuous. The Soviet program of resocialization to create the 'new Soviet man' was not successful; rather, the Communist system was able to utilize elements that already existed in the traditional society (White, 1979).

There is widespread agreement among both historians and political scientists that Russian politics is stamped with a history of autocratic rule (Inkeles and Baurer, 1959; Tucker, 1973; Pipes, 1974; White, 1977, 1978, 1979; Brown, 1989). A more recent work by Nicolai Petro (1995), in contrast, argues that Russian history displays democratic elements that evolved over time, and that it is this evolution that explains the transition to democracy in 1991. However, Petro's dissenting argument is not convincing; Russian history clearly displays a politics of authoritarianism, bureaucratization, and lack of democratic representative bodies.

The pattern of political development in Russia differs greatly from both the Western and the Central and Eastern European states. Russia's size and lack of natural boundaries have continually left it open to foreign invasion. This, as well as its economic isolation from Europe, resulted in an emphasis on centralized control and an almost xenophobic suspicion of foreigners. The social fabric of Russia, characterized by collectivism and linked to autocracy, is also quite distinct from the West in its development. The serfs' bondage to the land and Russia's modified form of feudalism foreshadowed the collective farms of the Soviet regime. A brief survey of Russia's historical development will readily demonstrate the authoritarian characteristics that link traditional Russian political culture, Soviet political culture, and the recent lack of support for democracy.

Kievan Russia (850-1240) The formation of Russian political society, centered at Kiev in the South and Novgorod in the north, began in the 9th century (Florinsky, 1953; Riasanovsky, 1969; Pipes, 1974; Mackenzie and Curran, 1986). This early period of political development differs from later periods in that it contained rudimentary elements of democracy. The political structure was confederal in nature and consisted of decentralized principalities. As Mackenzie and Curran remark, 'within Kievan Russia, political power was divided among the ruling princes, noble advisory council (*boyar* duma) and town councils (*veche*), reflecting respectively monarchical, aristocratic and democratic principles' (Mackenzie and Curran, 1986, 9).

The Prince of Kiev maintained a special status within this system and from the 12th century carried the title of 'Grand Prince'. Princely power was largely concentrated in military leadership, justice, and administration (Riasanovsky, 1969, 55). The *boyar* duma evolved in this period as an advisory board to the prince. The *veche*, or town council, was a much more interesting political development. The decentralization of the political structure allowed for localized political institutions, and, in fact, Riasanovsky asserts that 'princely government came relatively late and had to be superimposed on rather well developed local institutions, notably so in towns' (Riasanovsky, 1969, 55). A *veche* entailed a town meeting made up of all the heads of households who would 'decide such basic issues as war and peace, emergency legislation, and conflicts with the prince or between princes' (Riasanovsky, 1969, 56). Although the *veche* was not fully developed representative body, it did have the power to elect the local princes and limit their power regarding taxation (Florinsky, 1953, 28, 34). Historians deem the emergence of the *veche* as being very similar to developments taking place in Western Europe at the same time.

It was during the Kievan period that Russia was converted to Christianity. While such conversion was taking place across the whole of Europe, for Russia the Christian influence was Byzantine, not Roman. Although the jurisdictional distinctions were of negligible importance at this time (the Church did not split until 1054), this development marked an important cultural break with the West. The adoption of the Byzantine Church meant isolation from Latin civilization and all its offerings. And, as Riasanovsky points out, 'it helped notably to inspire Russian suspicions of the West and the tragic enmity between the Russians and the Poles' (Riasanovsky, 1969, 39). Apart from its spiritual role, the Church also took on important societal functions such as operating hospitals and hostels, distributing charity, and administering education. Overall, the Byzantine Church had a major impact upon Kievan education, literature, and the arts (Riasanovsky, 1969, 54, 57-66).

The Kievan Russian state is often noted for its foreign commerce (Kliuchevskii, 1958; Riasanovsky, 1969; Pipes, 1974). Its economic activities led to the development of a class system. The prince, of course, stood at the top. The retainers of the prince, known as the *druzhina,* were below the princely family. This group eventually merged with the local aristocracy and became known as the *boyars*. The middle class, or *liudi*, followed the *boyars* and had significant numbers at this time. In fact, the middle class was larger in Russia at this time than it was in Europe. However, in later periods of Russian history this class all but disappeared. Finally, the lowest class consisted of Kievan peasants who made up the bulk of the population. The peasants were not bound to the land at that time and the emphasis on towns and trade meant that Russia did not have feudalism in the same sense as the West (Riasanovsky, 1969, 53-54).

Tartar Invasion – Appanage Russia (13th century to 15th century) The history of Russia was deeply affected by the Mongol invasions from central Asia led by Genghis Khan. The rule of the Mongol khans, known as the Golden Horde, introduced absolute rule into the Russian principalities and stifled the early democratic political development of the *veche*. The Tartars' chief interest in European Russia was the exaction of revenue. The Russian princes acted as tax collectors for the Mongols directly at the expense of the people. As Florinsky notes, 'the [princes] frequently appeared in part not only [as]

Tartar agents but even defenders of Tartar interests against those of the people they were supposed to represent' (Florinsky, 1953, 60). In addition, the Russian princes were no longer elected by the *veche*; rather, the Mongol khans assumed power of appointment. 'The *veche*, whose influence was on the decline even before the Tartar invasion, lost under the rule of the Golden Horde two of its most important functions: the right to choose and to expel the princes, this right passing into the hands of the khans. The *veche* itself then sank into insignificance' (Florinsky, 1953, 63).

Traditionally, the common perception of the Mongol invasions is one of destruction, which retarded the development of Russia and inflicted wholesale devastation and massacre. However, it is important to recognize that the Mongols had a long-lasting effect that was both social and political in nature. The Tartar influence extended itself into the social structure of Russian society through a process of upper class assimilation. Marriage between Russian princes and Mongol princesses was not uncommon. In fact, 'at the end of the seventeenth century about 17 percent of the Moscow upper class was of Tartar or eastern origin' (Florinsky, 1953, 64).

The most important effect of the Tartars was the establishment of absolutism. The Muscovite state was a direct successor of the Mongol khanate. Thus, Riasanovsky emphasizes 'the influence of the Mongols in transforming weak and divided Appanage Russia into a powerful, disciplined, and monolithic autocracy. Institutions, legal norms, and the psychology of Muscovite Russia have all been described as a legacy of Genghis Khan' (Riasanovsky, 1969, 81).

The Church consolidated its position during the Appanage period. In a time of political divisions and invasions, the Church benefited from its central organization. In addition, the Mongols tolerated and were benevolent toward the Church. The Muscovite princes protected the Church and the center of religion shifted from Kiev to Moscow. The strength of the Church also stemmed from its accumulation of land and possessions, resulting from donations and the bequeathing of estates. Riasanovsky estimates that 'at the end of the Appanage period the Church in Russia owned over 25 percent of all cultivated land in the country' (Riasanovsky, 1969, 130-131). Moreover, the ecclesiastical lands were not subject to tax.

The social structure of the Appanage period is linked to the question of Russian feudalism. Historians have debated whether Russia experienced a true type of feudal society[1]. Suffice it to say that Appanage Russia had a rudimentary type of feudalism, which remained weak in the face of the rising power of the grand princes. Thus, the class system that emerged under

Kievan Russia continued, although there was a large decline in the middle class.

The political and cultural development that had begun in the Kievan period was halted by the Mongols in the Appanage period. Riasanovsky states that 'the Mongol devastation and the relative isolation and poverty characteristic of the age led to a diminution in culture and learning' (Riasanovsky, 1969, 144). In fact, education was virtually nonexistent. Politically, it was during this period that autocracy first established itself as the form of political rule. The Muscovite period would further consolidate this development.

Muscovite Russia (15th century to 17th century) As a result of the Tartar invasion of the 13th century, the Muscovite principate emerged as the primary political structure. The rise of Moscow at the center of Russia was accompanied by the formation of a centralized authoritarian state. Moscow's geographic location was critical for the expansion of the Muscovite state (Soloviev, 1959; Kliuchevskii, 1958; Riasanovsky, 1969). Expansion begun by the Muscovite princes and continued by the Czars led to increased centralization of the administration and the weakening of local self-rule. In Riasanovsky's words, 'Bureaucracy continued to proliferate on both the central and the local levels' (Riasanovsky, 1969, 212).

White asserts that 'a central characteristic of the Muscovite state was the absence of political institutions in any way constraining the exercise of monarchical power' (White, 1979, 24). The *boyar* duma, which had existed alongside the princes during both the Kievan and Appanage periods, had a perfunctory role. In 1550, a law stipulated legislative functions to the duma; however, the duma was at no time independent of the monarch, or Czar (the term used after 1547). Thus, White (1979, 25) characterizes the duma's role throughout this period of the Russian Empire as follows:

> Its purpose was simply to execute the instructions of the Czar, who appointed its members. It had no area of competence of its own, its composition and size were extremely unstable, it maintained no records, and it had no fixed procedures. It was an advisory, not a representative institution.

By the mid-16th century, the influence of the duma declined and the Czar's influence increased. An 'inner duma' was formed which consisted of nobles loyal to the Czar. Most significant issues were delegated to the inner duma. In fact, the Czar largely dictated legislation in the form of decrees or *ukazy* (White, 1979, 24). This consolidation of power in the hands of the monarch was accomplished during the reign of Ivan IV (1547-84), who claimed full autocratic powers. In addition to territorial expansion, Ivan initiated a Machiavellian domestic policy of *Oprichnina* (1564-72), or 'reign of terror', against the *boyars* and the clergy (Pipes, 1974, 94).

The legislative body from the mid-16th to the mid-17th centuries, known as the *Zemskii Sobor*, 'resembled an institution of an embryonically parliamentary character' (White, 1979, 25). Myers argues that it is only at this time that any comparison to the West can be made (Myers, 1975, 41). However, unlike Western representative bodies, the *Sobor* acted as an advisory institution. According to Florinsky (1953, 196),

> Its members were not elected but were appointed by the government. It was not, as Kliuchevsky has made clear, in any sense a national assembly, but a consultation of the government with its agents. The members of the sobor were not spokesmen of local interests; they were government officers familiar with the situation in the provinces, and they were called together to supply information, to answer questions, and to carry out decisions. Although this gathering is sometimes described as democratic in character, such was not the case.

The *Sobor* was of considerable size and held the power to elect the Czar. However, the *Sobor* was convened by the Czar, and its decisions had limited effectiveness. Thus, debate surrounds the true power of the *Sobor* (Kliuchevskii, 1958; Riasanovsky,1969). The most famous *Sobor*, of 1613, ended what is known as the Time of Troubles and established the Romanov Dynasty (Riasanovsky, 1969, 211). The Time of Troubles (1598-1613) was characterized by peasant revolts and foreign intervention. The impetus for the Time of Troubles was the death of Czar Theodore; for the first time there was no successor to the Muscovite throne. The *Sobor* emerged as the highest authority in the Muscovite state; however, it willingly forfeited its power to the newly appointed Romanov Czar, and autocracy survived unimpaired. The *Sobor*, however, 'from the middle of the seventeenth century ... became less and less inclusive and representative in character; finally, in 1722, the *Sobor* was deprived of its right to elect to the throne and fell altogether into desuetude' (White, 1979, 25).

An important point of contrast between Russian and Western European political development is that the Russian nobility was not an independent political force. As noted above, the nobility lacked formal political power in the duma, and in fact, the landed aristocracy was unable to assert any type of political or economic check on the Czar. Moreover, it was during the Muscovite period that the basis for aristocratic landholdings was transformed from hereditary to service. Under the Appanage system, the *boyar* landlords inherited their estates. Under the *votchiny* system, the *boyars* made contracts with their prince and were free to leave a prince's service and enter into a contract with another prince. In the Muscovite period, the system of *pomestie* emerged in which an estate was granted by the prince during the term of service. This system put the landed gentry directly under the Czar's control. Thus, the aristocracy no longer had an independent claim to the land through inheritance. This system extended and standardized state service, and the aristocracy gradually became a homogenous class of service gentry.

In addition, the *pomestie* system promoted the bondage of the serfs to the land. Risanovsky states that 'serfdom was the mainstay of Muscovite agriculture. Serf labor supported the gentry and thus the entire structure of the state' (Riasanovsky, 1969, 204). Before this period, the peasant-landlord relationship, like the *boyar*-prince relationship, was based on contracts. However, the peasants became increasingly dependent upon the landlords because they could seldom meet their obligations. Under the *pomestie* system, the Czar granted lands and bound peasants to the aristocracy. This underscores an important difference between Russian and West European serfs. Russian serfdom did not emanate from the feudal structure itself but, rather, appeared collaterally with a centralized monarchy (Riasanovsky, 1969, 204-206).

Alongside the consolidation of the state, the Church rose in stature. Attempts to improve organization and practice lead to a schism, or *raskol*, in the Russian Church in the 17th century. The schism did not develop over dogmatic or doctrinal issues; rather, it involved the correction of errors in the translation of texts and minor changes in rituals. What is fascinating about the *raskol* is how it differed from the Reformation. The Reformation occurred because of the need to reform and halt Church abuses. The *raskol*, on the other hand, occurred as a reaction against reform (Florinsky, 1953, 293-294; Riasanovsky, 1969, 219-223).

The Muscovite period was characterized by the consolidation of autocratic rule and a centralization of administration. Changes in the social structure furthered the concentration of power in the hands of the Czar and established a caste system. Moreover, the service requirements of the *boyar* landlords greatly reduced the power of the aristocracy. In addition, the bulk of the population consisted of uneducated serfs bound to the land. Russia lagged behind the West. It experienced neither Renaissance nor Reformation.

Imperial Russia (17th century to 1917) The period of Imperial Russia, beginning with the reign of Peter the Great (1682-1725), 'began a new epoch in Russian history' (Riasanovsky, 1969, 235). This period broke with Muscovite Russia in that the state came to include more and more peoples other than the Great Russians or Muscovites. Russia, as MacKenzie and Curran write, was transformed into 'a vast Eurasian multinational empire' (MacKenzie and Curran, 1986, 12). The entire period can be depicted as one of reform (short of liberalization) on the one hand and concentration of autocratic power and centralization on the other. This period lasted until the Communist revolution of 1917. The reign of Peter the Great was characterized by attempts to reform Russia so that its development corresponded to Western patterns. Peter's reforms stretched across a broad spectrum of areas including the military, education, society, economics, and politics. However, in spite of the enormity of reform, the basic autocratic nature of the political structure remained unchanged.

Peter the Great's domestic reforms were largely an outgrowth of the need to exact money to support a modern military. For most of his reign, Peter was preoccupied with the Great Northern War, and 'only a single year in Peter the Great's whole reign, 1724, passed entirely without war, while no more than another thirteen peaceful months could be added for the entire period' (Riasanovsky, 1969, 251). Moreover, as Pipes notes, 'his military expenditures regularly absorbed 80-85 percent of Russian revenues, and in one year (1705) as much as 96 percent' (Pipes, 1974, 120). The strain of war made it necessary to improve the administrative system to address the increased financial demands that confronted the state. But while most of Peter's reforms stemmed from his war efforts, his long-term goals were to Westernize and modernize Russia's society and culture (Riasanovsky, 1969, 251).

Peter's political reforms helped organize central and local government as well as Church administration. Peter brought to Russia the European ideas of the Age of Reason, and he ruled as an enlightened despot, thereby having no use for either the *boyar* duma or the *Zemskii Sobor*. In terms of institutional reforms, at the national level, he created the Governing Senate. 'The Senate was founded as the highest state institution to supervise all judicial, financial, and administrative affairs' (Riasanovsky, 1969, 255). The Senate played a particularly important role in administration and law; however, no decision could go into effect without the emperor's signature. Peter also reformed the unwieldy and overlapping national ministries by creating reorganized agencies, or *collegia*. In addition, administrative reforms were made at both the provincial and local level. The provincial reform, modeled after the Swedish system, gave the 'provincial bodies responsibility for local health, education, and economic development' (Riasanovsky, 1969, 256). Thus, the state became responsible for the basic social needs of the people. Provincial reform also helped to facilitate tax collection and the generation of money. In fact, the constant need for money led to one of the emperor's lasting innovations — the method of direct taxation. Peter replaced the household tax with the head, or poll tax. This was done by conducting a census to ensure that no one failed to pay the tax. It is important to note that the poll tax was exacted upon the masses (both serf and slave) (Florinsky, 1953, 362-364; Riasanovsky, 1969, 259-260; Pipes, 1974, 120-122).

Although the poll tax affected the lower classes, the aristocracy was also subject to Peter's reforms. The nobility, as mentioned earlier, had to fulfill a service requirement to the state. The service requirements for the gentry began at age 16 and continued for the rest of their lives. Peter standardized service by creating a 'Table of Ranks' that established a hierarchical order for military, civil, and court service positions (Riasanovsky, 1969, 260). Pipes calls this 'one of the most important pieces of legislation in the history of imperial Russia' (Pipes, 1974, 124). The Table provided the organizational framework for the Russian bureaucracy, and it remained in place until 1917. In addition, non-gentry who reached a particular rank were able to enter the gentry class and acquire hereditary membership (Riasanovsky, 1969, 260-261).

Peter also tightened state control of the Orthodox Church. The Church was reorganized and the seat of the patriarch was replaced by the Holy Synod, an organization eventually consisting of twelve clerics. This change 'enable[d] the government to exercise effective control over Church organization, possessions, and policies' (Riasanovsky, 1969, 257). In fact, Peter's general charter, known as Ecclesiastical Regulation 'provided in the minutest detail for the operations of the parish and monastic clergy ... and was a veritable bureaucratic constitution of the Russia church' (Pipes, 1974, 241). Government domination over religious institutions continued until 1917. As a result, Church and state became inextricably linked, transforming the Church into a compartment of the state, in contrast to the parochial, ecclesiastical, Church-centered society of the Muscovite period. This shift was due to the cultural reforms begun by Peter and continued under Catherine the Great (Riasanovsky, 1969, 257, 317).

The cultural reforms of the 18th century, known as the Russian Enlightenment, emphasized secularism, reason, and education. Modeled after the West and directed by the so-called enlightened despots, Russian culture emerged as a gentry culture. In the area of education, Peter sought reform at the fundamental level. He replaced the Slavonic alphabet with the civil Russian alphabet composed of Slavonic, Greek, and Latin letters. In addition to sending hundreds of Russians to the West to study, Peter established a number of secondary schools as well as the Imperial Academy of Science. Catherine the Great extended educational opportunities, largely to the middle class, through the establishment of 'popular' schools patterned after the Austrian Empire's educational system (Riasanovsky, 1969, 317-322).

Under the reign of Catherine the Great (1762-96), Russian literary expression developed fully, and this was clearly linked with the growth of state-supported social criticism. Catherine, influenced by the French *philosophes*, promoted social criticism as part of the Enlightenment. Of the many social problems that were criticized, serfdom was probably the most profusely denounced. However, Catherine's promotion of secular philosophy and social criticism stopped short of allowing criticism of the monarchy and despotism. In other words, social and cultural development was allowed until it threatened the autocratic political structure (Riasanovsky, 1969, 325-328).

The liberal ideas of the Enlightenment later brought about the first revolutionary group in Russia – the Decembrists. The Decembrists made an unsuccessful attempt to seize power after the death of Alexander I and the succession of Nicholas I in 1825. Following the Decembrist rebellion, Nicholas I was determined to fight revolution and to defend the existing autocracy. In fact, Florinsky (1953, 753) argues that under Nicholas I 'Russian nineteenth century absolutism reached its fullest development.' Nicholas, while aware of the problems of serfdom, feared that the emancipation of the serfs would lead to revolution. His reign was reactionary rather than reform-minded. Riasanovsky notes that Nicholas I was 'determined to preserve autocracy, afraid to abolish serfdom, and suspicious of all independent initiative and popular participation.' As a result, 'the emperor and his government could not introduce in their country the much-needed fundamental reforms' (Riasanovsky, 1969, 364). He rolled back liberal advances and implemented repressive measures such as large-scale censorship and restrictions on travel and academic freedom.

Although Nicholas I introduced strict control of the Ministry of Education, the upper classes continued to be educated. Thus, despite Nicholas's repressive policies, the first half of the 19th century saw the development of a Russian intelligentsia and gentry culture. This was reflected in the 'golden age of Russian literature', which included such great Russian figures as Pushkin and Dostoevsky (Riasanovsky, 1969, 385-386).

Alexander II succeeded Nicholas in 1855, and another era of reform ensued. Riasanovsky asserts that Alexander II implemented 'fundamental reforms unparalleled in scope in Russian History since Peter the Great' (Riasanovsky, 1969, 409). Following the end of the Crimean War, Alexander began what is known as the 'great reforms', and he became known as the 'Czar-Liberator' (Florinsky, 1953, 879). The most significant of these reforms was the emancipation of the serfs in 1861. Economic, political, and moral issues played a role in the emancipation. In the face of a growing money economy and market competition, landlords found it increasingly difficult to support serfs, and they accumulated enormous debts to the state. Politically, serfdom sparked numerous peasant uprisings in the 18th and 19th centuries (Riasanovsky, 1969, 209-215; Pipes, 1974, 162-165).[2] Moreover, as education advanced, the notion that serfdom was evil became widespread, and, by the mid-1800s it was generally recognized that the institution 'had outlived all usefulness' (MacKenzie and Curran, 1986, 21).

The emancipation reform, which granted liberty to the serfs, did not improve the situation of the peasants. They received less land for themselves than they had under the landlords, were required to repay the landlords for the land they received, had to pay the head tax, and were tied to communes. With few exceptions, land was not granted to individual peasants; rather, the state established peasant communes known as *obshchina* or *mir*. *Mir* is a term that 'emphasizes the communal gathering of peasants to settle their affairs – when it divided the land among its members and was responsible for taxes, the provision of recruits, and other obligations to the state' (Riasanovsky, 1969, 413). Although the communes offered protection for the peasants, they reinforced economic stagnation at a time when Russia was greatly in need of agricultural modernization. Thus, the misery of the peasants continued long after emancipation (Riasanovsky, 1969, 415).

In addition to freeing of the serfs, Alexander II reformed local government with the establishment of the *zemstvo* system, which sought to strengthen the historically weak local governments and introduced an element of democracy in them. The representation in the *zemstvo* assemblies was proportional to the amount of landholdings; thus, the gentry was overrepresented. However, Alexander's reforms did address many of the needs of the peasantry with improvements coming in the areas of education, health, roads, insurance, and food reserves. In particular, Riasanovsky notes that 'Russia obtained a kind of socialized medicine through the *zemstvo* long before other countries, with medical and surgical treatment available free of charge' (Riasanovsky, 1969, 417).

The peasant communes and the *zemstvo* established collectivism and reliance on the state as basic characteristics of modern Russia. The *mir*, as the basic social unit above the family, displayed the collectivist nature of Russian society. The Soviets would utilize this collectivist nature not only in agriculture but also in the promotion of Marxist ideology. The *zemstvo* also demonstrated the extent of the scope of the Russian state in the lives of the masses. Soviet socialism would continue this tradition of state intervention in society coupled with large-scale bureaucracy and centralized rule.

Both Alexander III (1881-94) and Nicholas II (1894-1917) were reactionaries. Not only did they not further reforms begun by Alexander II, but they also instituted 'counterreforms'. They sought to roll back the changes that had been made and to reinforce the centralized bureaucracy and class structure of the Russian system. The late 19th and early 20th centuries witnessed religious persecution and Russification of the multinational empire. Repression resulted in sporadic peasant uprisings culminating in a general strike in 1905. The revolution of 1905 forced Nicholas II to issue the October Manifesto, which granted civil liberties to Russian citizens, established a legislative duma, and seemingly transformed Russia into a constitutional monarchy. However, the Fundamental Laws, issued in 1906, circumscribed the power of the duma and allowed the emperor to retain many powers. On the other hand, the Fundamental Laws did specify an electoral law for the duma that emphasized representation and allowed almost all Russian men to participate in the election. The first two dumas of 1906 and 1907 clashed with the government and the Czar. In 1907 Czar Nicholas arbitrarily and unconstitutionally changed the electoral law, thereby reasserting his autocratic powers (Riasanovsky, 1969, 433-467).

The Imperial period leading up to the 1917 revolution was a continuation of a long history of autocracy, weak representative bodies, centralization, illiteracy of the masses, collectivism, and agrarian society. Russian society at the beginning of the 20th century, in spite of attempts at reform, was far from modern. The traditional elements of society persisted, and 'the new Soviet regime inherited a large, heterogeneous and backward Empire from its Tsarist predecessors' (White, 1979, 64).

Soviet Union (1917-1985) Czarist Russia fell when Nicholas II abdicated his powers in February 1917. Since Alexander II's reform efforts in the 1860s, the Russian state had become increasingly isolated from the society. Industrialization had produced a new technical and professional class as well as a critical intelligentsia. These classes, coupled with a dissatisfied peasantry, posed a direct opposition to the regime. In addition, anti-Czarist groups, such as the Socialist Revolutionaries (SR) and the Russian Social Democratic Labour Party (RSDLP)[3], became increasingly radicalized. The state's inability to adapt its autocratic political system to changing social and economic conditions led, ultimately, to a crisis of authority and breakdown of the old order. The impetus of the breakdown was WW I.

It is widely agreed that Russia experienced two revolutions in 1917: the bourgeois March revolution and the socialist November revolution. The social conditions precipitating the March revolution made the event unsurprising. Crouch (1989, 13) describes the circumstances prior to March 1917:

> The collapse of Tsarism in March was not unexpected. There had been repeated military disasters in the war with Germany, there were food shortages in the capital, St. Petersburg (whose Germanic name had been Russified to Petrograd in 1914), frequent and widespread strikes, demonstrations and bread riots. Accusations of treason were leveled openly at the German-born Empress. Finally, troops in Petrograd mutinied, the government panicked and the Tsar abdicated.

Following the March Revolution, the Provisional Government, consisting largely of liberals from the Duma, took control of Russia. It promised both a democratically elected National Assembly and land reform for the peasantry. However, there was slow movement toward both elections and land reforms. In addition, it misread the political climate in terms of Russian participation in the War, which lacked popular support. The Bolsheviks capitalized on the weakness of the Provisional Government by not supporting the government or the war and by using organizational and propaganda skills. Slogans such as 'Bread, land, and peace', which caught the public mood, were especially effective. On November 25, 1917, the Bolsheviks staged a bloodless coup against the Provisional Government (Riasanovsky, 1969, 507-508; Crouch, 1989, 14-15).

The Bolsheviks delivered what the Provisional Government could not: elections, land, and peace. However, the Bolsheviks were in a minority – as demonstrated by the subsequent election results for the Constituent Assembly. The Bolsheviks received 25 percent of the vote and the peasant-based SR received 38 percent. The Assembly met only once (in January 1918), after which it was forcibly disbanded by the Bolshevik Red Guard (Riasanovsky, 1969, 528; Crouch, 1989, 16). As revolutionary sentiment spread across Russia so did support for the Bolsheviks.

For the next three years, Russia was engaged in civil war. Until the Bolshevik consolidation of power in 1921, there were no specific Soviet policies addressing either economy or culture. However, the consequences of the Bolshevik revolution spanned politics, economics, and culture. The most significant political consequence was the establishment of the one-party centralized state. This stemmed directly from Lenin's notion, stated in *State and Revolution* (1917), 'that the socialist revolution could only survive if it smashed the old ruling apparatus and replaced it with the dictatorship of the proletariat, exercised in practice by the Bolshevik vanguard' (Crouch, 1989, 19). The structure of the one-party system took on the form of what was known as 'democratic centralism'. Dissent and opposition outside of the party were crushed; however, debate and discussion within the party were tolerated so long as the party maintained a united front. However, independent, intraparty debate gradually declined with the increased bureaucratization of the rapidly expanding party machine. And, it ceased all together under Stalin.

In 1921, Lenin initiated the New Economic Policy (NEP) to avoid economic collapse. The NEP liberalized agricultural policy to reestablish prewar production levels and to appease the peasantry. Lenin argued that the NEP was a necessary retreat to capitalism to prepare for the socialist society to come. The NEP not only privatized agriculture but also ended grain requisitioning and restored private ownership in consumer sectors. By 1927, 98.3 percent of all agricultural units were individual farms; however, the peasant communes, with their village assemblies, dominated rural life. Ninety percent of the peasantry continued to belong to *mirs*. In other words, privatization increased production, but the traditional communities were not disrupted. Moreover, although a degree of economic freedom existed under the NEP, 'political controls were tightened' (MacKenzie and Curran, 1986, 161-164).

Economic liberalization under Lenin allowed some experimentation and diversity in cultural life. Culture from the Marxist perspective is merely part of the superstructure of the society and cannot be altered unless the base (mode of production) is changed. In other words, for the Marxist, culture cannot be modified until a new economic system is in place. However, this is not to suggest that the Bolsheviks were uninterested in developing policies addressing culture and the arts. The first task faced by Lenin was to provide basic education to the illiterate masses, which comprised an estimated 70 percent of the population (MacKenzie and Curran, 1986, 223). An educational policy of 'ideological reorientation' sought to integrate ideological loyalty and Soviet patriotism into the curriculum. The new curriculum acted as an economic and political instrument of the party to promote Marxist ideology and teach social responsibility. Lenin's Commissariat of Education was quite successful, and by 1926, 51 percent of the population was literate (Riasanovsky, 1969, 631; MacKenzie and Curran, 1986, 225). MacKenzie and Curran contend education had two primary purposes: 'to train a new generation in socialist thinking and counteract lingering bourgeois influences; and to establish a solid foundation for a new socialist culture expressed in all the arts and sciences' (MacKenzie and Curran, 1986, 236). Reorientation efforts in the arts and sciences, however, did not begin until Stalin was in power. Under Lenin, the arts and science enjoyed relative freedom of expression.

Lenin's foundation of the 'party-state regime' enabled Stalin to consolidate his autocratic powers (Mawdsley, 1998, 15). Crouch (1989, 28) describes the party as 'a monolithic vehicle for Stalin's industrialization and collectivization drive', and he argues that after 1928 Stalin 'simply ceased to tolerate any dissent'. Stalin's rule can be characterized as a return to Czarist autocracy. The regime used systematic terror and force under the veil of a democratic constitution. In addition, Stalin successfully created a cult of personality. Like the Czars, Stalin became known as 'the beloved father and teacher – savior of the Soviet people'. White argues that one characteristic of traditional Russian political culture is that popular political attachments were highly personalized under the Czars (1979).[4] Stalin was able to use such personalized political attachments to his advantage and to persuade the populace that 'the chaos and the brutality were despite rather than because of the dictator' (Crouch, 1989, 28).

Stalin's 'revolution from above' transformed the Soviet Union economically and culturally more so than the revolution of 1917. He abandoned the NEP and launched a nationwide program of forced collectivization of agriculture, thereby destroying all private farms. Collectivization was coupled with a rapid and extensive industrialization drive. The forced collectivization enabled Stalin to crush any peasant opposition and gain control of the countryside. The Five-Year-Plans, which forced high industrial output, initiated what was to become a command economy with bureaucratically set prices. In other words, Stalin replaced the market economy of the NEP with a socialist system of centralized control. The plans were handed down from Gosplan, the state planning committee, and by the central ministries to the state-owned enterprises. This economic organization continued to exist until Gorbachev's reforms of 1989 (Riasanovsky, 1969, 545-563; Crouch, 1989, 28-35; Mawdsley, 1998, 27-41).

Stalin's complete control of Russian society was aided by the People's Commissariat of Internal Affairs (NKVD), the secret police. NKVD, forerunner to the KGB, established a 'state within a state' that controlled political, regular, and criminal police (MacKenzie and Curran, 1986, 184). During the Great Purge (1936-38), Stalin used the NKVD to consolidate his dictatorship by eliminating all in-party opposition. The Great Purge decimated Soviet political and military leadership. Mackenzie and Curran estimate that about half of the officers corps was shot or imprisoned (14 of 16 army generals were purged), and approximately 70 percent of the Central Committee members were purged. Total estimates of purge victims vary from 8 million to 20 million (MacKenzie and Curran, 1986, 187). Through maximum use of force and terror, Stalin created a powerful centralized state with a vast bureaucracy. Stalin continued the pattern of authority that harkened back to the Oriental despotism established by the Mongols.

As agriculture and industrialization moved forward, Stalin began to extend his control over the cultural lives of the citizens. Stalin continued Lenin's educational efforts to create a 'New Soviet Man'. The educational and cultural environment had to be consistent with the regime's objectives of adherence to Marxist ideology. This program of political socialization embraced formal political instruction in the schools and informal instruction by means of subordinating cultural life to political orthodoxy. Party control tightened over literature, and attacks were made on any work considered anti-Soviet, which included works hostile to the regime as well as those that took a neutral position. A new doctrine of 'socialist realism' was implemented for literature, the cinema, and the arts. The goal of 'socialist realism' was to portray the 'real' life of socialist society and promote ideological reorientation. Cultural life was to present a positive model for the proletarian. In addition, the cinema and the media (newspapers, television, radio) became powerful tools for the Party for the transmission of propaganda and mass information. Given the scale and intensity of this socialization, it would be surprising if a lasting impact upon the population was not achieved.

Soviet leadership from Stalin to Gorbachev was characterized by a fluctuation between reformism and conservatism (Crouch, 1989, 36). The need for change was evident throughout this period; but, as in the case of the reform-oriented Czars, the approach of controlled change from above was all that was permitted. The Khrushchev Era (1953-64) is depicted as a period of reform and rehabilitation. The Khrushchev regime continued the pattern of autocratic rule, but not to the extent of Stalin's dictatorship. In 1953 Khrushchev abolished arbitrary arrest in order to prevent more party purges; thus, the ending of terror limited his powers (Crouch, 1989, 37-38).

Khrushchev's most significant political reform was his de-Stalinization campaign. He criticized Stalin to the 20th Party Congress in March 1956 in what is known as the 'secret speech'. Khrushchev's attack was leveled at

Stalin's 'cult of personality' and the 'illegal repression' of party comrades (Medvedev and Medvedev, 1976; Crouch, 1989, 41). Although only a limited number of purge victims were formally rehabilitated, the speech stirred passions and brought the suffering of Stalin's victims to the surface. Khrushchev attempted to disassociate the party from Stalin's actions. 'He absolved the party from blame, even suggesting that the party had retained some precarious independent existence as a Leninist organization under Stalin' (Crouch, 1989, 42). The 'secret speech' signaled a wider cultural thaw in Russia and the Eastern bloc. This is evidenced by Khrushchev's consent, in 1962, to the publication of dissident writer Alexander Solzhenitsyn's *One Day in the Life of Ivan Denisovitch*, which detailed life in the *gulag* or prison camp system (Breslauer, 1982, 130; Crouch, 1989, 43).

In addition to acknowledging Stalin's reign of terror, Khrushchev addressed the flaws of the command economic system. He was critical of 'uneven development' in the USSR and sought to rectify this by agricultural reform. He embarked on the Virgin Lands project in Kazakhstan and was able to boost peasant morale as well as grain output (Medvedev and Medvedev, 1976, 58-60; McCauley, 1987, 19; Crouch, 1989, 40). Khrushchev also reformed the economic structure by decentralizing economic power from the central ministries to the local *sovnarkhozy*. By doing this he hoped to introduce greater flexibility into the rigid and inefficient economy. And in 1962 he split the party organizations into two hierarchies: one for industry and one for agriculture. These reforms created much confusion between the ministries and the *sovnarkhozy*, and management was chaotic (Medvedev and Medvedev, 1976, 104-107; MacKenzie and Curran, 1986, 307). Furthermore, Khrushchev adopted the doctrine of 'different roads to socialism', stipulating that the Soviet model was not necessarily applicable to all socialist countries. This policy, coupled with the liberalization of de-Stalinization, led to crises in Poland and Hungary in 1956, Soviet military intervention ultimately being required to put down domestic uprisings in these two countries.

Khrushchev's reformism never emerged as a coherent program and as a result did not succeed. The agricultural reforms and the restructuring of economic control fell short of solving any of the inherent systemic flaws. Consequently, the economy began to slow. In 1963 Khrushchev was forced to import grain. In addition, he suffered major international defeats, reflected not only in the Polish and Hungarian Uprisings but also in the Cuban Missile crisis of 1962.

Following the removal of Khrushchev in 1964, Brezhnev returned to the conservative Stalinist approach. Brezhnev's rule reaffirmed the authority of the party. The invasion of Czechoslovakia in August of 1968 demonstrated the danger of reforms gone too far. All further attempts at political or economic reform were halted. De-Stalinization ceased. The economic situation worsened during the latter part of Brezhnev's rule with increasing imports of grain. Crouch (1989, 57) points out that 'between 1975 and 1982 about one quarter of all Soviet grain needs were met by imports'. Economic growth declined as 'national income rates fell from 41 percent 1966-70 to 16.5 percent 1981-85, even on official figures' (Aganbegyan, 1988, 2).

Liberalization (1985–present) Following the death of Brezhnev on November 10, 1982, hard-liner Yuri Andropov came to power, but his rule was cut short by his death on February 9, 1984. Konstantin Chernenko succeeded Andropov as general secretary. However, in little over a year he too was dead, and Mikhail S. Gorbachev was named general secretary on March 11, 1985. Gorbachev, age 54, represented a generational transition in Russian leadership. He immediately began to make changes in both governmental and party leadership, replacing older, hard-line Communists with younger reform-minded technocrats. Most importantly, Gorbachev soon announced a campaign for radical reform of the Soviet system. His proposed political and economic reforms were based upon his ideas of openness (glasnost) and restructuring (perestroika). Centralized one-party rule remained intact until 1989; however, this period was characterized by a general relaxation of censorship, open criticism of the party and government, the development of independent political organizations, the release of political prisoners, and the easing of emigration restrictions. In 1988 Gorbachev rehabilitated old Bolshevik leaders who were victims of the Stalinist purges, and he called for a reformation of Marxist-Leninism that permitted a 'socialist pluralism of views'. In addition, he encouraged the 'free development' of national cultures within the Soviet Union.

Political liberalization became a reality with the implementation of constitutional amendments in December 1988, December 1989, and March 1990, which stipulated a parliamentary system, competitive elections, an independent judiciary, the right to private property, and free enterprise. Moreover, the 1990 amendments officially ended the Communist Party's monopoly of power. However, although political liberalization proceeded at a rapid pace, economic reform was stalled. Attempts at implementing an economic reform package were delayed by buying panics that resulted from notification of the reforms.

In late 1990 and early 1991 a conservative backlash against the pluralistic reforms ensued. Gorbachev also seemed to backslide on the reform effort. In October 1990 he failed to execute a market reform package, and in March 1991 he cracked down on demonstrators who supported Boris Yeltsin. (Yeltsin, elected president of the Russian Republic on May 29, 1990, had come under the attack of conservatives who were attempting to remove him from power.)

Gorbachev's hard-line approach came to an abrupt end in April 1991 with the 'Nine-plus-One' conference, which 'endorsed a new treaty that called for extensive decentralization in the social, political, and economic spheres' (Banks, 1993). The treaty acted as the impetus for the August 1991 failed coup attempt by hard-line conservatives. In June 1991 Yeltsin was directly elected president of the Russian Federation. Yeltsin claimed that his powers had to be increased if efforts at economic reform were to be successful. Later that year he assumed the powers of the chairman of the Council of Ministers, banned the Communist Party, and nationalized its assets. On December 21, 1991, the Russian Federation declared independence and the Soviet Union was dissolved in conjunction with the creation of the Commonwealth of Independent States (CIS). Most of the former republics had declared independence by that time.

Yeltsin began radical 'shock therapy' in January of 1992 by eliminating all price controls, which led to a dramatic increase in inflation. In March 1992 additional economic shocks resulted from trade liberalization and currency convertibility. These economic reforms resulted in legislative disputes and an attempt to strip Yeltsin of most of his powers. Yeltsin was consequently prevented from pursuing privatization and land reform. In October 1992 the National Salvation Front (NSF), a coalition of former Communists and nationalists, attacked Yeltsin and indicated that it would seek power. Subsequently, Yeltsin banned the NSF.

Executive-legislative relations worsened throughout 1993. Yeltsin campaigned for a referendum that called for the adoption of a new constitution that would expand presidential powers. He also sought early legislative and executive elections. Yeltsin suggested he would seek the referendum without legislative approval, and the Supreme Soviet responded with a declaration of emergency rule and a reduction of presidential powers. Yeltsin responded that the Supreme Soviet had overstepped its authority. Yeltsin's new constitution gave the president the ability to dissolve the legislature. The Supreme Soviet's Constitutional Commission rejected the constitution on May 7, and Yeltsin called his own constitutional conference that approved the constitution on July 12. In September Yeltsin suspended the legislature and called for elections in December. The legislature moved to impeach Yeltsin, and Yeltsin retaliated by militarily sealing off the White House. The anti-Yeltsin leaders were defeated. The December elections included a referendum on the new constitution. The constitution was approved and the reformist party, Russia's Choice, won a plurality of seats in the State Duma. Interestingly, the nationalist Liberal Democratic Party, headed by Vladimir Zhirinovsky, finished second in the balloting. Thus, the Russian people indicated a preference, both in the passage of the new constitution and their party choice, for authoritarianism.

The pace of economic reform slowed in 1994 and 1995 as the crisis in Chechnya took precedence. The Chechnyan situation and his own health problems significantly weakened Yeltsin. The legislative election of December 1995 resulted in a plurality victory by the Communist Party of the Russian Federation (KPRF), which was viewed as a backlash against economic reforms. Yeltsin responded by slowing reforms further, particularly privatization. The presidential elections of August 1996, however, resulted in a win for Yeltsin and the promise of renewed reform.

The history of the Russian state reveals a pattern of autocracy, extensive state intervention in society, and collectivism. The despotism begun by the Mongol khans, maintained by the Czarist succession, and continued by the Communist Party leadership and apparatus, demonstrates a clear continuity of autocratic rule. The lack of a check on this autocratic power by a representative institution resulted in a paternalistic state. Mass commitment to this type of political structure was achieved through personalized attachment to the ruler. Over time, this created passivity in the Russian people toward politics.

This passivity in terms of political control has been matched by an expectation of state intervention. The huge bureaucratic edifice established under the Czars underwent many organizational reforms; however, it was never curtailed. Over-bureaucratization went hand and hand with the centralization of political control. Moreover, local government failed to establish a link between the populace and leadership throughout the history of the Russian state. The Soviet regime continued this pattern of centralization and bureaucracy in its ministry system.

The collective orientation of Russian society can be traced from the peasant communes, or *mirs*, to the collectivized farms of the Soviet Union. The forced collectivization of agriculture, however, was a perversion of the traditional local communal setting. Traditional Russian society was of the *gemeinschaft* type in which citizens are responsible to the community as a whole. The Soviet regime effectively used this traditional community-based orientation to promote Marxist ideology. More recently, under democracy, Russia has elected Communists who campaign on a platform emphasizing the needs of the people over market reform.

It can be argued that traditional Russian political culture is playing itself out in the present politics of Russia. Yeltsin has demonstrated authoritarian tendencies and repeatedly overridden the legislature since coming to power. Moreover, the Russian people have freely elected Yeltsin despite these authoritarian tendencies, and legislative elections have displayed a preference for Communists rather than reformists.

Survey Data

Survey data for the Soviet era are extremely scarce. Much of the research on Soviet attitudes was limited to studies of Soviet émigrés (Miller and Hesli; 1993). These studies have been criticized because it is uncertain how representative the sample of émigrés is to the Soviet public at large (White, 1979; Miller and Hesli, 1993). Thus, because the respondents in the émigré studies were not a scientifically selected cross-section, a conclusion regarding the continuity of Soviet values is not possible. However, the major studies of Soviet émigrés (Inkeles and Baurer,1959; White, 1978; Millar, 1987) provide an indirect means of collecting data on Soviet attitudes during the Communist regime. Moreover, they do give us valuable insight into Soviet attitudes and beliefs toward the political system.

Inkeles and Baurer's (1959) *The Soviet Citizen* examined more than 2700 Soviet refugees in Western Europe at the end of WW II. Their findings reveal that, on the whole, Soviet citizens demonstrated 'strong hostility towards the "absolutist" character of the political system and towards the "terror and injustice" associated with the secret police' (White, 104). However, as Inkeles and Baurer (1959) and White (1979) argue, absolutism and terrorism were regarded as abuses of the system rather than inherent defects. And, White further argues, 'there was no suggestion that the citizen might best be protected from such abuses by a series of constitutional limitations upon the actions of government such as existed in most liberal democracies' (104). Thus, the hostility was aimed at the abuses rather than the institutions. In addition, the Soviet respondents supported a wide degree of state intervention in social life and in the economy. Over 50 percent of respondents strongly supported the educational and medical systems. Inkeles and Baurer con-

Russia 173

cluded that the wish to live in a welfare state was 'rooted in deep values of the Soviet citizen' (236). In other words, a very high level of state intervention into the society was expected by the populace.

A mere 14 percent of respondents in the Inkeles and Baurer survey supported the establishment of a capitalist economy, while four-fifths preferred a socialist system with extensive public ownership and control over most areas of economic life. 'More than 86 percent, for instance, favored state ownership of heavy industry, and many specified the inclusion of light industry as well' (White, 100). However, the Inkeles and Baurer surveys show that, on the whole, Soviet citizens thought agriculture should be in private hands, or organized on some kind of cooperative basis. Thus, we see that in both the social and economic realms, Soviet citizens displayed broadly collectivist responses and widespread agreement regarding the extent of state control.

More recent research, using public opinion polls at the beginning of transition in 1990, examines the role of political culture in Russia (Miller, 1993; Gibson, Duch, and Tedin, 1992; Gibson and Duch, 1993). Arthur H. Miller (1993) investigated the legitimacy of the Communist regimes in the Russian Federation, the Ukraine, and Lithuania. This research is particularly useful in determining the level of legitimacy and support for the Soviet regime and for the new democratic institutions. Miller used the New Soviet Citizen Survey (NSCS) conducted in June 1990 to assess the level of political alienation of citizens toward the Communist regime. He constructed an index of political alienation using seven survey questions asking respondents to evaluate Soviet leadership, the Communist Party, the Supreme Soviet, the Soviet military, multiparty system, and the freedom to demonstrate publicly. In addition, Miller used factor analysis to conduct an index of level of alienation. The following table presents a breakdown of responses for Russia and Lithuania.[5]

The responses reported in Table 8.5 reveal an interesting pattern of Soviet attitudes. Although liberalization had begun at the time of the survey, we see that Soviet citizens were more alienated from leadership than from the institutions of the old regime, with 72.7 percent believing that leaders don't care and 68.2 percent never trusting or only sometimes trusting Soviet leaders. However, the responses for rating the institutions (Communist Party, Supreme Soviet, and Military) were mixed. Less than half of the respondents negatively rated the Communist Party and less than a third negatively rated the Supreme Soviet and the military. New political parties had already emerged in Russia by 1990; however, only slightly more than half of the respondents agreed that multiple parties are good for the system. And, in terms

Table 8.5 Russian Response to Systems Support/Alienation Items (1990)

	Russia	Lithuania
Trust Soviet Leaders		
Always/Most of the Time	25.7	13.7
Only some of the time	54.5	50.9
Never*	13.7	31.9
DK	6.1	3.5
Leaders Don't Care		
Agree*	72.7	85.4
Pro/Con	16.1	9.6
Disagree	6.0	2.2
DK	5.2	2.8
Rating of CPSU		
Negative*	46.4	79.3
Neutral	24.3	10.6
Positive	24.3	7.7
DK	5.1	2.4
Rating of Supreme Soviet		
Negative*	30.0	63.2
Neutral	34.1	23.1
Positive	26.6	8.5
DK	9.3	5.2
Rating of Military		
Negative*	28.4	78.5
Neutral	23.8	10.1
Positive	39.9	9.4
DK	8.0	2.0
Multiple Political Parties Good for the System		
Agree*	52.5	55.0
Pro/Con	17.8	22.0
Disagree	20.0	12.4
DK	9.8	10.6
Orderly Society More Important than Freedom to Demonstrate		
Agree	54.1	21.6
Pro/Con	20.9	17.0
Disagree*	19.2	51.9
DK	5.8	9.6

*Response indicating alienation when conducting alienation index
Source: New Soviet Citizen (NSC) Survey, June 1990

of freedom, more than half of the Russian respondents agreed that an orderly society is more important than freedom to demonstrate.

The Lithuanian responses differ sharply from the Russians. The Lithuanians reject the leaders and the institutions. They also tend to favor multiple parties and freedom over order. The difference in preferences is a reflection of the difference in political culture between the two nations.

Prospects for Democracy

Consolidation of democracy will not be successful without a modification of Russian political culture and a complete transition to the market. Although Russia has democratic institutions and has conducted free and fair elections, rule of law has not been fully accepted, as demonstrated by Yeltsin's unconstitutional change in the constitution in order to increase his own executive power in 1993. Cavalier treatment of the new constitution by Yeltsin was also evident in his announcement not to run for the presidency again. The implication of his statement was that he had a choice; however, the constitution clearly states that the president is 'directly elected for no more than two consecutive terms'. If Russia is to change its political culture toward more pluralistic values, the leadership must alter its political behavior and fully adopt the notion of rule of law.

Russia is faced with obstacles from all sides. Poor economic conditions, slowdown of economic reforms (especially privatization), authoritarian tendencies in leadership, Communists in control of the legislature, and a non-democratic political culture all threaten democracy. Russia needs to push radical economic reform, without which it faces protracted economic dislocations, and will be unable to compete in the world economy. In addition, the democratic regime will not be consolidated without economic recovery.

Notes

1   For further discussion of the debate on Russian feudalism, see: Blum, *Lord and Peasant*, pp. 90-2; George Vernadsky, 'Feudalism in Russia', *Speculum*, XIV (1939) 300-23; Marc Szeftel, 'aspects of feudalism in Russian history', in R. Colbourn (ed.), *Feudalism in History* (Princeton, 1956); and Pipes, *Russia under the Old Regime*, pp. 48-54.
2   Semevsky counted 550 peasant uprisings in the 19th century prior to emancipation. Ignatovich counted 1467 uprisings and rebellions from 1801 to 1862. For further discussion see Nicholas V. Riasanovsky, *A History of Russia* pp. 408-422.

3   The RSDLP split into two factions in 1902: the majority Bolshevik and the minority Menshevik.
4   Stephen White argues, in *Political Culture and Soviet Politics* (pp. 31-33), that the Russian populace conceived the political authority of the Czars in very personalized terms. He cites some Russian proverbs to demonstrate this point. For example, 'without the Czar the land cannot be ruled'; 'God in the sky, the Czar on earth'; 'Without the Czar, the country is widowed'; 'The people are the body, and the Czar is the head'.
5   The table presents both Russia and Lithuania for comparative purposes. The same data for Lithuania are presented in the Lithuanian case study. The table is taken from Arthur H. Miller's 'In Search of Regime Legitimacy' in Arthur H. Miller, William M. Reisinger, and Vicki L. Hesli (eds) *Public Opinion and Regime Change: The New Politics of Post-Soviet Societies* Boulder: Westview Press 1993.

Conclusion

Social scientists have long been interested in why some new democracies flourish while others slip back into authoritarianism. That question has been addressed with even greater intensity recently as the result of the collapse of communism, which has provided researchers with a unique opportunity to investigate a 'real experiment' in democratic consolidation as it occurs. The Central and Eastern European region represents a particularly rich research vein for such study because of the relatively large number of countries involved and the magnitude of their political and economic transitions.

Cross-national empirical research in this field has largely concentrated on the role of institutions in determining the fate of fledgling democracies. However, in this study I have chosen instead to focus on how the people of a country feel about the new political system, on the theory that a lack of popular support can lead to a breakdown in democratic governance. Overall, my research finds that the citizens in most of the Central and Eastern European countries do not appear sufficiently satisfied with democracy, indicating the potential for reversal. In that context, I have attempted to discern the influence of the economy upon public sentiment regarding democracy, while also exploring the political culture in several countries as an explanation of why their levels of support are higher or lower than anticipated by the regional economic model.

Empirical Findings

Chapter Three tests a Policy Outputs approach by examining the effect of economic factors on popular support for democracy. The hypotheses state that a worsening of the economic environment leads to a decline in support and, conversely, an improvement in the economy results in an increase in support. Evidence for this analysis is found in both the relationship between citizens' evaluations of their financial well-being and popular support as well as the relationship between the level of economic reform and popular support. Interestingly, my research suggests that the actual state of the economy does not affect support levels. Instead, the dominant factor is how people perceive economic conditions, particularly in terms of their own financial well-being. Strategically, then, governments would be well-advised to devote significant energy to instilling confidence in their populations regarding their current and future economic status.

In addition to citizens' evaluations of financial well-being, the extent of economic reform also has a significant impact on democratic support. The broad implication of this finding is that the new democracies should move toward the market as quickly as possible in order to foster long-term regime support. This remains the case even though drastic reforms can have immediate negative effects and, ironically, generate short-term dissatisfaction with democracy. Thus, governments must tread a fine line in pushing forward with reforms, while, at the same time, reassuring their citizens that their economic well-being is being served.

Economic factors are not alone in determining support levels for new democracies. Political values, norms, and attitudes (political culture) are also influential. Past research suggests that states with citizens who have pluralistic values have stable democratic regimes. Therefore, in order to assess the role of political culture, I have employed a most similar systems design, which allows, among other things, control for the unique characteristics of the region.

Case Studies

The case studies are utilized to supplement the empirical analysis and to examine the differences in political culture among the countries in Central and Eastern Europe. Chapters Five through Eight examine the Czech Republic, Slovakia, Lithuania, and Russia, investigating how their particular political cultures have hindered or assisted democratic consolidation. Differences are most clearly seen in the cases of the Czech Republic and Slovakia, despite their shared history. The Czech Republic demonstrates a positive impact on support, while Slovakia displays a negative impact, a phenomenon which, in part, could be explained by their varying historical political development and differing perceptions of historical figures and time periods. The Czech Republic's favorable economic situation, coupled with a pluralistic political culture, makes the likelihood of democratic consolidation quite high. However, Slovakia appears to be at greater risk, even though its economic transition is nearly complete and its economy, although not as strong as the Czech Republic's, is in better shape than many other Central and Eastern European states. The problem may rest with a lack of overt democratic values. Despite this deficiency in pluralistic standards, however, Slovakia may still be successful in consolidating democracy as long as its economy strengthens. Economic success may override traditional political culture by conveying to the populace the benefits of the new economic and political systems.

Like the Czech Republic, Lithuania has high support levels for democracy. However, unlike the Czech Republic, Lithuania does not exhibit a long-term continuity of pluralistic values. Rather, Lithuania's regime support seems to stem from nationalism and the need to be free from foreign (specifically Russian) domination. Democratic support is high because the new democracy offers an alternative means of governing and self-determination. A favorable economic environment and the pursuit of closer ties with the West should cultivate more pluralistic attitudes in the populace.

On the other hand, the level of support for democracy is, not surprisingly, lower in Russia, which can be attributed to both the continued economic problems and the long history of authoritarian rule and collectivism. The lack of pluralistic values and the harsh economic realities appear to make democratic consolidation in Russia particularly difficult. Of the four case studies examined, Russia has the poorest prospects in this regard. It appears that its success in maintaining democratic governance will depend upon not only complete economic restructuring, but also its ability to foster long-term, or even intergenerational, change in its political culture.

Future Research

Future research on democratic consolidation in Central and Eastern Europe could take a variety of directions. My investigation employed a systems level of analysis that has helped to identify patterns across the post-Communist states. The systems analysis aggregated the Central and Eastern Euro-Barometer surveys on popular support for democracy. However, the same theoretical framework could also be applied to the individual level of analysis without aggregating the data. For instance, one could search for patterns across the separate surveys for a particular country or a particular year, providing for a fuller picture of citizen support by including additional societal characteristics such as educational level, social status, and ethnicity. Moreover, an individual level analysis would allow for a closer examination of citizens' economic evaluations, and collateral hypotheses could be tested regarding citizens' retrospective and prospective evaluations of their own financial situation.

Related to the explanation of popular support for the regime is an understanding of support for specific governments. Easton's model of support addresses not only regime support but also support for government elites. The effect of economic factors on support for governments is particularly interesting in regard to the current politics in these states. The Policy Outputs approach has long been used to explain Western electoral results (particularly in the United States and Western Europe). Hypotheses regarding 'economic voting' and the likelihood of reelection for incumbents could now be tested in the Central and Eastern European cases. In addition, hypotheses regarding specific parties could be tested. For example, one could examine the influence of economic factors on the election of former Communist parties. Thus, my research could be extended to include explanations of governmental support in conjunction with regime support.

Further research could also examine other aspects of the consolidation process, such as the development of democratic institutions and the emergence of civil society. My work assumed that the institutions were in place and functioning. However, systematic analysis could be done to examine the types of institutions that have been constructed. Finally, a Culturalist approach would be particularly useful in assessing how societal characteristics, political development, and political culture might explain differences in institutional arrangement.

Appendix One: Economic Reform Index

The Economic Reform Index was provided by the European Bank for Reconstruction and Development. The following data were used in Chapter Three's cross-sectional analysis.

Country	Economic Reform Index
Albania	15
Armenia	11
Bulgaria	10
Czech Republic	21
Estonia	20
Georgia	8
Hungary	20
Latvia	17
Lithuania	18
Macedonia	17
Moldova	15
Poland	20
Russia	16
Slovakia	20
Slovenia	19
Ukraine	8

The above Economic Reform Index is a summary index of expert ratings in six types of economic reforms. On the next two pages is a table describing the categories used in the index.

Type of Reform	Category	Description of Category
Large-scale Privatization	4	More than 50 percent of state-owned enterprise assets privatized.
	3	More than 25 percent of state-owned enterprise assets privatized.
	2	Advanced comprehensive scheme almost ready to be implemented.
	1	Little Done.
Small-scale Privatization	4	Comprehensive and well-designed program implemented.
	3	Nearly comprehensive program implemented.
	2	Substantial share privatized.
	1	Little Done.
Enterprise Restructuring	4	Restructuring Program; corporate governance in operation; strong financial discipline at enterprise level; large conglomerates broken up.
	3	Structure created to promote corporate governance; strong action taken to break up conglomerates.
	2	Moderately tight credit and subsidy policy; weak enforcement of bankruptcy legislation; little action to break up conglomerates.
	1	Lax credit and subsidy policies weakening financial discipline at the enterprise level.
Price Liberalization and Competition	4	Comprehensive price liberalization and competition; anti-trust legislation in place.
	3	Comprehensive price liberalization and competition.
	2	Price controls remain for several important products.
	1	Prices controlled by government.

Appendix One 183

Trade and Foreign Exchange System	4	Few import or export quotas; almost full currency convertibility at unified exchange rate.
	3	Few import quotas; almost full currency convertibility at exchange rate.
	2	Few import quotas; almost full current account convertibility in principle but with a foreign exchange regime which is not fully transparent.
	1	Widespread import controls or very limited legitimate access to foreign exchange.
Banking Reform	4	Well-functioning banking competition and prudential supervision.
	3	Significant presence of private banks; full interest rate liberalization; bank auditing.
	2	Interest rates significantly influencing the allocation of credit.
	1	Little progress beyond establishment of a two-tier system.

Appendix Two: Data

The following data were used in the analyses in Chapter Three. Democratic satisfaction, Financial Evaluations, and Financial Expectations are reported as calculated weighted averages for each country/year.

Name	Code	Year	Demo Satisf.	Fin Eval	Fin Exp	% DK	% Δ GDP	Inflat	log Inflat
POL	290	1990	2.4842	2.5757	2.9354	20.80	-11.6	249.3	5.5186
POL	290	1991	2.1764	2.1629	2.6801	18.60	- 8.0	60.0	4.0943
POL	290	1992	2.1818	2.2419	2.6946	15.42	3.0	44.0	3.7841
POL	290	1993	2.3692	2.2781	2.9729	15.44	4.0	38.0	3.6375
POL	290	1994	2.0773	2.3734	2.7172	17.23	5.0	30.0	3.4011
HUN	310	1990	1.9076	-999	1.9233	2.00	- 3.5	33.4	3.5085
HUN	310	1991	2.1307	2.1224	2.6251	9.52	-12.0	32.0	3.4657
HUN	310	1992	1.9620	2.0101	2.3517	7.60	- 3.0	22.0	3.0910
HUN	310	1993	1.9205	2.0993	2.5028	8.33	- 1.0	21.0	3.0445
HUN	310	1994	2.0343	2.1369	2.3553	10.71	2.0	21.0	3.0445
CZE	315	1990	3.2094	-999	2.5989	6.70	- 0.4	18.4	2.9123
CZE	315	1990	2.2541	2.1742	2.0307	8.40	- 0.4	18.4	2.9123
CZE	315	1991	2.1508	2.2213	2.7744	7.71	-14.0	52.0	3.9512
CZE	315	1992	2.3086	2.5337	2.7728	4.11	- 6.0	13.0	2.5649
CZR	316	1993	2.4037	2.6927	2.8983	3.67	- 1.0	18.0	2.8903
CZR	316	1994	2.3333	2.7020	2.6947	6.40	3.0	10.0	2.3025
SLO	317	1992	2.0854	2.2851	2.4163	2.86	- 7.0	9.0	2.1972
SLO	317	1993	2.0030	2.2521	2.6468	3.95	- 4.0	25.0	3.2188
SLO	317	1994	1.9285	2.4686	2.8231	4.52	5.0	12.0	2.4849
ALB	339	1991	2.4045	2.9744	3.8799	21.60	-28.0	104.0	4.6443
ALB	339	1992	2.3735	3.5064	3.7811	4.96	-10.0	237.0	5.4680
ALB	339	1993	2.3751	3.4765	3.6656	10.63	11.0	31.0	3.4339
ALB	339	1994	2.2333	3.4173	3.5800	12.86	7.0	16.0	2.7725
MAC	343	1992	2.3760	2.1590	3.0186	12.86	-14.0	1935.0	7.5678
MAC	343	1993	2.3255	2.4024	2.9990	8.88	-14.0	230.0	5.4380
MAC	343	1994	2.1294	2.7941	3.3196	6.11	- 7.0	55.0	4.0073
SLV	349	1992	2.4643	2.6587	3.2641	8.28	- 5.0	93.0	4.5325
SLV	349	1993	2.2523	2.5438	3.1356	7.10	1.0	23.0	3.1354
SLV	349	1994	2.2053	2.8497	3.2178	5.34	6.0	18.0	2.8903
BUL	355	1990	2.1316	2.2423	2.8359	0.30	- 9.1	64.0	4.1588
BUL	355	1991	2.3421	2.1008	3.0350	13.55	-12.0	339.0	5.8260
BUL	355	1992	2.1964	2.3786	2.9266	13.80	- 7.0	79.0	4.3694
BUL	355	1993	1.8159	2.1136	2.4845	11.02	- 2.0	64.0	4.1588
BUL	355	1994	1.5359	2.0332	2.6620	10.24	1.0	122.0	4.8040

MLD	359	1992	2.2247	2.2472	2.5580	7.70	-29.0	2198.0	7.6953
RUM	360	1991	2.3600	2.8453	3.1239	18.50	-13.0	223.0	5.4071
RUM	360	1992	2.0661	2.6333	3.2739	8.89	-10.0	199.0	5.2933
RUM	360	1993	2.2037	2.3914	2.9078	9.52	1.0	296.0	5.6903
RUM	360	1994	2.1257	2.5771	3.1073	3.98	3.0	62.0	4.1271
RUS	365	1991	1.8685	2.2737	2.3361	14.56	-13.0	144.0	4.9698
RUS	365	1992	1.7497	2.2515	2.5697	22.50	-19.0	2318.0	7.7484
RUS	365	1993	1.8279	2.4500	2.7145	26.22	-12.0	841.0	6.7345
RUS	365	1994	1.5948	2.2864	2.4801	19.60	-15.0	203.0	5.3132
EST	366	1991	2.2106	2.5219	2.7546	18.42	-11.0	304.0	5.7170
EST	366	1992	2.0561	1.9082	2.6760	17.90	-14.0	954.0	6.8606
EST	366	1993	2.2818	2.5410	2.9711	17.80	-7.0	36.0	3.5835
EST	366	1994	2.1555	2.7700	3.0419	16.77	6.0	42.0	3.7376
LAT	367	1991	2.3280	2.5458	2.5702	14.51	-8.0	262.0	5.5683
LAT	367	1992	1.9456	1.9128	2.4561	19.10	-35.0	958.0	6.8648
LAT	367	1993	2.1822	2.3763	2.9127	19.15	-15.0	35.0	3.5553
LAT	367	1994	2.0348	2.5625	2.9534	16.20	2.0	26.0	3.2580
LIT	368	1991	2.6009	2.7910	2.7256	13.60	-13.0	345.0	5.8435
LIT	368	1992	2.5075	2.1556	2.6795	11.70	-38.0	1175.0	7.0690
LIT	368	1993	2.2646	2.2354	2.6783	10.39	-24.0	189.0	5.2417
LIT	368	1994	2.2067	2.5149	2.7486	9.62	2.0	45.0	3.8066
UKR	369	1992	1.9102	2.1751	2.6895	24.07	-17.0	2000.0	7.6009
UKR	369	1993	1.6885	1.6793	2.0458	18.10	-17.0	10155	9.2257
UKR	369	1994	1.7365	1.7633	2.2541	25.58	-23.0	401.0	5.9939
BLR	370	1992	1.7709	2.2052	2.3667	13.69	-10.0	1558.0	7.3511
BLR	370	1993	1.8909	2.0992	2.4030	14.70	-12.0	1994.0	7.5978
BLR	370	1994	1.8029	2.0552	2.5883	20.20	-22.0	1875.0	7.5363
ARM	371	1992	1.6888	1.8557	2.3235	18.19	-52.0	1341.0	7.2011
ARM	371	1993	1.5620	1.8790	2.1698	16.40	-15.0	10996	9.3052
ARM	371	1994	1.5995	2.0993	2.2920	12.70	5.0	1885.0	7.5416
GRG	372	1992	2.3276	2.3768	3.0279	13.87	-40.0	1463.0	7.2882
GRG	372	1994	1.6763	1.9037	2.1207	17.20	-35.0	7380.0	8.9065

Data source for Democratic Satisfaction, Financial Evaluations, Financial Expectations, and *% Don't Know* is the Central and Eastern Euro-Barometer 1-5: 1990-1994.

Data for inflation and percentage change in real GDP are published in *Economics of Transition*, Volume 3 (4), 1995. These data were compiled from national authorities, IMF, OECD, the World Bank, PlanEcon, and the Economist Intelligence Unit.

Bibliography

Aganbegyan, A. (1988), *The Challenge: Economics of Perestroika*, Hutchinson, New York.
Allison, G.T. and Beschel, R.P. (1992), 'Can the United States Promote Democracy?', *Political Science Quarterly*, vol. 107, pp. 81-98.
Almond, G.A. and Coleman, J.S. (1960), *The Politics of Developing Areas*, Princeton University Press, Princeton.
Almond, G.A. and Powell G.B. (1966), *Comparative Politics: A Developmental Approach*, Little, Brown, Boston.
Almond, G.A. and Verba S. (1963), *The Civic Culture: Political Attitudes and Democracy in Five Nations*, Princeton University Press, Princeton.
Almond, G.A. and Verba S. (1980), *The Civic Culture Revisited*, Little, Brown, Boston.
Anderle, J. (1980), 'Uncharted Areas for Research on the History of Slovakia and the Slovaks', *East Central Europe*, vol. 1, pp. 49-88.
Anderson, C. J. (1997), 'System Support in Old and New Democracies', Paper presented at the American Political Science Association's Annual Meeting, 28-31 August 1997, Washington D.C.
Anderson, C. J. and Guillory C.A. (1997), 'Political Institutions and satisfaction with democracy: a cross-national analysis of consensus and majoritarian systems', *American Political Science Review*, vol. 91, pp. 66-81.
Arat, Z. F. (1988), 'Democracy and Economic Development: Modernization Theory Revisited', *Comparative Politics*, vol. 21, pp. 21-36.
Arat, Z. F. (1991), *Democracy and human rights in developing countries*, Lynne Rienner Pubilshers, Boulder.
Åslund, A. (1994), 'The Case for Radical Reform', *Journal of Democracy*, vol. 5, pp. 63-74.
Balcerowicz, L. (1994a), 'Democracy Is No Substitute for Capitalism', *Eastern European Economics*, March-April, pp. 39-49.
Balcerowicz, L. (1994b), 'Understanding Postcommunist Transitions', *Journal of Democracy*, vol. 5, pp. 75- 89.
Balcerowicz, L. (1995), 'Understanding Postcommunist Transitions', in L. Diamond and M.F. Plattner (eds), *Economic Reform and Democracy*, Johns Hopkins University Press and the National Endowment for Democracy, Baltimore.
Banks, A.S. (1971), *Cross-Polity Times Series Data*, The MIT Press, Cambridge.
Banks, A.S. (ed.) (1992), *The Political Handbook of the World*, CSA Publications, Binghamton.

Banks, A.S. (ed.) (1993), *The Political Handbook of the World*, CSA Publications, Binghamton.
Banks, A.S. (ed.) (1994-1995), *The Political Handbook of the World*, CSA Publications, Binghamton.
Banks, A.S., Day A.J. and Muller T.C. (eds) (1995-1996), *The Political Handbook of the World*, CSA Publications, Binghamton.
Banks, A.S., Day A. J. and Muller T.C. (eds) (1997), *The Political Handbook of the World*, CSA Publications, Binghamton.
Banks, A.S. and Textor, R.B. (1963), *A Cross-Polity Survey*, The MIT Press, Cambridge.
Barghoorn, F.C. (1965), 'Soviet Russia: Orthodoxy and Adaptiveness', in L. Pye and S. Verba (eds), *Political Culture and Political Development*, Princeton University Press, Princeton.
Benes, E. (1944), 'Czechoslovak Policy for Victory and Peace', in *Czechoslovak Documents and Sources*, No. 10, Czechoslovak Ministry of Foreign Affairs, Information Service, London.
Beneš, V. (1973), 'Czechoslovak Democracy and Its Problems', in V.S. Mamatey and R. Luza (eds), *A History of the Czechoslovak Republic, 1918-1948*, Princeton University Press, Princeton.
Berglund, S. and Dellenbrant, J.A. (1994), *The New Democracies in Eastern Europe: party systems and political cleavages*, Edward Elgar Publishing Co., Brookfield.
Bird, G. and Bird, H. (1992), 'Economic Reforms in Eastern Europe: Central Issues in the Move to Market Economies', in G. Bird (ed.), *Economic Reform in Eastern Europe*, Edward Elgar Publishing Co., Brookfield.
Blalock, H.M. (1979), *Social Statistics*, 2nd ed., McGraw-Hill, New York.
Bollen, K.A. (1979), 'Political Democracy and the Timing of Development', *American Sociological Review*, vol. 45, pp. 370-90.
Bollen, K.A. (1980), 'Issues in the comparative measurement of political democracy', *American Sociological Review*, vol. 50, pp. 438-57.
Bollen, K.A. and Jackman, R.W. (1985), 'Political Democracy and the Size Distribution of Income', *American Sociological Review*, vol. 48, pp. 468-79.
Bova, R. (1991), 'Political Dynamics of the Post-Communist Transition: A Comparative Perspective', *World Politics*, vol. 44, pp. 113-38.
Breslauer, G.W. (1982), *Khrushchev and Brezhnev as Leaders: Building Authority in Soviet Politics*, Allen & Unwin, London.
Brittan, S. (1975), 'The Economic Contradictions of Democracy', *British Journal of Political Science*, vol. 5, pp. 129-59.
Brown, A. (1984), *Political Culture and Communist Studies*, The Macmillan Press, London.
Brown, A. (1989), 'Ideology and Political Culture', in S. Bialer (ed.), *Politics, Society, and Nationality Inside Gorbachev's Russia*, Westview Press, Boulder.
Brown, A. and Wightman, G. (1979), 'Czechoslovakia: Revival and Retreat', in A. Brown and J. Gray (eds), *Political Culture and Political Change in Communist States*, Holmes & Meier Publishers, New York.

Brunk, G.G., Caldeira, G.A. and Lewis-Beck, M.S. (1987), 'Capitalism, Socialism, and Democracy: An Empirical Inquiry', *European Journal of Political Research*, vol.15, pp. 459-70.
Brzezinski, Z. (1990), *The Grand Failure: the birth and death of communism in the twentieth century*, Collier Books, New York.
Budreckis, A.M. (1968), *The Lithuanian National Revolt of 1941*, Lithuanian Encyclopedia Press, Boston.
Bunce, V. and Csanadi, M. (1993), 'Uncertainty in the Transition: Post-Communism in Hungary', *East European Politics and Societies*, vol. 7, pp. 240-75.
Burkhart, R.E. and Lewis-Beck, M.S. (1994), 'Comparative Democracy: The Economic Development Thesis', *American Political Science Review*, vol. 88, pp. 903-10.
Burton, M., Gunther R. and Higley, J. (1992), 'Introduction: Elite Transformations and Democratic Regimes', in J. Higley and R. Gunther (eds), *Elites and Democratic Consolidation in Latin America and Southern Europe*, Cambridge University Press, New York.
Butora, M. and Butorova, Z. (1993), 'Slovakia: the identity challenges of the newly born state', *Social Research*, vol. 60, pp. 705-36.
Butora, M., Butorova Z. and Rosova, T. (1991), 'The Hard Birth of Democracy in Slovakia: The Eighteeen Months Following the "Tender" Revolution', *Journal of Communist Studies*, vol. 7, pp. 453-59.
Chase, T. (1946), *The Story of Lithuania*, Harcourt, Brace & World, New York.
Coleman, J.S. (1960), 'Conclusion: The political systems of the developing areas', in G. Almond and J.S. Coleman (eds), *The Politics of Developing Areas*, Princeton University Press, Princeton.
Conradt, D.P. (1980), 'Changing German Political Culture', in G. Almond and S. Verba (eds), *The Civic Culture Revisited*, Little, Brown, Boston.
Conradt, D.P. (1981), 'Political Culture, Legitimacy, and Participation', *West European Politics*, vol. 4, pp. 18-34.
Cook, K. (1977), 'Expectations, evaluations, and equity', *American Sociological Review*, vol. 40, pp. 372-88.
Couter, P.B. (1975), *Social mobilization and liberal democracy: a macroquantitative analysis of global and regional models*, Lexington Books, Lexington.
Crouch, M. (1989), *Revolution and Evolution: Gorbachev and Soviet Politics*, Philip Allan, New York.
Cutright, P. (1963), 'National political development: Its measures and analysis', *American Sociological Review*, vol. 28, pp. 253-64.
Cutright, P. and Wiley J.A. (1969), 'Modernization and Political Representation: 1927-1966', *Studies in Comparative International Development*, vol. 5, pp. 23-44.
Dahl, R.A. (1971), *Polyarchy: participation and opposition*, Yale University Press, New Haven.
Dahl, R.A. (1989), *Democracy and Its Critics*, Yale University Press, New Haven.
Dahrendorf, R. (1990), *Reflections on the Revolution in Europe: in a letter intended to be sent to a gentleman in Warsaw*, Times Books, New York.

Dalton, R.J. (1996), *Citizen Politics*, Chatham House Publishers, Chatham.
Diamond, L. (1992), 'Economic Development and Democracy Revisited', *American Behavioral Scientist*, vol. 35, March, p. 450.
Diamond, L. (1993), *Political culture and democracy in developing countries*, Lynne Rienner Publishers, Boulder.
Diamond, L., Linz J.J. and Lipset S.M. (1988), *Democracy in Developing Countries*, Lynne Rienner, Boulder.
Dielman, T.E. (1989), *Pooled Cross-Sectional and Time-Series Data Analysis*, Marcel Dekker, New York.
Di Palma, G. (1990), *To Craft Democracies: An Essay on Democratic Transitions*, University of California Press, Berkeley.
Dogan, M. (1988), *Comparing pluralist democracies: strains on legitimacy*, Westview Press, Boulder.
Dogan, M. (1994), 'The Pendulum between Theory and Substance: Testing the Concepts of Legitimacy and Trust', in M. Dogan and A. Kazancigil (eds), *Comparing Nations: Concepts, Strategies, Substance*, Blackwell Publishers, Oxford, pp. 292-313.
Duch, R. (1993), 'Tolerating Economic Reform: Popular Support for Transition to a Free Market in the Former Soviet Union', *American Political Science Review*, vol. 87, pp. 590-609.
Duch, R. (1995), 'Economic chaos and the fragility of democratic transition in former communist regimes', *Journal of Politics*, vol. 57, pp. 121-58.
Easton, D. (1965), *A Systems Analysis of Political Life*, Wiley, New York.
Easton, D. (1975), 'A re-assessment of the concept of political support', *British Journal of Political Science*, vol. 5, pp. 435-57.
Ekiert, G. (1991), 'Democratization Processes in East Central Europe: A Theoretical Reconsideration', *British Journal of Political Science*, vol. 21, pp. 285-313.
Fagen, R.R. (1969), *The Transformation of Political Culture in Cuba*, Stanford University Press, Stanford.
Felak, J.R. (1994), *At the Price of the Republic: Hlinka's Slovak People's Party, 1929-1938*, University of Pittsburgh Press, Pittsburgh.
Fiorina, M.P. (1978), 'Economic Retrospective Voting in American National Elections: A Micro Analysis', *American Journal of Political Science*, vol. 22, pp. 426-43.
Fiorina, M.P. (1981), *Retrospective Voting in American National Elections*, Yale University Press, New Haven.
Florinsky, M.T. (1953), *Russia: A History and an Interpretation*, Macmillan, New York.
Frentzel-Zagorska, J. (1992), 'Patterns of Transition from a One-Party State to Democracy in Poland and Hungary', in R.F. Miller (ed.), *The Development of Civil Society in Communist Systems*, Allen & Urwin, Boston.
Fukuyama, F. (1992), *The End of History and the Last Man*, Free Press, New York.
Gastil, R.D. (1978), *Freedom in the World: Political Rights and Civil Liberties 1978*, Freedom House, New York.

Gastil, R.D. (1987), *Freedom in the World: Political Rights and Civil Liberties 1986-1987*, Greenwood Press, Westport.
Geddes, B. (1995), 'Challenging Conventional Wisdom', in L. Diamond and M.F. Plattner (eds), *Economic Reform and Democracy*, The Johns Hopkins University Press and the National Endowment for Democracy, Baltimore.
Geremek, B. (1992), 'Problems of Postcommunism: Civil Society Then and Now', *Journal of Democracy*, vol. 3, pp. 3-12.
Gibson, J.L. and Duch, R. (1993), 'Emerging Democratic Values in Soviet Political Culture', in A.H. Miller, W.M. Reisinger and V.L. Hesli (eds), *Public Opinion and Regime Change: The New Politics of Post-Soviet Societies*, Westview Press, Boulder.
Gibson, J.L., Duch M. and Tedin K. (1992), 'Democratic Values and the Transformation of the Soviet Union', *The Journal of Politics*, vol. 54, pp. 329-71.
Gitelman, Z.Y. (1970), 'Power and Authority in Eastern Europe', in C. Johnson (ed.), *Change in Communist Systems*, Stanford University Press, Stanford.
Gitelman, Z.Y. (1977), 'Public Opinion in Communist Political Systems', in W.D. Connor and Z.Y. Gitelman (eds), *Public Opinion in European Socialist Systems*, Praeger, New York.
Gonick, L.S. and Rosh, R.M. (1988), 'The Structural Constraints of the World-Economy on National Political Development', *Comparative Political Studies*, vol. 21, pp. 171-99.
Gramsci, A. (1971), *Selections from the Prison Notebooks of Antonio Gramsci*, Q. Hoare and G.N. Smith (eds), Lawerence and Wishart, London.
Grey, R.D. (ed.) (1997), *Democratic Theory and Post-Communist Change*, Prentice Hall, Upper Saddle River.
Haggard, S. and Kaufman, R.R. (1992), *The Politics of Economic Adjustment: International Constraints, Distributive Conflicts, and the State*, Princeton University Press, Princeton.
Haggard, S. and Kaufman, R.R. (1994), 'The Challenges of Consolidation', *Journal of Democracy*, vol. 5, pp. 5-16.
Hajda, J. (1964), 'The Role of the Intelligentsia in the Development of Czech Society', in M. Rechcigl (ed.), *The Czechoslovak Contribution to World Culture*, Mouton, Hague.
Halecki, O. (1952), *Borlerlands of Western Civilization: A History of East Central Europe*, Ronald Press Co., New York.
Han, S.J. (1990), 'South Korea: Politics in Transition', in L. Diamond, J. Linz, and S.M. Lipset (eds), *Politics in Developing Countries: Comparing Experiences with Democracy*, Lynne Rienner, Boulder.
Higley, J. and Gunther R. (1992), *Elites and Democratic Consolidation in Latin America and Southern Europe*, Cambridge University Press, New York.
Hoensch, J.K. (1973), 'The Slovak Republic, 1939-1945', in V.S. Mamatey and R. Luza (eds), *A History of the Czechoslovak Republic, 1918-1948*, Princeton University Press, Princeton.
Höhmann, H., Meier H.C. and Timmerman H. (1993), 'The European Community and the Countries of the CIS: Political and Economic Relations', *The Journal of Communist Studies*, vol. 9, pp. 151-76.

Huntington, S.P. (1968), *Political Order in Changing Societies*, Yale University Press, New Haven.
Huntington, S.P. (1974), 'Postindustrial Politics: How Benign Will It Be?', *Comparative Politics*, vol. 6, pp. 163-91.
Huntington, S.P. (1984), 'Will more countries become democratic?', *Political Science Quarterly*, vol. 99, pp. 193-218.
Huntington, S.P. (1991), *The Third Wave: Democratization in the Late Twentieth Century*, University of Oklahoma Press, Norman.
Huntington, S.P. (1991/1992), 'How countries democratize', *Political Science Quarterly*, vol. 106, pp. 579-616.
Iglehart, R. (1990), *Culture Shift in Advanced Industrial Countries*, Princeton University Press, Princeton.
Inkeles, A. (1991), *On measuring democracy: its consequences and concomitants*, Transaction Publishers, New Brunswick.
Inkeles, A. and Bauer, R.A. (1959), *The Soviet Citizen. Daily Life in a Totalitarian Society*. Harvard University Press, Cambridge.
Iwaskiw, W.R. (ed.) (1996), *Estonia, Latvia, and Lithuania*, Federal Research Division, Library of Congress, Washington D.C.
Jackman, R. (1973), 'On the Relationship of Economic Development to Political Performance', *American Journal of Political Science*, vol. 17, pp. 611-21.
Jelinek, Y. (1976), *The Parish Republic: Hlinka's Slovak People's Party*, East European Quarterly, Boulder.
Johnson, O.V. (1985), *Slovakia, 1918-1938: Education and the Making of a Nation*, Columbia University Press, New York.
Jusaitis, A. (1918), *The History of the Lithuanian Nation and its Present National Aspirations*, The Lithuanian Catholic Truth Society, Philadelphia.
Kamenec, I. (1992), 'The Deportation of Jewish Citizens from Slovakia in 1942', in D. Toth (ed.), *The Tradegy of the Slovak Jews*, DATEI, Banska Bystrica.
Karatnycky, A. (1994), 'Freedom in Retreat', *Freedom Review*, vol. 25, pp. 4-9.
Karl, T.L. (1990), 'Dilemmas in Democratization in Latin America', *Comparative Politics*, vol. 23, pp. 1-21.
Karl, T.L. and Schmitter, P.C. (1991), 'Modes of Transition and Types of Democracy in Latin America, Southern and Eastern Europe', *International Social Science Journal*, vol. 128, pp. 269-84.
Kavanagh, D. (1983), *Political Science and Political Behavior*, Allen & Unwin, London.
Keane, J. (1988), *Democracy and Civil Society: on the predicaments of European socialism, the prospects for democracy, and the problem of controlling social and political power*, Verso, London.
Key, V.O. (1966), *The Responsible Electorate: rationality in Presidential Voting, 1936-1960*, Belknap Press, Cambridge.
Kiewiet, D. R. (1983), *Macroeconomics and Micropolitics: The Electoral Effects of Economic Issues*, University of Chicago Press, Chicago.
Kinder, D. R. and Kiewiet, D.R. (1979), 'Economic Discontent and Political Behavior: The Role of Personal Grievances and Collective Economic Judgments in

Congressional Voting', *American Journal of Political Science*, vol. 23, pp. 495-527.

Kinder, D. R. and Kiewiet, D.R. (1981), 'Sociotropic Politics: The American Case', *British Journal of Political Science*, vol. 11, pp. 129-41.

Kirby, D. (1995), *The Baltic World: 1772-1993: Europe's Northern Periphery in an Age of Change*, Longman, London.

Kirschbaum, S.J. (1995), *A History of Slovakia: the Struggle for Survival*, St. Martin's Press, New York.

Kirschbaum, S.J. and Roman, A. (1987), *Reflections on Slovak History*, Slovak World Congress, Toronto.

Kitschelt, H. (1992), 'Review Essay: Structure and Process Driven Explanations of Political Regime Change', *American Political Science Review*, vol. 86, pp. 1028-34.

Kliuchevskii, V.O. (1958), *Peter the Great*, Vintage Books, New York.

Koch, B. (1993), 'American and German Approaches to East-Central Europe: A Comparison', *World Affairs*, vol. 156, pp. 86-96.

Korbel, J. (1977), *Twentieth-century Czechoslovakia: The Meanings of Its History*, Columbia University Press, New York.

Kornai, J. (1980), *Economics of Shortage*, North-Holland, New York.

Kornai, J. (1990), *The Road to a Free Economy: Shifting from a Socialist System: The Example of Hungary*, Norton, New York.

Kramer, G.H. (1983), 'The Ecological Fallacy Revisited: Aggregate-versus Individual-level Findings on Economics and Elections and Sociotropic Voting', *American Political Science Review*, vol. 77, pp. 92-111.

Kusin, V.V. (1982), 'Husak's Czechoslovakia and Economic Stagnation', *Problems of Communism*, vol. 31, pp. 24-37.

Lavigne, M. (1995), *The Economics of Transition: from socialist economy to market economy*, St. Martin's Press, New York.

Lawson, S. (1993), 'Conceptual Issues in the Comparative Study of Regime Change and Democratization', *Comparative Politics*, pp. 183-205.

Leff, C.S. (1988), *National Conflict in Czechoslovakia: the Making and Remaking of a State, 1918-1987*, Princeton University Press, Princeton.

Leff, C.S. (1997), *The Czech and Slovak Republics: Nation Versus State*, Westview Press, Boulder.

Lerner, D. (1958), *The Passing of Traditional Society: Modernizing the Middle East*, Fress Press, Glencoe.

Levin, D. (1990), 'Lithuania', in I. Gutman (ed.), *Encyclopedia of the Holocaust*. vol. 3, Macmillan, New York, pp. 895-99.

Lewin, M. (1988), *The Gorbachev Phenomenon: A Historical Interpretation*, University of California Press, Berkeley.

Lewis-Beck, M.S. (1988), *Economics and Elections: the Major Western Democracies*, University of Michigan Press, Ann Arbor.

Lieven, A. (1993), *The Baltic Revolution: Estonia, Latvia, Lithuania, and the path to independence*, Yale University Press, New Haven.

Lijphart, A. (1977), *Democracy in Plural Societies: A Comparative Exploration*, Yale University Press, New Haven.
Lijphart, A. (1984), *Democracies: Patterns of Majoritarian and Consensus Government in Twenty-One Countries*, Yale University Press, New Haven.
Lijphart, A. (1991), 'Constitutional Choices for New Democracies', *Journal of Democracy*, vol. 2, pp. 72-84.
Lijphart, A. (1992), 'Democratization and Constitutional Choices in Czechoslovakia, Hungary and Poland, 1989-91', *Journal of Theoretical Politics*, vol. 4, pp. 207-23.
Linz, J.J. (1978), *The breakdown of democratic regimes: crisis, breakdown, and reequilibration*, Johns Hopkins University Press, Baltimore.
Linz, J.J. (1988), 'Legitimacy of democracy and the socioeconomic system', in M. Dogan (ed.), *Comparing pluralist democracies: strains on legitimacy*, Westview Press, Boulder.
Lipset, S.M. (1959), 'Some Social Requisites of Democracy: Economic Development and Political Legitimacy', *American Political Science Review*, vol. 53, pp. 69-105.
Lipset, S.M. (1960), *Political Man: The social bases of politics*, Doubleday, Garden City.
Lipset, S.M. (1981), *Party Coalitions in the 1980s*, Institute for Contemporary Studies, San Francisco.
Lipset, S.M. (1990), 'The Centrality of Political Culture', *Journal of Democracy* vol. 1, pp. 80-83.
Lipset, S.M. (1993), 'Reflections on Capitalism, Socialism, and Democracy', *Journal of Democracy*, vol. 4, pp. 41-56.
Lipset, S.M. (1994), 'The Social Requisites of Democracy Revisited', *American Sociolgical Review*, vol. 59, pp. 1-22.
Lipton, D. and Sachs, J. (1990), 'Creating a Market Economy in Eastern Europe: The Case of Poland', *Brookings Papers on Economic Activity*, 1.
Lowenthal, A.F. (1991), *Exporting Democracy: The United States and Latin America*, The Johns Hopkins University Press, Baltimore.
MacKenzie, D. and Curran, M.W. (1986), *A History of the Soviet Union*, The Dorsey Press, Chicago.
Maddala, G.S. (1971), 'The Use of Variance Component Models in Pooling Cross Section and Times Series Data', *Econometrica*, vol. 39, pp. 341-58.
Maddala, G.S. (1983), *Limited-dependent and Qualitative Variables in Econometrics*, Cambridge University Press, New York.
Maher, K.H. (1997), 'The role of mass values', in R.D. Grey (ed.), *Democratic Theory and Post-Communist Change*, Prentice Hall, Upper Saddle River.
Mainwaring, S. (1992), 'Transitions to Democracy and Democratic Consolidation: Theoretical and Comparative Issues', in S. Mainwaring, G. O'Donnell and J.S. Valenzuela (eds), *Issues in Democratic Consolidation: the new South American democracies in comparative perspective*, University of Notre Dame Press, Notre Dame.

Mamatey, V.S. and Luza, R. (eds) (1973), *A History of the Czechoslovak Republic: 1918-1949*, Princeton University Press, Princeton.

Maoz, Z. and Russett B. (1993), 'Normative and Structural Causes of Democratic Peace, 1946-1986', *American Political Science Review*, vol. 87, pp. 624-39.

Markus, G. (1988), 'The Impact of Personal and National Economic Conditions on the Presidential Vote: A Pooled Cross Sectional Times Series Analysis', *American Journal of Political Science*, vol. 32, pp. 137-54.

Mawdsley, E. (1998), *The Stalin Years: The Soviet Union 1929-1953*, Manchester University Press, Manchester.

McAuley, M. (1984), 'Political Culture and Communist Politics: One Step Forward, Two Steps Back', in A. Brown (ed.), *Political Culture and Communist Studies*, Macmillan Press, London.

McCauley, M. (1976), *Khrushchev and the Development of Soviet Agriculture*, Macmillan Press, London.

McCauley, M. (1987), *Khrushchev and Khrushchevism*, Indiana University Press, Bloomington.

McColm, B.R. (1993), 'The Comparative Survey of Freedom', *Freedom Review*, vol. 3, February.

Mead, M. (1979), *Soviet Attitudes toward Authority*, Random House, New York.

Medvedev, R.A. and Medvedev, Z.A. (1976), *Khrushchev: The Years in Power*, Columbia University Press, New York.

Mikula, B. (1944), *Progressive Czech [Bohemian]*, Czechoslovak National Council of America, Chicago.

Miliband, R. (1973), *The State in Capitalist Society*, Quartet Books, London.

Millar, J. (ed.) (1987), *Politics, Work, and Daily Life in the USSR: a Survey of Former Soviet Citizens*, Cambridge University Press, New York.

Miller, A.H. (1993), 'In Search of Regime Legitimacy', in A.H. Miller, W.M. Reisinger and V.L. Hesli (eds), *Public Opinion and Regime Change: The New Politics of Post-Soviet Societies*, Westview Press, Boulder.

Miller, A.H., Reisinger, W.M. and Hesli, V.L. (eds) (1993), *Public Opinion and Regime Change: The New Politics of Post-Soviet Societies*, Westview Press, Boulder.

Mishler, W. and Rose, R. (1996), 'Trajectories of Fear and Hope: The Dynamics of Support for Democracy in Eastern Europe', *Comparative Political Studies*, vol. 28, pp. 553-81.

Mishler, W. and Rose, R.. (1997), 'Trust, Distrust and Skepticism: Popular Evaluations of Civil and Political Institutions in Post-Communist Society', *Journal of Politics*, vol. 59, pp. 418-51.

Misiunas, R.J. and Taagepera, R. (1993), *The Baltic States, Years of Dependence, 1940-1990*, University of California Press, Berkeley.

Montesquieu, C. (1977), *The Spirit of the Laws*, University of California Press, Berkeley.

Moore, B. (1966), *Social Origins of Democracy and Dictatorship: Lord and Peasant in the Making of the Modern World*, Beacon Press, Boston.

Mousseau, M. (1997), 'Democracy and Militarized Interstate Collaboration', *Journal of Peace Research*, vol. 34, February, pp. 73-88.
Mroz, J.E. (1992/93), 'Russia and Eastern Europe: Will the West Let Them Fail?', *Foreign Affairs*, vol. 72, pp. 44-57.
Muller, E.M. (1988), 'Democracy, Economic Development and Income Inequality', *American Sociological Review*, vol. 53, pp. 50-68.
Muravchik, J. (1991), *Exporting Democracy: Fulfilling America's Destiny*, The American Enterprise Institute Press, Washington, D.C.
Muravchik, J. (1992), 'Eastern Europe's "Terrible Twos"', *Journal of Democracy*, vol. 3, pp. 65-72.
Myers, A.R. (1975), *Parliaments and Estates in Europe to 1789*, Harcourt, Brace, New York.
Nelson, J.M. (1994), 'Linkages between Politics and Economic', *Journal of Democracy*, vol. 5, pp. 49-61.
O'Donnell, G. (1973), *Modernization and Bureaucratic Authoritarianism; Studies in South American Politics*, University of California Institute of International Studies, Berkeley.
O'Donnell, G. (1994), 'Delegative Democracy', *Journal of Democracy*, vol. 5, pp. 155-69.
O'Donnell, G., Schmitter, P. and Whitehead, L. (eds) (1986), *Transitions from Authoritarian Rule*, The Johns Hopkins University Press, Baltimore.
Offe, C. (1991), 'Capitalism by Democratic Design? Democratic Theory Facing the Triple Transition in East Central Europe', *Social Research*, vol. 58, pp. 865-902.
Oldenburg, F. (1993), *Germany's Interest in Russian Stability*, International Studies, Koln.
Pacek, A.C. (1994), 'Macroeconomic Conditions and Electoral Politics in East Central Europe', *American Journal of Political Science*, vol. 38, pp. 723-44.
Pastor, M. (1987), *The International Monetary Fund and Latin America*, Westview Press, Boulder.
Paul, D.W. (1979), *The Cultural Limits of Revolutionary Politics: Change and Continuity in Socialist Czechoslovakia*, East European Quarterly, Boulder.
Paul, D.W. (1985), 'Slovak Nationalism and the Hungarian State, 1870-1910', in P. Brass (ed.), *Ethnic Groups and the State*, Croom Helm, London.
Pereira, L., Bresser, C., Maravall, J.M. and Przeworski A. (1993), *Economic reforms in new democracies: a social-democratic approach*, Cambridge University Press, New York.
Petro, N.N. (1995), *The Rebirth of Russian Democracy: An Interpretation of Political Culture*, Harvard University Press, Cambridge.
Piekalkiewicz, J. (1972), 'Public Opinion in Czechoslovakia during the Dubcek Era', in E.J. Czerwinski and J. Piekalkiewicz (eds), *The Soviet Invasion of Czechoslovakia: Its Effects on Eastern Europe*, Praeger Publishers, New York.
Pipes, R. (1974), *Russia under the Old Regime*, Charles Scribner's Sons, New York.
Pithart, P. (1995), 'From Autonomy to Federation, 1938-89', in J. Musil (ed.), *The End of Czechoslovakia*, Central European University Press, New York.

Powell, G.B. (1982), *Contemporary Democracies: Participation, Stability and Violence*, Harvard University Press, Cambridge.

Pridham, G. and Vanhanen, T. (1994), *Democratization in Eastern Europe: Domestic and International Perspectives*, Routledge, New York.

Pridham, G., Herring, E. and Sanford G. (1994), *Building Democracy: The International Dimension of Democratization in Eastern Europe*, St. Martin's Press, New York.

Przeworski, A. (1986), 'Some Problems in the Study of the Transition to Democracy', in G. O'Donnell, P.C. Schmitter and L. Whitehead (eds), *Transitions from Authoritarian Rule: Prospects for Democracy*, Johns Hopkins Press, Baltimore.

Przeworski, A. (1988), 'Democracy as a Contingent Outcome of Conflicts', in J. Elster and R. Stagstad (eds), *Constitutionalism and Democracy*, Cambridge University Press, New York.

Przeworski, A. (1991), *Democracy and the Market: Political and Economic Reforms in Eastern Europe and Latin America*, Cambridge University Press, Cambridge.

Przeworski, A. and Teune, H. (1970), *The Logic of Comparative Social Inquiry*, Wiley-Interscience, New York.

Putnam, R. (1993), *Making Democracy Work: Civic Traditions in Modern Italy*, Princeton University Press, Princeton.

Pye, L.W. and Verba, S. (eds) (1965), *Political Culture and Political Development*, Princeton University Press, Princeton.

Reisinger, W.M. (1997), 'Establishing and strengthening democracy', in R.D. Grey (ed.), *Democratic Theory and Post-Communist Change*, Prentice Hall, Upper Saddle River.

Riasanovsky, N.V. (1969), *A History of Russia*, 2nd ed., Oxford University Press, New York.

Rogowski, R. (1974), *Rational legitimacy. A theory of political support*, Princeton University Press, Princeton.

Rose, R. and Mishler W. (1994), 'Mass Reaction to Regime Change in Eastern Europe: Polarization or Leaders and Laggards?', *British Journal of Political Science*, vol. 24, pp. 159-82.

Rothschild, J. (1974), *East Central Europe Between the Two World Wars*, University of Washington Press, Seattle.

Rueschemeyer, D., Stephens, E.H. and Stephens, J.D. (1992), *Capitalist Development and Democracy*, University of Chicago Press, Chicago.

Rychlik, J. (1995), 'From Autonomy to Federation, 1938-68', in J. Musil (ed.), *The End of Czechoslovakia*, Central European University Press, Budapest.

Sachs, J.D. (1990), 'Charting Poland's Economic Rebirth', *Challenge*, January-February.

Sayrs, L.W. (1989), *Pooled Times Series Analysis*, Sage Publications, Beverly Hills.

Scalapino, R.A. (1992), *The Last Leninists: the Uncertain Future of Asia's Communist States*, Center for Strategic and International Studies, Washington, D.C.

Schmitter, P.C. (1994), 'Dangers and Dilemmas of Democracy', *Journal of Democracy*, vol. 5, pp. 57-74.

Senn, A.E. (1959), *The Emergence of Modern Lithuania*, Columbia University Press, New York.
Senn, A.E. (1990), *Lithuania Awakening*, University of California Press, Berkeley.
Seton-Watson, R. W. (1943), *Masaryk in England*, Cambridge University Press, Cambridge.
Seton-Watson, R. W. (1965), *History of the Czechs and Slovaks*, Archon Books, Hamden.
Seton-Watson, H. (1967), *The Russian Empire, 1801-1917*, Clarendon P., Oxford.
Shawcross, W. (1970), *Dubcek*, Weidenfeld and Nicolson, London.
Shin, D.C. (1994), 'On the Third Wave of Democratization: A Synthesis and Evaluation of Recent Theory and Research', *World Politics*, vol. 47, pp. 135-70.
Skilling, H.G. (1976), *Czechoslovakia's Interrupted Revolution*, Princeton University Press, Princeton.
Skilling, H.G. (1977), 'Stalinism and Czechoslovak Political Culture', in R.C. Tucker (ed.), *Stalinism: Essays in Historical Interpretation*, W.W. Norton and Company, New York.
Skilling, H.G. (1981), *Charter 77 and Human Rights in Czechoslovakia*, George Allen & Unwin, London.
Skilling, H.G. (1991), *Czechoslovakia, 1918-1988: seventy years from independence*, St. Martin's Press, New York.
Skocpol, T. (1979), *States and Social Revolutions: A Comparative Analysis of France, Russia, and China*, Cambridge University Press, Cambridge.
Skocpol, T. and Somers M. (1980), 'The Uses of Comparative History in Macrosocial Inquiry', *Comparative Studies in Society and History*, vol. 22, pp. 174-97.
Smith, G. (ed.) (1994), *The Baltic States: the national self-determination of Estonia, Latvia and Lithuania*, St. Martin's Press, New York.
Soloviev, A. (1959), *Holy Russia: The History of a Religious-Social Idea*, Mouton, Gravenhage.
Sorbell, V. (1988), 'Czechoslovakia: The Legacy of Normalization', *East European Politics*, vol. 2, pp. 36-69.
Starr, H. (1991), 'Democratic Dominoes: Diffusion Approaches to the Spread of Democracy in the International System', *Journal of Conflict Resolution*, vol. 35, pp. 356-81.
Suda, Z. (1980), *Zealots and Rebels. A History of the Ruling Communist Party of Czechoslovakia*, Hoover Institution Press, Stanford.
Temperley, H.W.V. (1921), *A History of the Peace Conference of Paris*, vol. 5, Henry Frowde and Hodder & Stoughton, London.
Thomson, S.H. (1953), *Czechoslovakia in European History*, 2nd ed., Princeton University Press, Princeton.
Tocqueville, A.de. (1961), *Democracy in America*, Schocken Books, New York.
Toká, G. (1996), 'Political Support in East-Central Europe', in H.D. Klingemann and D. Fuchs (eds), *Citizens and the State*, Oxford University Press, Oxford.
Trochim, W.M.K. (1984), *Research Design for Program Evaluation: the Regression-discontinuity Approach*, Sage Publications, Beverly Hills.

Trochim, W.M.K. (1986), *Advances in Quasi-experimental Design and Analysis*, Jossey-Bass, London.
Tucker, R.C. (1973), 'Culture, Political Culture, and Communist Society', *Political Science Quarterly*, vol. 88, pp. 173-90.
Tucker, R.C. (1974), 'Communist Revolutions, National Cultures and the Divided Nations', *Studies in Comparative Communism*, vol. 7, pp. 235-45.
Tucker, R.C. (1987), *Political Culture and Leadership in Soviet Russia: From Lenin to Gorbachev*, W.W. Norton & Co., New York.
Ulč, O. (1974), *Politics in Czechoslovakia*, Freeman and Company, San Francisco.
Ulč, O. (1979), 'The Normalization of Post-Invasion Czechoslovakia', *Survey*, vol. 24, pp. 3.
Vanhanen, T. (1990), *The Process of Democratization: A Comparative Study of 147 States, 1980-88*, Crane, Russak, New York.
Vanhanen, T. (1994), *Democratization in Eastern Europe: domestic and international perspective*, Routledge, New York.
Vardys, V.S. (1978), *The Catholic Church, Dissent and Nationality in Soviet Lithuania*, Columbia University Press, New York.
Vardys, V.S. and Sedaitis, J.B. (1997), *Lithuania: The Rebel Nation*, Westview Press, Boulder.
Volgyes, I. (1975), *Political Socialization in Eastern Europe: A Comparative Framework*, Praeger Publishers, New York.
Walkin, J. (1962), *The Rise of Democracy in Pre-Revolutionary Russia*, Praeger, New York.
Walsh, E.A. (1931), *The Fall of the Russian Empire: the story of the last of the Romanovs and the coming of the Bolsheviki*, Blue Ribbon Books, New York.
Ware, A. (1988), *Citizens, Parties and the State: a Reappraisal*, Princeton University Press, Princeton.
Warwick, C. A. and Lininger, D.P. (1975), *The Sample Survey: Theory and Practice*, McGraw-Hill, New York.
Weil, F. (1989), 'The Sources and Structure of Legitimation in Western Democracies: A Consolidated Model Test with Time-Series Data in Six Countries Since World War II', *American Sociological Review*, vol. 54, pp. 682-706.
White, S. (1977), 'The USSR: Patterns of Autocracy and Industrialism', in A. Brown and J. Grey (eds), *Political Culture and Political Change in the Communist States*, Holmes & Meier Publishers, New York.
White, S. (1978), 'Continuity and change in Soviet political culture: an emigre study', *Comparative Political Studies*, vol. 11, pp. 381-95.
White, S. (1979), *Political Culture and Soviet Politics*, Macmillan, London.
White, S. (1985a), 'Soviet Political Culture Reassessed', in A. Brown (ed.), *Political Culture and Communist States*, Macmillan, London.
White, S. (1985b), 'Propagating Communist values in the USSR', *Problems of Communism*, vol. 34, pp. 1-18.
White, S., Rose R. and McAllister I. (1997), *How Russia Votes*, Chatham House Publishers, Chatham.

Whitehead, L. (1986), 'International Aspects of Democratization', in G. O'Donnell, P. Schmitter, and L. Whitehead (eds), *Transitions from Authoritarian Rule: Comparative Perspectives*, The Johns Hopkins University Press, Baltimore.

Wolchik, S. (1989), 'Prospects for Political Change in Czechoslovakia', Paper presented at the 1989 meeting of the Midwest Political Science Association, Chicago, April.

Wolchik, S. (1990), 'The Crisis of Socialism in Central and Eastern Europe and its Future', Paper presented at Conference on the Future of Socialism in Eastern Europe, University of North Carolina, April.

Wolchik, S. (1991), *Czechoslovakia In Transition: Politics, economics and society*, Pinter Publishers, London.

Wolchik, S. (1993), 'The Repluralization of Politics of Czechoslovakia', *Communist and Post-Communist Studies,* vol. 26, pp. 412-31.

Yin, R.K. (1994), *Case Study Research: design and methods*, 2nd edition, Sage Publications, Thousand Oaks.